SEALs

THE US NAVY'S ELITE FIGHTING FORCE

OSPREY
PUBLISHING

THE AUTHORS

Mir Bahmanyar was born in Iran, educated in Germany and received his BA in History from the University of California at Berkeley. He served in the US Army's 75th Ranger Regiment and has written several books on their history including *US Army Ranger 1983–2002, Darby's Rangers 1942–45*, and *Shadow Warriors: A history of the US Army Rangers*. Mir is also a feature film producer and scriptwriter. In 2006 he produced and co-wrote the multi-award-winning *Soldier of God*. He currently resides California.

Chris Osman is a former US Marine and US Navy SEAL. He was on active duty for 11 years, and has two honorable discharges from the Marine Corps and the Navy. Chris is the founder of Tactical Assault Gear (www.theoperatorschoice.com), a multi-million-dollar company that supplies tactical equipment to military and law-enforcement units around the world. He lives in San Diego, CA with his wife and daughter.

SEALs

THE US NAVY'S ELITE FIGHTING FORCE

MIR BAHMANYAR *with* **CHRIS OSMAN**

First published in Great Britain in 2008 by Osprey Publishing.
This paperback edition published in 2011 by Osprey Publishing.
Midland House, West Way, Botley, Oxford, OX2 0PH, United Kingdom.
44-02 23rd St, Suite 219, Long Island City, NY 11101, USA
Email: info@ospreypublishing.com
Osprey Publishing is part of the Osprey Group.

A CIP catalog record for this book is available from the British Library

ISBN: 978 1 84908 477 2

Mir Bahmanyar and Chris Osman have asserted their right under the Copyright, Designs and Patents Act, 1988, to be identified as the authors of this book.

Page layout by Myriam Bell Design, France
Index by Alison Worthington
Typeset in Minion Pro
Originated by United Graphic Pte Ltd., Singapore
Printed in China through Bookbuilders

11 12 13 14 15   11 10 9 8 7 6 5 4 3 2

The Woodland Trust
Osprey Publishing is supporting the Woodland Trust, the UK's leading woodland conservation charity, by funding the dedication of trees.

www.ospreypublishing.com

Front cover and title page images from the authors' collections.

CONTENTS

AUTHORS' PREFACES

MIR BAHMANYAR

Former US Marine and US Navy SEAL Chris Osman rang me in my Los Angeles home one afternoon, not to catch up as he does on occasion, but to see if I would be interested in writing a book on Navy SEALs. SEAL is an acronym for SEa, Air, and Land and refers to the methods of insertion and ability to perform missions in these environments. I had previously written a rather dry monograph on SEALs and had vowed never to write about them again. They had struck me as pompous and over-rated, with an exceedingly active and well-oiled public relations spin machine. That, coupled with the fact that I had served in the US Army's 75th Ranger Regiment, which had recently taken a few casualties in Afghanistan when Rangers acted as a Quick Reaction Force (QRF) for a Navy SEAL mission gone horribly wrong, made me less than enthusiastic about the prospect. Nonetheless, Chris' enthusiasm and candor were refreshing and he persuaded me to take on the project.

This book focuses solely on the US Navy SEALs. It does not cover anyone else associated with Naval Special Warfare. Chris had the task of organizing interviews with the mostly reclusive SEALs and this took many, many months. Operational tempo for active-duty SEALs is at best demanding and at worst straining. Many spoke openly about their experiences without compromising comrades, operations, tactics or procedures. The SEALs were forthcoming with their time, when they had any, and their audio/visual collections. Sometimes, though, a "… can't put that in the book" followed a remarkable story.

Whenever possible real names are used. The accuracy of the book rests with the SEALs as very few official reports or news stories are available to the public. In that sense this cannot be an historical book. The story begins in 1987 with the creation of the Naval Special Warfare Command and ends with actions in Iraq around 2007. We could not research every detail or cover every operation. These first-hand accounts are, of course, individual perspectives, based on personal recollections, beliefs, and desires to express certain issues. No audio recordings of the interviews were made except for one, and follow-up telephone conversations took place over many more months.

It is nearly impossible to do justice to history, as almost all SEAL operations are classified and will remain so for decades to come. We did not interview anyone who had any active participation in Somalia, the Philippine Islands, or Peru, to name but a few places. Furthermore we do not cover in detail some of the well-known incidents involving SEALs. The majority of coverage of US Navy SEALs comes in the aftermath of a SEAL mission gone wrong, always resulting in the deaths of American servicemen. The most widely reported of these were the fights around Neil Roberts, who fell out of a helicopter after a Taleban rocket-propelled grenade hit in 2003, and the destruction of a small SEAL reconnaissance team and the follow-on QRF in Afghanistan in 2005. Both of these "failures" resulted in enormous coverage. Neil Roberts' tragic death was covered in many newspapers and several books, one of which painted an unflattering portrait of the SEALs during Operation *Anaconda*. The only survivor of the SEAL reconnaissance team, Marcus Luttrell, wrote an account of his experiences titled *Lone Survivor*. Subsequently, the book was purchased by a Hollywood studio and is scheduled to be a major motion picture.

These exceptions should never be used to detract from the fact that the overwhelming number of special operations missions go unreported and most operations are highly successful: missions such as hostage rescues, target interdiction or planting tracking devices on foreign vessels in foreign harbors, to name but a few.

Although the Navy SEALs' reputation in some military circles varies, the SEALs are a professional and competent force who undergo a great deal of technical training and usually spend a year in pre-deployment before executing a six-month combat tour. In recent years they have on occasion been deployed without the necessary equipment, which they have had to obtain from other special operations forces. The SEALs discussed their opinions on the Global War on Terrorism, and the role they have played in it. Finally, many Navy SEALs were concerned that the public remember that these wars are difficult for the spouses and families of servicemen, particularly those in the special operations forces. The long deployments for training and combat tours, coupled with the news reporting the death of an un-named special operations soldier, send shivers down the spines of wives and girlfriends alike.

The majority of the book attempts to represent the Navy SEALs as they really are, with language kept intact as far as possible and with very little analysis of or alterations to the tone and intent of the person interviewed.

I break away from Prussian military theorist Carl von Clausewitz's (1780–1831) astute statement "that war is nothing but the continuation of policy with other means" and thus do not cover the political nature of and reasons for entering wars.[1] I shall also not comment on the scourge that is the private contracting business and the politicians responsible for thinning our ranks in the special operations community. This book is simply a mirror reflecting the values and actions of some of the most highly trained men in the world.

I should thank SOvV and Chickenfarmer and the following SEALs for their time and efforts: Chris Dye, Tony Duchi, Marcus Luttrell, and many other nameless sailors.

Thanks to Michelle Ricci, who is from Canada, for her selfless work on this project and for suffering through being exposed to violence, American style.

My editors, Anita Baker and Ruth Sheppard, were extremely supportive. It is because of them that the book was ultimately approved, and their hard work helped to make this a much better text.

Lastly, and most importantly, I dedicate this book to Peanut 41, my beloved pitbull, who suffered a most cruel and untimely death, and to my friend and mentor Franklin Delano Nastasi who passed away on December 18, 2007. Both are sorely missed. Frank was the greatest admirer and supporter of the founding father of modern American and British special operations – Robert Rogers of the Rangers (1731–95). Some believe Frank to have been Rogers reincarnated.

Mir Bahmanyar, Los Angeles, CA, 2008

CHRIS OSMAN

The idea for this book came from my desire to provide a new look at Naval Special Warfare and more specifically the men who operate in and fill the ranks of the SEAL platoons and task units. Without them there is no mission. It is these men, not the medals on their chests, which make the teams what they are.

Mir and I have spent many months and hundreds of hours putting this book together, and dozens of operators from both the East and West Coast teams were interviewed. Some of them are longtime friends whom I have known or operated with for more than ten years. Others are operators whom I had not met before. All of them were more than willing to help me out with this project. I cannot thank them enough. When I asked for their help, the answer was always "Sure, anything for a fellow Frogman," or "Sure dude, whatever I can do for you," or "Of course! You're a team guy." The brotherhood of the teams is a living, breathing thing that cannot be explained to those who have not been a part of it.

There is one common goal that ties all SEALs together. That goal is to be the best. SEALs want to be the best at everything they do, all of the time. It is what separates us from all others and it is the reason all of us went to BUD/S (Basic Underwater Demolition/SEAL). BUD/S is known for being the hardest military training and selection process of any armed force anywhere in the world. All SEALs regard the accomplishment of graduating BUD/S as one of the highest honors a man can achieve in his lifetime. BUD/S is a selection process to see who has what it takes to move on and actually begin advanced training and move into a SEAL platoon. For a Navy SEAL, being in a platoon and operating in a task unit is the ultimate goal. It is what drives all of us to push ourselves beyond what most believe is possible and keeps all operators focused on mission success.

Since September 11, 2001, much has changed in the teams. All SEALs in all platoons and task units are now likely to undertake real world missions. From the late 1970s through 9/11, very few missions were carried out compared to today's operational tempo.

This book will focus on some of the modern-day SEAL missions and the men who operate in the platoons and task units. It is impossible to discuss all of the missions and those who were a part of them. Operational security must be protected at all times. As a result, few real names are used in the book and many of the photographs used have been modified to conceal the identities of the individuals depicted in them.

This book is a written tribute to all of the men I have been lucky enough to serve with and to know. There are men in the world to whom all SEALs bow their heads, the men who have paid the ultimate price and selflessly sacrificed their lives in training and in combat for God, country, and their fellow team mates. It is to them that I dedicate this book.

Chris Osman, San Diego, CA, 2008

FOREWORD BY MARCUS LUTTRELL

NCDUs, UDTs or SEALs – whatever the names given to our profession throughout history, people have spent countless hours and thousands of pages simply trying to explain our way of life. The hardships we face, the adversity we overcome, the death we encounter, the brothers we lose, our way of life on and off the battlefield. Since the birth of the frogman, history buffs and action junkies have tried to write or emulate our lifestyle. In my opinion very few have been able to capture it correctly.

Perhaps that is the reason we are so reluctant to speak openly to outsiders about anything dealing with the teams and the type of work we do. However, if and when stories are told they should be told by the men who were there and are directly affected by them. Simply put, stories of SEALs should be told by SEALs or not at all. Cover to cover, this book chronicles and gives an upfront and in-your-face testimony of what life in the teams is all about, from the most credible source you can have... It comes from the operator himself.

Describing BUD/S, the command structure, weapons, work-up, deployment and the battles we have fought, *SEALs* creates a unique insight into our community and gives the reader a mental workout on the modern day frogman. From Bosnia to Panama across the battlefields of Iraq into the unforgiving mountains of Afghanistan, this narrative is a no-nonsense look at the way we do and have done business for the past forty plus years. It's a must read for anyone wanting to be a SEAL or wanting to have a real understanding of today's modern frogman.

Osman sets the record straight and brings a reality check to the reader. Contrary to popular belief SEALs are not bullet proof, we don't wear capes, and our blood is just as red as the people we fight: the only difference between us and the enemy is that we refuse to lose and when knocked down we get back up every time, we are never out of the fight... For those readers looking to become SEALs I suggest you read this book cover to cover and then read it again. If you still think you have what it takes then we will see you on the beach (chances are you won't make it anyway). For those readers just wanting to gain knowledge and an understanding about the SEALs and the SEAL community there is no other book you need read... Good job Oz.

Marcus Luttrell, US Navy SEAL and author of *Lone Survivor*, May 2008

FOREWORD BY ETHAN REIFF

I first met Mir Bahmanyar through his writing. I don't mean that in a poetic or existential manner but in the most simple, matter-of-fact way possible. He wrote a book about contemporary US Army Rangers and my partner, Cyrus Voris, and I were producing a TV pilot we had written, in which the FBI hero had previously served in the Ranger Regiment. Wanting our show to be as "real" as possible, I contacted Mir and asked if he would be interested in working as a technical advisor on Ranger-related matters, which would principally entail spending some time with Michael Ealy – the actor playing our hero – and explaining to him what his character would have experienced during Ranger training and service in a Ranger battalion. Mir was busy writing books and producing movies, so he was not very excited at the idea of "advising" us. But he agreed to do so – mostly, I believe, out of a sense of obligation to his old unit. If we, the lousy Hollywood producers, were going out of our way attempting to make our television portrayal of Rangers a bit more accurate, how could he – one-time active duty Ranger himself – refuse?

The pilot went on to become a show called *Sleeper Cell*. It ran for two seasons on the Showtime cable network, becoming a critical hit and something of a popular success as well. During season two Mir introduced us to former Navy SEAL Chris Osman, who did an outstanding job helping us stage a scene in which US Special Operations troops delivered a terrorist detainee into the custody of his native government and then helped us choreograph a prison raid/firefight set in Saudi Arabia, which is one of my favorite scenes of the entire series. Needless to say, the reason Chris was able to help us make both those scenes feel so real is that while on active duty he had participated in similar ones for which there had been no script at all, other than an operations order.

Sleeper Cell maintains something of a cult following among members of the law-enforcement, intelligence-gathering and military communities. We have it on good authority that a copy of the DVD boxed-set was for some time carried on the private jet which ferries officers of the Central Intelligence Agency (CIA) from Virginia to Afghanistan and back again. When my partner and I heard that from a reliable source, we agreed it was better than if we had won all the Emmys and Golden Globes we had been nominated for. The generally unrecognized contributions of Mir, Chris and other real life military, law-enforcement and intelligence veterans helped make *Sleeper Cell* as good as it was. I am happy to have this opportunity to thank them for that in public.

But as far as Mir is concerned, I'm shocked at the venue which he has provided for me to express those thanks. He served with the Second Battalion, 75th Regiment. As such, Navy SEALs have never been at the top of his "all-time favorite elite fighting unit" list. Roger's Rangers of the French & Indian War? Yes. Darby's Rangers of WWII? Yes. The Immortals of the ancient Achaemenid Persian empire? Maybe (fearsome as Herodotus reports them to have been, they never wore a "Battalion Scroll" on their shoulder). But Squids…? Well, Mir was raised in Germany until high school and has lived his entire life primarily for soccer – or, as he calls it, "football" – so him writing a book about SEALs is like him choosing to watch the Super Bowl over a World Cup final: not bloody likely.

But inter-service rivalry notwithstanding, that is what he has done. And once I stopped to think about it, I realized the SEALs could not have asked for a more perfectly appropriate author. As a society, the United States at the dawn of the 21st century is a peculiar animal in military terms. After seven years of protracted and ongoing war on several fronts, we remain one of the least militarized societies and least martial cultures in history. Less than 10 percent of our current population has ever served in the military. Even if you include all reserve components, the full strength of our entire military establishment is a little under three million, fielded by a nation of over three hundred million, meaning less than 1 percent of our overall population wears the uniform. One result of this state of affairs is that certain aspects of military reality fall prey to mythologization.

Mir Bahmanyar has not treated the US Navy SEALs like the Legion of Superheroes or the Justice League. He has treated them like who and what they are: one of the best-trained, best-equipped and hardest-fighting Special Operations units in the world, made up of some of the most intelligent, competent and tough servicemen in the US military (Ridley Scott's Demi Moore movie *GI Jane* aside, there are no female SEALs). The very best of men occasionally make an error or come up short. This does not make them any less deadly to our enemies, nor should it make them any less impressive to the rest of us. Even under the rigorous glare of Mir Bahmanyar's Army Ranger eyes, the US Navy SEALs presented in these pages are a mighty impressive bunch.

Ethan Reiff, writer/producer *Sleeper Cell*, *Kung Fu Panda*, *Eleventh Hour*, and *Nottingham*, Valley Village, CA, April 2008

IN PRAISE OF THE SEALS

Let there never be a moment that you are not aware of our support, gratitude, and prayers. In all that you do and all that you are, because of your example we as Americans can live a life inspired to do good for mankind. You are our beacon of light in a sometimes misty world. We are painfully aware of the sacrifices made by you, your families, and loved ones. For this, our heartfelt thanks.

Wayne Newton

During our 30 years of visiting deployed troops overseas, it has been infrequent that our Cheerleaders have had the opportunity to thank members of the SEALs, and other SF forces. Their areas of operations are usually further "out front" than logistical operations for entertainers can support. That made our 2001 visit to Afghanistan all the more unique and rewarding. Thank you for helping SEAL team members tell their story. We are honored to have been remembered.

The Dallas Cowboys Cheerleaders

Thanks to the Navy SEALs for everything they, and all of our troops, have done for our country. I cannot begin to imagine the depth of dedication that job would take.

Neal McCoy

PART I

COMMAND STRUCTURE AND TRAINING

THE US SEALS AND NAVAL SPECIAL WARFARE COMMAND

The Birth of a Command

THE HISTORY OF THE US NAVY SEALS

The father of all British and American commandos was Robert Rogers, born in the colonies, who recruited, trained, and led "Roger's Rangers" during the French and Indian War (1754–63). His basic Rules of Discipline (rules of combat patrolling) are taught to all special operations personnel, including Navy SEALs, to this day.

The first organized use of underwater special operations personnel occurred with the onset of World War II. American volunteers began training for beach reconnaissance missions in Little Creek, VA, on August 15, 1942.[2] These amphibious scouts and raiders participated in major combat operations in the European and Mediterranean theaters as well as in the Pacific. During Operation *Torch* in North Africa in 1942, naval commandos cut cables allowing US Navy vessels to insert American Rangers. Subsequent training included demolition coursework at the Naval Combat Demolition Unit established in 1943. When the Marines were preparing to assault Tarawa in the Pacific theater of operations, these frogmen conducted hydrographic reconnaissance missions detailing any and all obstacles the American assault force could encounter. Later that year Underwater Demolition Teams (UDT) One and Two were founded, comprised of approximately 30 officers and 150 enlisted sailors.[3] During the Korean War (1950–53) UDT conducted mine-clearing operations as well as riverine combat operations.

SEALs and Ranger M pose for a celebratory picture after Fallujah was taken in 2004. (Authors' collections)

THE RISE OF THE NAVY SEALS

From the 1950s through the 1970s unconventional warfare was on the rise, most notably demonstrated by revolutionary activities in Central and South America, the Middle East, and Europe. With the decline of imperialism, nationalist movements became a perceived threat. Some of these revolutionaries are as well-known as Fidel Castro, who, in 1959, overthrew a US-supported dictatorship in Cuba. Another example is seen in Gamal Abdel Nasser, who in 1952 led the Egyptian Revolution against King Farouk I and became a major supporter of Arab nationalism. Although large conventional forces were abundant and capable of dealing with the threat of the Warsaw Pact in Europe, conventional tactics proved unsuitable for countering small groups of men and women dedicated to a specific cause. It became evident that smaller, elite units were required to combat these unconventional tactics. As a result, several American special operations units were raised, including the Navy SEALs, who were founded by presidential order under John F. Kennedy in January 1962. All existing frogmen were absorbed into the SEALs, whose primary missions were to conduct unconventional warfare in the maritime and riverine areas of operation. SEALs participated in the Vietnam War between 1966 and 1973, where they executed aggressive direct action and reconnaissance missions.

On May 1, 1983, all UDTs were redesignated as SEAL Teams or Swimmer Delivery Vehicle Teams (SDVTs). SDVTs have since been redesignated SEAL Delivery Vehicle (SDV) Teams.[4] SEALS have participated in Operations *Urgent Fury* (Grenada, 1983), *Earnest Will* (Persian Gulf, 1987–90), *Just Cause* (Panama 1989–90), *Desert Shield/Desert Storm* (Middle East/Persian Gulf, 1990–91), *Enduring Freedom* (Afghanistan, 2001–ongoing) and *Iraqi Freedom* (Iraq, 2003–

This is the current day SEAL MK48 7.62mm machine gun. It has a collapsible stock, as well as improved combat optics. The optic used on this particular MK48 is an EOTECH Holographic sight. Note the short barrel, and brass deflecting device built into the weapon. This version can now be employed by right- and left-handed shooters. The older-style M60s could only be used right-handed. A left-handed shooter will still get hot brass on their arms when using the MK48, but it no longer hits them in the face as was the case with the M60. (Authors' collections)

ongoing). SEAL missions were and, in some cases, continue to be conducted in Somalia, Bosnia, Bolivia, Haiti, Liberia, the Philippines and the Horn of Africa.

NAVAL SPECIAL WARFARE COMMAND

The United States Special Operations Command (USSOCOM) was founded on April 16, 1987 as a direct result of a failed hostage rescue mission in Iran in 1980. Iranian students had seized 66 hostages at the US Embassy in Tehran, Iran. A joint task force attempted a rescue but met with tragedy without enemy action, resulting in the death of eight servicemen.[5] The United States Congress recognized that in order to conduct successful joint special operations, a joint special operations headquarters was required. It took seven years to realize this command.

USSOCOM was created by the passing of the Nunn–Cohen Amendment to the Goldwater–Nichols Act in 1986 and remains the only Combatant Command established by Congress.[6] All branches of the US military, the Army, Navy including Marines, and Air Force, have their elite forces commanded and controlled by a single headquarters that is responsible for the recruitment, training, and mission planning, to name just a few areas of responsibility standardized within USSOCOM.

Silhouette photo of a SEAL in a Humvee turret. (Authors' collections)

Navy SEALs rehearsing Immediate Action drills and building-clearing techniques. (Authors' collections)

The Naval Special Warfare Command (NAVSPECWARCOM) was commissioned on April 16, 1987 at the Naval Amphibious Base in Coronado, CA, and is the naval component to the USSOCOM. Naval Special Warfare (NSW) personnel comprise less than one percent of the entire US Navy. NSW forces conduct numerous missions in special operations, although more specific tasks have been assigned in the wake of the Global War on Terrorism (GWOT) in 2001, but in principle they comprise Unconventional Warfare (UW), Direct Action (DA), Special Reconnaissance (SR), Foreign Internal Defense (FID), Sniper Overwatch, Security Assistance, Personal Security Detachment-capable (PSD), Counter-Terrorism, Counter-Drug operations, Combat Search and Rescue (CSAR) and Special Activities (or SUPPACT – Support Activities).

Naval Special Warfare Command underwent several changes to meet the needs of the strategic requirements of the United States. Much like the rest of USSOCOM, naval special operations units were geographically specific – meaning each SEAL team had a geographic area of responsibility. By 1998/99 a new doctrine, called Naval Special Warfare (NSW) 21 or Force 21, was implemented, which resulted in the elimination of specific areas of operations and enabled other NSW components to deploy together. "Before the development of the NSW squadron concept, SEAL teams would not be joined by the other NSW detachments until they deployed, and therefore lacked interoperable training."[7]

NSW 21 was a result of the US Army's own transformation philosophy called Force XXI. The transformation was based on years of research, actual combat experience, and a desire to streamline the heavier, conventional fighting forces and thus align them with the rise of technological assets within the military as a whole. The guiding philosophy was one of rapid worldwide deployment of combat-capable brigades. NSW 21 followed that guiding philosophy. Greater efficiency and more effective in-theater control by regional commanders were envisioned. In effect a basic house-cleaning operation was conducted by streamlining the various NSW components into units that were more easily controlled.

A key part of NSW 21 was the formation of new NSW squadrons by joining each SEAL team with a SEAL Delivery Vehicle detachment, a special warfare boat detachment, a mobile communications detachment, tactical cryptology support, and explosive ordnance disposal (EOD) experts. The squadron elements are now going through a four-phase, two-year cycle of six months of individual-level training, six months of unit training, and six months of squadron training before beginning an all-hands six-month operational deployment.[8]

US Navy SEAL practicing breaching techniques during pre-deployment work-up. (Authors' collections)

Another core component in the restructuring was that senior command personnel would accompany the deploying NSW task units.

NSW 21's major Naval Special Warfare command structure is arranged into four major operational commands: Naval Special Warfare Group One, Coronado, CA; Naval Special Warfare Group Two, Little Creek, VA; Naval Special Warfare Group Three, Coronado, CA; and Naval Special Warfare Group Four, Little Creek, VA (see also Appendix 1 for complete organizational charts of NSW).

Under NSW 21, the squadron is built around the entire SEa, Air and Land (SEAL) team deploying and includes its senior leadership, SEAL Vehicle Delivery Teams and Special Boat Teams, as well as personnel detachments such as mobile communications teams, tactical cryptology support, and explosive ordnance disposal. Additionally, the squadrons receive support from five permanently deployed NSW units overseas.

NSW forces can operate independently or in conjunction with other US special operations forces or within US Navy Carrier Battle Groups and Amphibious Ready Groups. There are approximately 5,000 total active duty personnel.

At the heart of the NSW realignment are the NSW Squadrons and a new two-year, four-phase deployment cycle. The deployment schedule is facilitated by the establishment of new SEAL teams created from the restructuring of current continental US-based forces. Following a year of individual and unit-level training, the squadron receives six months of interoperability training prior to its six-month deployment. The NSW Squadron provides the same tactical forces and assets, but they arrive in theater more completely trained and integrated with enhanced command and control forward. This greatly increases the squadron's ability to organize NSW forces to meet specific requirements. Consolidating the SEAL teams' administrative and support functions under the Logistics Support Units and shifting the training functions from the teams to training detachments assigned to the

This is one of the most commonly used weapons in the teams. The machine gun is the Navy SEALs version of the SAW or Squad Automatic Weapon. It was developed a few years ago and is produced by Fabrique Nationale de Herstal. Developed to add more fire power to a SEAL platoon, this weapon shoots a 5.56mm bullet, the same as the M4. Newer versions have collapsible stocks, and rails on the feed tray covers allowing the user to add advanced optics. The Army and Marine Corps call this weapon the M249 SAW or Para SAW. The nomenclature for it in the teams is the MK46. This weapon also has a big brother. The MK48 is also made by FN and fires a 7.62mm round. This version has replaced the old M60-style machine guns. Both weapons are used by one operator. All other forces use the 7.62mm version (the 240G) as a crew-served weapon. (Authors' collections)

This is the latest version of the M14 used by the SEAL teams. It uses the same barrel and bolt group as the original version but all the other components are different. The upper receiver is dropped into a Sage International stock. This has a collapsible stock, as well as a cheek piece that can be elevated allowing the shooter the proper eye relief for his chosen optics. This battle rifle shoots a 7.62mm round. This weapon is very effective, but is not used that often. Most operators prefer to use the MK11 instead, which is the 7.62 semi-automatic sniper rifle. (Authors' collections)

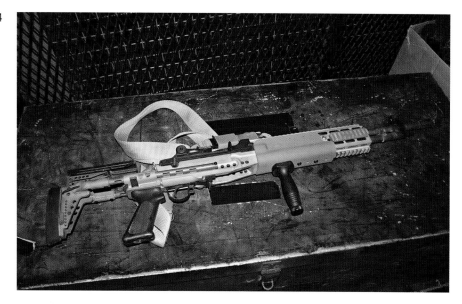

groups has created a more efficient organization. This consolidation allows NSW operators to maintain a strong operational focus… and provides unity of command for these systems and optimal support to the operational commanders.[9]

Subsequent to the terrorist attacks on September 11, 2001 on the mainland of the United States, the military as a whole re-evaluated its previous philosophy and command structures. The US Navy created Sea Power 21, a major transformational initiative to address the new challenges presented by global terrorist networks.[10]

MAJOR NAVAL SPECIAL WARFARE COMPONENT COMMANDS

There are two NSW component commands. The Naval Special Warfare Center, Coronado, CA, provides basic and advanced instruction and training in maritime special operations to US military and government personnel and members of other allied armed forces.

The Naval Special Warfare Development Group Dam Neck, VA (DevGru aka Dam Neck), is responsible for the testing, evaluation, and development of technology and maritime, ground, and airborne tactics applicable to NSW forces, with possible applicability throughout the Department of Defense.[11] DevGru has a structure of five teams. Red, Blue and Gold are all assault teams, Grey Team is vehicles and boats, while Black Team is a sniper team. One former member of DevGru describes his old unit:

THE TRANSFORMATION OF NAVAL SPECIAL WARFARE FROM 2000 TO 2008

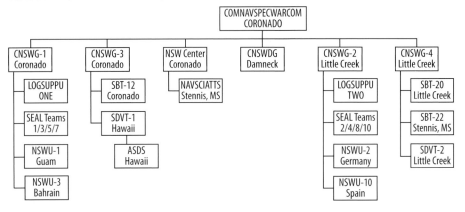

COMNAVSPECWARCOM CORONADO

CNSWG-1 Coronado
- LOGSUPPU ONE
- SEAL Teams 1/3/5/7
- NSWU-1 Guam
- NSWU-3 Bahrain

CNSWG-3 Coronado
- SBT-12 Coronado
- SDVT-1 Hawaii
  - ASDS Hawaii

NSW Center Coronado
- NAVSCIATTS Stennis, MS

CNSWDG Damneck

CNSWG-2 Little Creek
- LOGSUPPU TWO
- SEAL Teams 2/4/8/10
- NSWU-2 Germany
- NSWU-10 Spain

CNSWG-4 Little Creek
- SBT-20 Little Creek
- SBT-22 Stennis, MS
- SDVT-2 Little Creek

NAVAL SPECIAL WARFARE COMMAND TODAY[12]

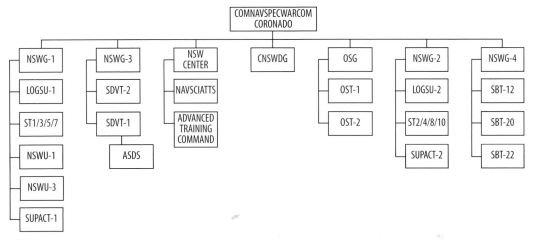

COMNAVSPECWARCOM CORONADO

NSWG-1
- LOGSU-1
- ST1/3/5/7
- NSWU-1
- NSWU-3
- SUPACT-1

NSWG-3
- SDVT-2
- SDVT-1
  - ASDS

NSW CENTER
- NAVSCIATTS
- ADVANCED TRAINING COMMAND

CNSWDG

OSG
- OST-1
- OST-2

NSWG-2
- LOGSU-2
- ST2/4/8/10
- SUPACT-2

NSWG-4
- SBT-12
- SBT-20
- SBT-22

DPV (Desert Patrol Vehicle).
(Authors' collections)

The SEAL Special Operation Peculiar Modification kit (SOPMOD) is issued to everyone in the teams. It is the most widely used weapon system in SOCOM today. This M4 has a 14in. barrel on it, used for land warfare missions. In the upper right-hand corner of the case is the 10in. barrel used for CQB missions. The two uppers have two different types of sights. On the 14in. barrel there is a 1x–4x power scope optic, on the hand rail there is a visible and IR laser aiming device. The 10in. upper has an EOTECH holographic sight, as well as a light. There is also a P226 9mm handgun in the case. In the lower left-hand corner is the pistol light which can be quickly attached as well as the suppressor for the M4, and a back up iron sight. There is also a binocular set and monocular set of night vision goggles. The small cases are for long-term storage of some of the components to the kit. (Authors' collections)

We research training, tactics and procedures, and conduct research and development for SEAL SOPs [standard operating procedures]. We really love our jobs and are professional and have a great ethic and dedication to our unit and although we are super-patriotic we have no desire to lay down our lives for our country. We are all cut of the same cloth. It's about commitment, cohesion, and your brothers-in-arms. Part of our job is examining SEAL teams and their training cycles and deployments. How can we gain efficiencies, shorten things, and yet retain the same amount of knowledge and Tactics, Training, and Procedures (TTP)? At DevGru you have also two duties; primary and collateral. You might be a communicator and your collateral might be optics, just to give one example. You can easily travel for 240 days out of the year conducting research.[13]

MAJOR SUBORDINATE COMMANDS

SEAL TEAMS

SEAL teams are "maritime, multi-purpose combat forces organized, trained and equipped to conduct a variety of special missions in all operational environments and threat conditions. They infiltrate their objective areas by fixed- and rotor-winged aircraft, Navy surface ships, combatant craft and submarines."[14]

Traditionally, a SEAL platoon is comprised of 16 members, who are subdivided into two squads, and is commanded by a Navy lieutenant (O-3). An AOIC (Assistant Officer in Charge, an O-2), a platoon chief (E-7), and an LPO (Leading Petty Officer, E-6) comprise the rest of the leadership of the platoon.

US NAVY RANKS AND RATES

Pay Grade	Rank	Abbreviation
O-1	Ensign	ENS
O-2	Lieutenant Junior Grade	LTJG
O-3	Lieutenant	LT
O-4	Lieutenant Commander	LCDR
O-5	Commander	CDR
O-6	Captain	CAPT
O-7	Rear Admiral (lower half)	RDML
O-8	Rear Admiral (upper half)	RADM
O-9	Vice Admiral	VADM
O-10	Admiral	ADM
O-11	Fleet Admiral*	FADM

* The rank of Fleet Admiral has been reserved for war-time use only. The last fleet admirals were in World War II.

Pay Grade	Rank	Abbreviation
W-1*	Warrant Officer	WO1
W-2	Chief Warrant Officer	CWO2
W-3	Chief Warrant Officer	CWO3
W-4	Chief Warrant Officer	CWO4
W-5*	Chief Warrant Officer	CWO5

* The grade of Warrant Officer (W-1) is no longer in use. W-5 was established in the Navy in 2002.

A typical SEAL team's table of organization and equipment requires three 40-man task units (TU). Each TU is composed in turn of two SEAL platoons and a headquarters (HQ) element commanded by an O-5. The HQ element consists of a Senior Enlisted man (E-8), an Operations Officer (O-2/3), and an Operations Leading/Chief Petty Officer (E-6/7). Additional personnel, from Explosive Ordnance Disposal (EOD) or Air Force Special Tactics (AFST) for example, are included subject to mission requirements and can increase the size of a SEAL task unit.

SEAL DELIVERY VEHICLE (SDV) TEAMS

SDV teams are "specially trained SEALs and support personnel who operate and maintain the SDVs and Dry Deck Shelters (DDS). SDVs are wet submersibles that are designed to conduct clandestine reconnaissance, direct action and passenger delivery missions in maritime environments. DDS deliver SDVs and specially trained forces from modified submarines."[15]

Marcus Luttrell during special reconnaissance training. (Marcus Luttrell)

Very little is ever written about SDV missions. An SDV is an insertion platform, home to SEALs who consider themselves the real deal. There is rivalry between them and the land-based SEAL teams, whose platoons are mockingly called "vanilla teams" by SDV SEALs.[16] SDV platoons comprise between 12 and 15 men who spend all their time underwater. During Advanced Operator Training (AOT), which is SDV training and lasts for three months, the average dive and time spent underwater is six hours per day. SDVs concentrate on maneuvering their subs, practicing swimmer cast and are the genuine frogmen of the SEALs. Swimmer cast is "an old UDT technique for getting men into and out of the water rapidly. An IBS [Inflatable Boat Small] was made fast to the side of a motor launch. Then men climbed into the IBS and rolled – were *cast* – into the water while the launch maintained its speed. For the recovery, a snare man in the middle of the IBS used a figure-eight loop to snatch swimmers out of the water as the launch roared past."[17]

Marcus Luttrell is well known for being the sole survivor of an SDV reconnaissance element compromised and over-run by Taleban/Al Qaeda fighters in Afghanistan in June 2005. Luttrell is a big man, 6ft 5in. of muscle. He describes the tiny spaces and claustrophobic conditions that SDV personnel operate in. Some transits to objectives are so long that SEALS even sleep underwater. "The worst part is diving where you can get arterial gas metabolism on ascent, and diving injuries are somewhat common. SDV is the coldest most miserable place you'll ever be, crammed into small spaces all the time. That is what suck is all about."[18]

RATE INSIGNIA OF NAVY ENLISTED PERSONNEL

The use of the word "rank" for Navy enlisted personnel is incorrect. The term is "rate." The rating badge – a combination of rate (pay grade) and rating (specialty) – is worn on the left upper sleeve of all uniforms in grades E-4 through E-6. E-1 through E-3 have color-coded group rate marks based upon their occupational field. Group rate marks for E-1 (optional) through E-3 are worn on dress uniforms only. Chief petty officers (E-7 through E-9) wear collar devices on their white and khaki uniforms, and rate badges on their service dress blues.

Pay Grade	Rate	Abbreviation
E-1	Seaman Recruit	SR
E-2	Seaman Apprentice	SA
E-3	Seaman	SN
E-4	Petty Officer Third Class	PO3
E-5	Petty Officer Second Class	PO2
E-6	Petty Officer First Class	PO1
E-7	Chief Petty Officer	CPO
E-8	Senior Chief Petty Officer	SCPO
E-9	Master Chief Petty Officer	MCPO
E-9	Master Chief Petty Officer of the Navy	MCPON

(Source: http://www.navy.mil/navydata/navy_legacy_hr.asp?id=260)

Marcus jokingly said that SOCOM did not think they [Seal Delivery 1] were cool enough to be called ST-11. SDVT-1 and SDVT-2 are located in Pearl Harbor and Virginia respectively, and each team has four platoons. Their mission in general is that of special reconnaissance. The SEAL Delivery Vehicle is just a means of insertion. The SEALs cast out, swim ashore, go inland, recon the area, and swim back to their SDVs, which may wait for them on the sea floor. Missions on land can last from mere hours to a week. The SDV allows insertion where large submarines cannot go. SDV personnel waterproof all their gear and since their primary mission is SR they carry all the extra weight of their intelligence gathering equipment. "All we do is recon, dive, recon, dive…"[19]

The support teams are comprised of divers and various technical operatives, such as electricians. The average platoon comprises 12 frogmen, five technical operatives per platoon and a lieutenant. The best part of being an SDV SEAL is the camaraderie as they are always by themselves and thus form tighter bonds than other SEALs. "SDV does not have a high turn-rate as once you get to the teams you really no longer have a choice – you wear the Trident on your chest."[20]

SDV Team 1. (Marcus Luttrell)   SDV platoons also can augment regular SEAL teams.

SPECIAL BOAT TEAMS

SDV transport. (Marcus Luttrell)

NSW platforms include the 11-meter Rigid Hull Inflatable Boat, MK V Special Operations Craft, Special Operations Craft – Riverine. Special Boat Units are located in San Diego, California; Little Creek, Virginia; and Stennis, Mississippi. Special Warfare Combatant-craft Crewmen (SWCC) operate and maintain these state-of-the art, high performance boats used to conduct coastal patrol and interdiction and support special operations missions. Focusing on clandestine infiltration and exfiltration of SEALs and other special operations forces, SWCC provide dedicated rapid mobility in shallow water areas where larger ships cannot operate.[21]

Today all NSW elements can form task units to fulfil any and all operational needs.

TRAINING

The Only Easy Day was Yesterday

BASIC UNDERWATER DEMOLITION/SEAL

Although the organization chart of Naval Special Warfare has transitioned over the years, the basic selection process remains unchanged. Any sailor wishing to become a SEAL has to go through BUD/S – Basic Underwater Demolition/SEAL. In order to attend BUD/S one must request it and receive orders for the course. All those wishing to attend must pass the SEAL Physical Screening Test (PST), which comprises a number of different timed exercises. A 500yd swim using breast and/or sidestroke has to be completed in under 12 minutes and 30 seconds. A ten-minute rest is then followed by a minimum of 42 push-ups in two minutes, a two-minute rest, a minimum of 50 sit-ups in two minutes, a two-minute rest, then a minimum of 6 pull-ups with no time limit. After another ten-minute rest candidates must run one and a half miles wearing running shoes and shorts in under 11 minutes.[22]

BUD/S lasts six months. The instructors are both officers and enlisted men and they are addressed by the trainees as "instructor." The BUD/S yell is "Hooyah," pronounced "Who-yaw."

Upon successful completion of training, the graduate is then assigned to a SEAL team by the Naval Special Warfare Command. Should the individual fail the BUD/S course, he serves out his remaining enlistment according to the needs of the US Navy.

Below is arguably one of the best-written accounts of BUD/S, written more than 30 years ago by Richard Whiteside, a former Navy SEAL officer and Annapolis

Boats lined up in front of BUD/S Medical just before sunset. The students of the current First Phase class were at evening chow. After chow they would have run back, jocked up, and got ready for a night evolution of surf passage. (Authors' collections)

graduate, who went through this training from August 1975 through January 1976. Little has changed in BUD/S training in the years since then:

The principal goal of Basic Underwater Demolition School (BUD/S) training is to develop the individual physically and mentally while instilling a sense of team loyalty and unity. The course is intentionally demanding to weed out those who lack commitment, drive and, most importantly, self-motivation. Training runs 26 weeks and is reputed to be the most demanding military training worldwide. Attrition is typically 75-80%. My class started with 69 sailors and graduated 16 of that original group (plus a couple who were rolled back). For those who survive the six-month BUD/S training, there is then a six-month probation period in the teams. Only after successfully completing BUD/S and the six-month probation period does the individual receive the Navy Special Operations designation, the Budweiser [Trident]. Once you reach the teams you go on to further training such as Jump school, HALO training, Ranger training, Army Special Forces training, and SERE [Survival, Evasion, Resistance, Escape].

BUD/S training is divided into three phases that are under constant review and updated periodically to remain current with new concepts and Naval Special Warfare (SEAL team) operation requirements.

When I attended BUD/S, the first phase lasted six weeks and was essentially dedicated to breaking you down physically and mentally and then rebuilding you—solid, focused, more confident—with a strong sense of inner and outer strength and devotion to the team.

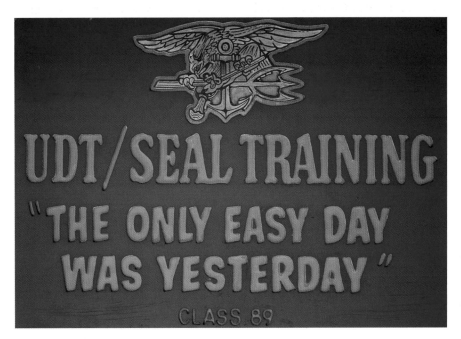

Every class donates a class gift to the BUD/S center. This is class number 89's gift. It is mounted on the wall facing the grinder for all the students to see. (Authors' collections)

In this phase you are pushed beyond any physical limits you dreamed possible. Then you are pushed further until you physically collapse to prove you that you do have limits, that you are mortal and that you must constantly be aware of these limits.

Phase One also includes the notorious Hell Week, which begins Sunday midnight following the fourth week of training. There is probably nothing more ominous to the BUD/S trainee than knowing he has to face Hell Week. This is a week of intense training. Evolutions run continuously, 24 hours a day from Sunday night until the following Saturday morning. My memories of this week are vivid despite getting a grand total of four hours' sleep between Sunday and Friday midnight. However, other than getting meals every six hours, you never know what evolution is next and you constantly question whether you have enough strength or will to survive the moment. You literally take things one evolution at a time repeatedly telling yourself – "I can make it through this evolution" – refusing to think beyond the task at hand for fear of being overwhelmed.

The second phase lasts ten weeks and focuses on those skills unique to Naval Special Warfare (NSW) – specifically: weapons, demolitions, team tactics, and beach surveys. In this phase you have to survive both San Clemente Island training – with the 3.5- and 6-mile ocean swims – and Water Week where you do two or three beach surveys a day. Water Week meant spending hours daily in the warm (ha! 50–55 degree) California ocean water.

The third phase, also ten weeks long, consists of SCUBA [self contained underwater breathing apparatus] and underwater tactics and includes some 100 dives – day and night – using both open-circuit and closed-circuit (re-breather) systems.

The front door of the Phil H. Bucklew Building Naval Special Warfare Center, better known as BUD/S. Photograph taken in 2008 (Authors' collections)

As I mentioned earlier, attrition typically runs 75–80%. Classes include both officers and enlisted men and everything is competitive. During Hell Week if your boat team comes in first in any event, you rest while everybody else is harassed. Dropping out is so simple it was difficult. All you have to say is "I quit." You are gone, and there is no taking it back. In classroom testing if you fail to make the required score you take a second, harder test, and failing this you are dropped from training. Starting day one, the trainee is instilled with two slogans, "THE ONLY EASY DAY WAS YESTERDAY" and "IT PAYS TO BE A WINNER!"

First Phase

Trainees are physically and psychologically broken down and then systematically restructured into confident and highly competent combat swimmers. One of the first evolutions, which seems to be standard for almost all military basic training, is to have your head shaved. In my case this was my third such occasion, first at Great Lakes boot camp when I enlisted in 1970, next at the Naval Academy during plebe summer (1971), and finally BUD/S (1975).

The phrase most often heard in First Phase is, "DROP," meaning "hit the floor and pump out 35 push-ups." There also is a corollary to this action – if one person is dropped, everybody drops. By my own count, each of us performed over 500 push-ups every day. In this phase when you are "dropped" you do 35 push-ups at a clip. In second phase it's 50 and 100 in third. In first phase it seems that all you do is "drop." By the end of this phase physical changes are dramatic. For us, it seemed like all we did was push-ups and run. Trainees run everywhere including to and from the mess hall in formation (about a mile each way). Physical Training (PT) runs are tough because the distance and pace are not predefined. Some runs are at a very fast pace for about a mile, while others involve varied paces covering distances ranging from 2 to 5 miles. In all cases, you are pushed to your physical limits, and you try to pace yourself to be sure to complete the evolution. It becomes a mind game as well as a demanding physical evolution and you are always reminded that it takes a team effort to survive.

The uniform for the day is khaki swim trunks, olive drab (OD) T-shirt, and jungle boots. Days begin at 0500 hours, at which time trainees are required to be in formation in the compound for an hour of PT. If you slack off during PT, you are directed to "Hit the bay," which means running some two hundred yards to the ocean, jumping in and running back. As an alternative, a tub in the compound is filled with water so you hit the tub and that way you don't miss any exercises. PT is followed by pull-ups and dips or a rope climb or all the above. Then it's off to breakfast. (I'll probably never see another eating frenzy quite like meals during BUD/S.) Everybody has huge appetites. One of the amazing things about training is that those arriving at training overweight, lost it and those, such as myself, who are on the thin side, gained weight.

One of the toughest parts of PT is flutter kicks, especially when you are required to do 350 four count flutter kicks. In order to build up stomach muscles we often did flutter kicks between evolutions. It seems that the more you do the more you can do. All I can say is it works. In fact I still do them from time to time.

Other weekly evolutions included two or three 4-mile timed runs on the hard packed sand, two 2-mile ocean swims, and the obstacle course.

Classroom training ranges from basic first aid, including emergency tracheotomy and stabilization of large wounds, to communications, prisoner handling, swimmer cast and recovery from speeding boats, and other basic combat training. There are swimming evolutions in the pool to teach basic combat swimmer technique. In the first week there is a requirement to swim 50 yards underwater in one breath. Most required several attempts to accomplish this, and those who could not make the required distance were dropped. Then there is Inflatable Boat Small (IBS) training (paddling in and out of surf zones), distance rowing, and stealth. Then there are the night drills: IBS rock portage, ocean swims, combat stealth and concealment.

The fifth week of training is Hell Week and this evolution is such an important part of the training that I have made it a separate section. In the week prior to Hell Week we had one memorable and humbling evolution, known as "Wet Suit Appreciation Day." Up to this point all ocean swims were conducted with wet suit tops as part of the standard uniform. On Wet Suit Appreciation Day we were pushed even harder than usual. The day started with an even more rigorous PT, followed by pull-ups, dips, and rope climb. Later that day we had a long run (16 miles) and we ran the O-course. The final evolution was a 2-mile ocean swim without wet suits. Only two swim pairs completed the full swim. It was truly an eye opening experience.

The physical difference wrought by BUD/S. The photo on the left was taken on the first day of BUD/S, the right-hand photo was taken post-Hell Week. (Richard Whiteside)

My partner and I started the swim and about a quarter mile into it we suddenly seemed to be caught in an unusually strong current running against us. I was stroking out with all my might but just wasn't gaining any headway. Then I got a cramp in my right calf and as I reached down to work it out my other calf cramped, then suddenly, my stomach and arms went into total cramps. From my partner's point of view the current wasn't getting stronger, I just started taking shorter and shorter strokes. I thought I was giving a full, long strong stroke, but I wasn't. My partner literally had to pull me to shore. I crawled out of the water onto the warm, dry sand and just laid there for a good five minutes before I started to recover. I felt exhaustion from the cramping for the next week. Believe me, I will always remember this day. The lesson was clear: cold water is deadly, it can alter your perception, and it can and will significantly diminish your ability to function on the rest of your mission. In reality, this was a day designed to keep us grounded because at this point we were starting to feel invincible.

Hell Week

Anticipation and tension build to a tremendous level a few days before the start. You know others have survived, but you don't know exactly what the evolutions are and you experience serious doubts about your ability to survive the week. Believe me, horror stories abound.

Lieutenant Junior Grade Richard E. Whiteside, Jr., January 4, 1978. (US Navy)

Just prior to the start of the week, most of us were busy hiding small caches of candy and brandy. Those in classes ahead of us had told us that this would be a smart move to ensure energy when between meals, and we were warned that the instructors look to find and then confiscate these caches. My sister, who was in San Diego with me during training, came out during Hell Week and sneaked in hot chocolate on one occasion. She and a friend did the same for the class after us, but her partner screwed up and got them caught. The trainees paid for it dearly.

We were put in boat crews of six or seven men based on height, and nearly every evolution was a competition for points. The boat crew with the most points on the last night of Hell Week was secured first, typically some six hours ahead of the last place crew. Additionally, the winning crew on most events or races got to rest while the others were harassed (it pays to be a winner!).

The week traditionally starts with the instructors bursting into the barracks shooting off M60s (with blanks), and throwing M80 firecrackers under bunks and in the hallways – a lot of smoke and confusion. However, our week started very quietly. Around 1:00am the

This is a brass plaque commemorating Captain Phil H. Bucklew (1914–91), after whom the BUD/S training center is named. Captain Bucklew is a legendary figure within Navy circles. He devoted his entire Navy career to scouting, raiding and intelligence. He was one of the Navy's first frogmen and a charter member of the Navy's Scouts and Raiders of World War II. Prior to the Allied invasions of Normandy, Salerno, and Sicily, Captain Bucklew was one of the men who scouted the beaches. He also conducted an overland scouting trip over 400 miles of Chinese coastline near Hong Kong, without being intercepted by Japanese occupation troops. In 1964, Captain Bucklew led a study team to investigate the Communist infiltration of South Vietnam. (Authors' collections)

instructors came and gently told us to form up in the bleachers in the rear of the barracks (near the ocean). We knew this was going to be trouble.

The first evolution was "Introduction to whistle drills," something that was not to make sense until the following Friday. We were required to perform this drill frequently during the week. The drill went like this: when you hear one blast from a whistle, everybody drops to the ground with mouth open and hands over your head. Two blasts on the whistle meant to crawl in a low profile on your elbows toward the person blowing the whistle. Three blasts on the whistle meant to resume what we were previously doing. To demonstrate this, our first orders were to strip down naked to our life jacket. Then we were lined up facing the ocean and told to march. About the time the water was to our knees a whistle was blown once. We all dropped into the water in the proper position, floating with the waves. Then two blasts, we started crawling toward the instructor. Then as we reached the point where the waves were just cresting over our shoulders the whistle was blown once. This meant to stay there, in place, in the proper position (hands over head and mouth open). Then they really played games. Three blasts on the whistle – meaning to continue what we were instructed to do, march to sea. All told, we spent a good 20 to 30 minutes marching in and out of the freezing surf zone. Talk about a case of tiny balls.

We were finally secured and given five minutes to be in the compound in formation at the bell wearing flippers, long green pants inside out, life jacket and face mask. We were late getting to formation and as a result the officers were sprayed down with water while the enlisted men had to run and jump into the ocean and return. It was obvious. After four weeks of instilling teamwork they now were trying to divide us, to challenge our unity.

The next evolution was supposedly a night swim without wet suits. However, we were not issued flares (required for all night water evolutions) nor was there a safety boat anywhere to be seen. Most of us knew this was only a threat, but it had the desired effect. As we entered the water the instructors told us we could secure from the evolution if at least one person quit. We never got to test who had the stronger will because two guys refused to enter the water and were dropped from training.

Next we were instructed to change into our greens with life jacket, meaning long green pants, OD T-shirt, and jungle boots. The standard issue life jacket is an inflatable gray type with double CO_2 cartridges. On night evolutions we attached to the life jacket a battery light and K-bar knife.

Thus our journey began. The next evolution started by paddling out into the ocean and down the beach toward the Hotel Del Coronado (about a mile). At that point we came back in through the surf zone and portaged across the strand into the bay (a hundred yards or so). Once in the bay we paddled to the base a short distance away. When we arrived we

BUD/S helmets. These examples belong to Marcus Luttrell, and are displayed on a shelf in his house in Texas. The blue helmet is from Second Phase and the red helmet is from Third Phase of BUDS. (Authors' collections)

had to tread water and sing songs while doing it for a good hour. At least the bay water was much warmer than the ocean.

During the few breaks allowed, trainees shot pool or called friends on the phone, anything to stay awake. The fear was that if you went to sleep it would be too difficult to wake up and go on. This was almost as difficult as any physical evolution. We ate every six hours. Some fell asleep in their food. It took a lot of discipline to stay awake, especially during meals. As a whole, we just refused to be bested by the training, especially knowing these instructors survived the same treatment.

Late in the week many people suffer from hallucinations. In one case while paddling on the bay one of our crews had a man who started yelling for everybody to stop and he started frantically back paddling. He swore there was barbed wire stretched across the bay directly in front of the IBS. Others threw their paddles away after they appeared to turn into snakes. Some would wander off.

To describe in detail all of the evolutions I can recall would fill too many pages. I will describe the most significant and list all the others. I can no longer recall the order of these, but I do remember: retaking the PT test required to gain access to BUD/S; a naked night pool swim, freezing, huddling to keep warm, portaging our IBS on our heads whenever traveling on land; banding the IBSs together to create Frog grottos, a home to huddle in and keep warm; the O-course; PT utilizing telephone poles – each boat crew carried a pole, raced around with a pole, did sit-ups with the pole on our chest, it took total team cooperation.

The ship's bell outside of the First Phase instructors' office. This bell serves two purposes. If a student wants to see the instructors about something, he will grab the bell with his hand and strike it only once, preventing the bell from ringing out. However a quitter rings it three times, then places his helmet right below it. (Authors' collections)

There were mud flat evolutions in the mud flats at the border between the US and Mexico. It was some 13 miles by IBS to reach this area where we spent the night. Team races such as boat crews sitting bunched up one behind the other in the mud stroking backwards as a team through the mud, or diving into mud that is 2ft deep – you got points for the best dive like a swan dive. It was a lot of fun and compared to the air the mud was warm. After the mud flats evolutions we would clean off in the ocean. There was also a night drill at the mud flats. Individually, we were to sneak into camp without getting caught. The instructors were very devilish at times. For example, one instructor noticed a trainee hiding in a bush, but instead of exposing him and sending him back to the start, he relieved himself into the bush. Well, maybe he really didn't see the trainee… sure!

One night we practiced landing our IBS on the rocks at the Hotel Del Coronado. Then we ran team races of quarter, half, and 1 mile with the IBS on your head. The winning team rested while the other teams hit the bay then had to roll in the dry sand (called making sugar cookies because that's what you looked like). It's amazing how much weight sand adds. It definitely paid to be a winner.

In the middle of the week, there was a 4-mile timed run. By this time you were so loose that it felt effortless, I didn't even sweat and ran my best time. By Wednesday, it felt like you were gliding on ice, everything was in automatic.

Friday was "So-sorry" day, pronounced "so-sollie" with a Japanese accent, an obvious carry over from training during WWII. On this day we went to the Black Lagoon, a pit of black standing water about a mile down the beach from BUD/S compound. [This no longer exists.] The area surrounding the pit is filled with millions of discarded oyster shells. Across the deep pit is a two-rope bridge. One rope to stand on and another at shoulder height used for balance.

In the area surrounding the pit the instructors had strategically located quarter lb block of demolitions (at least that's what I was told). The instructor in charge used one blast on the whistle to drop us then two to get us crawling combat style. They worked it so that we were crawling in a tight group. They led us by use of the whistle into areas where the demolition charges were staged on the outside. Then it came. One blast on the whistle to drop us face first to the ground, hands over the head, mouth open. Demolition charges were set off all around us, each time preceded by "Oh, So-sollie"… BOOM. We were moved from area to area followed by explosions, and all I recall is the instructor's voice "So sollie." (The reason your mouth was open was to allow the inner and outer ear to equalize as the pressure front passed.)

After they had their demolition fun with us we moved on to the rope bridge. Naturally, we had to cross the bridge while the instructors shook us off. Nobody made it across.

After we were all dropped into the water, we were given box lunches right there at the pit. This is when the final blow came. As we sat along side of the pit, in the middle of this great meal they set off a demolition charge hidden in the water. The charge blew the water up in the air and then it all rained down on us. We all hunched over our meals and waited

The latest victims of Class 267, 2007. These helmet liners belong to the sailors who have quit BUD/S. This photo was taken three days into First Phase. (Authors' collections)

for the water to stop falling. Then we went back to eating our lunch as if nothing had happened. It was so surreal.

On Friday afternoon we did a tour of the base, portaging the IBS on our heads. After five days of carrying the IBS, the pain down your spine made it feel like it was on fire, and the pain coupled with exhaustion brought uncontrollable tears to many.

Friday night brought a scavenger hunt. Boat crews in their delirium have to decipher riddles that are clues to a destination. When you think you understand the clue, you tell the instructor where you will meet him, then you take off. If you are right, there is an instructor waiting with another riddle. If you are wrong, he gives you the same clue again. Some trips were miles long. This continues all night. Boat crews are secured that night based upon the number of points accumulated during the week. My boat crew led the whole week by a large margin, and we were secured at midnight. The last boat crew was released about 0600 hours.

The following morning we did PT. Everybody had swollen joints. The swelling was so severe that most of us could not get our boots on without unlacing them completely. PT was a mixture of real exercises and jest: the exercises included "eye openers": opening and closing your eyes on command while lying on your back in the warm sun. The real trick was trying not to fall asleep when you closed your eyes; "Sky push-ups": lying on your back pushing the sky away. Believe me, by this time just lifting your arms was difficult. The final evolution was a threat by the instructors to make us row to the Mexican border and back (about 26 miles). They told us that we took so long to do this earlier in the week that we were doing it over again. Then they secured us just as we reached the edge of the ocean. Man, I never saw such jubilation as there was when it hit us that Hell Week was over. There just isn't a way to describe the feeling.

You'd think that most of the men quitting training would occur during Hell Week. In fact, we lost only a handful. Most losses were due to the daily grind and academics. However, the week or two following Hell Week was a time of deep depression for many, a result of the stress. I recall going through a brief period wondering if all this really had some meaningful purpose, but by the time Second Phase started I was up and ready to take on new challenges.

Second Phase

Emphasis during the next ten weeks is on the individual. Runs were done without formation (at your own stride) and you just had to keep up with the instructor. In general, these runs were further than the previous phase, but we no longer had to run in formation and sing. Training focused on UDT/SEAL skills, such as:

• Beach reconnaissance
• Beach surveys
• Special weapons (M60, M16, M203, grenade launchers, LAW [Light Antitank Weapon] rockets, etc.)
• Demolition training for land and water
• Platoon/ Squad tactics
• Ambush techniques
• Counter-ambush techniques
• Prisoner handling
• Beach insertions
• Beach obstacle clearance – (loading obstacles with demolition prior to an amphibious assault.)

TYPICAL FIRST PHASE DAILY ROUTINE

0500	PT
0630	Breakfast
0800	Classroom training
1100	O-course, run, or swim
1200	Lunch
1300	Classroom training
PM	O-course, run, or swim
1700	Secure

On average there was a night evolution about once a week. Also, each week there was at least one each of: timed four-mile run, two-mile ocean swim, and O-course run.

Second Phase also included Water Week where we planned and executed two to three beach surveys a day and prepared charts. This was prior to San Clemente.

During Second Phase we twice spent two weeks on San Clemente Island with its own air strip, tower and small facility. This is a stark, barren military training area used by Navy Air, the Marines, and Navy Special Warfare. There is also a Special Warfare compound and areas for both weapons and demolition training. The days were long and the training unbelievably rugged. PT was even more grueling and the longest swims in training were logged here. Swims of 3½ miles and 5 miles. The 3½-mile swim was run to and from a buoy near the shore and one far out.

The 5-mile swim took us around part of the island. This route was particularly difficult, because the currents around some of the bends kept you from making any progress until the tide changed. Naturally there were "rare" occasions when the current was with you and the shoreline whizzed past you. Then there were the kelp beds to deal with, which inevitably tangled your swim gear. It was hard to avoid without swimming way off shore which, of course, would make the swim that much further.

Next to the BUD/S bell hangs an air horn. It is painted green to signify that it belongs to First Phase. Students press it once to let a corpsman know that he is there to complain about a medical injury. Made by a First Phase corpsman, who put the sticker on the horn which says, "Suck it up." (Authors' collections)

Also mounted to a pole in front of the First Phase instructors' office is this tiny music box. Whilst giving the corpsman their medical complaint, students wind up the music box and play the music. (Authors' collections)

At the island, we mastered live-ammunition squad tactics, demolitions on land and in the water, beach reconnaissance and water insertions by boat, IBS, and swimming. All these evolutions were executed day and night. At the end of the island phase, we demonstrated our new skills in a full-blown WWII amphibious assault environment including beach recon, survey, identifying and locating obstacles by type and size and finally planning missions to destroy the obstacle field to ensure amphibious boat lanes to the beach are clear. We swam demolition packs from sea to the surf zone and then did free diving in the surging surf zone water to depths of 8–15ft to tie the demolitions to the varied shaped obstacles.

On this mission, one swim pair ran detonation cord (det cord) around the obstacle field (called a trunk line) while the other swim pairs used teamwork to properly secure the demolitions to the obstacle. (In the surf zone you often have to hang on for dear life while tying the demo packs on the obstacle to avoiding being impaled on the metal spikes protruding from the top of the obstacles.)

In preparation for this training, we practiced tying knots in a 50-foot water tower in the BUD/S compound. We started with knot tying in the water tower at depths of 10–15ft and worked up to 50 foot free dives. You dove down to a line stretched across the tower at the set depth, and an instructor in SCUBA gear had to approve the knots before you could untie it and surface. We were required to tie a number of types of knots used in different underwater situations. There are knots for tying det cord together, for tying the det cord to the trunk line and for tying demo packs to obstacles.

While at San Clemente Island if you screwed up in training they had a special harassment. Once a day they opened up the "Wooden Butterfly Terminal." Wooden

Butterflies are wood pallets that one puts on his shoulder and acts as if he is an aircraft. In the SEAL compound there is a terminal fully stocked. The trainee puts on a set of "wings" and runs in a large circle (called a holding pattern) awaiting permission to take off. When permission is granted, one flight consists of running up a hill around a water tower, a good third to half mile away, and back into a holding pattern waiting permission to land. Some had to make several flights before gaining permission to land.

Third Phase

This was the most enjoyable part of our training and it covered ten weeks of highly focused SCUBA. We completed over 100 dives using open-circuit, semi-closed-circuit and closed-circuit gear. Most dives were compass course drills. Some involved doglegs of 1000 yards on one heading then 500 to 1000 yards on another. Each swimmer memorized the time and how many kicks it took to go 10 yards, and during dives, this is how one judged his distance. We swam in pairs, tethered together by a six-foot line of rope with one swimmer acting as the navigator. The navigator carried an attack board, a neutrally buoyant board with a watch, depth gauge, and compass much like the kick boards used during beginning swimmer training. The navigator swims with his elbows pulled in tight to his side and holds the board so that, as he swims he can view the board. His buddy acts as a lookout, swimming slightly above and to one side and generally keeps some physical contact such as resting a hand on his partner's shoulder or holding lightly on to part of his life jacket.

Another gift from a graduating class, this is a model of the "Creature from the Black Lagoon" from the film of the same name. This was one of the nicknames given to "frogmen," the WWII predecessors of the modern-day SEALs. (Authors' collections)

THE SEAL CODE

Similar to other US military branches and units the Navy SEALs created a code of conduct for their personnel. This code is meant to best capture the essence of the Navy SEAL.

Loyalty to Country, Team and Teammate
Serve with Honor and Integrity On and Off the Battlefield
Ready to Lead, Ready to Follow, Never Quit
Take Responsibility for your Actions and the Actions of your Teammates
Excel as Warriors through Discipline and Innovation
Train for War, Fight to Win, Defeat our Nation's Enemies
Earn your Trident every day

(Source: US Navy)

Night swims are interesting especially in the bay. Day visibility is only a few feet, but at night if skies are clear and there is moonlight you can sense light but enjoy no real visibility.

Our objectives included navigating to a vessel at anchor. You start the dive by taking a bearing of the intended target then diving to 10–15ft down and staying on the heading. I found two ways to tell, in the murky water, when I was at the target. The first is that all remaining light suddenly disappears. If I put the illuminated compass dial to my facemask I couldn't read it. That's when you know you are then under your target. The other method is when you bump into it with your head. On my first dive I was the navigator, when everything suddenly went pitch black. I lifted my head to go up… and bong! We indeed were there. I was so startled that I laughed. Well, as best as I could with a regulator in my mouth.

Night swims are interesting evolutions. In clear, tropical waters during nights with clear skies and a full moon, everything has an eerie, science-fiction look. The water is filled with phosphorescent particles that glow as they hit you. As you swim, there is a constant glow over the top of the attack board. And fish swimming by leave their own phosphorescent trail. In general, fish are curious. You cannot really see them, but suddenly their light trails would flash in front of you. At first this is distracting. You start thinking about Jaws, but then you get used to it. Phosphorescence is very dramatic when submerged underwater on a moonless night.

We also practiced underwater beach surveys and other specific mission-oriented tasks.

Graduation finally came and 16 of the original 69, plus a few roll backs, enjoyed a small but rewarding ceremony in whites. The base CO gave a short address and we were handed our diplomas. Then it was off to the teams where the real training began. This six-month course truly weeds out the uncommitted and those not physically and/or mentally prepared to do whatever it takes to get the task completed successfully.

Picture of the grinder of Second Phase. The students are in Pool Week. The gear in the picture is twin 80s dive tanks, horse collar life jackets, and UDT fins. The deck is wet because the students have just finished practicing jock-up drills. (Authors' collections)

One final point, if you talk to those who have successfully completed BUD/S training, no matter how many years you go back, you will find that all the stories about training are similar. It's amazing. I have listened to others relate stories about their training ten or twenty years before me and I could have sworn they were in my class: the same Hell Week hallucinations, the same expressions and feelings. There is a certain unity in this feeling.[23]

BUD/S AT THE TURN OF THE TWENTIETH CENTURY

Chris Osman's training was spread over two different BUD/S classes after an injury side-tracked him. He entered BUD/S Class 213 in March 1997 and finally graduated in Class 215 in February of 1998. Consistency of the selection process is vital in maintaining the highest standards of any elite unit. Chris Osman wrote this account:

All of BUD/S training is now conducted at the Phil H. Bucklew Center, better known as the Naval Special Warfare Center, located on Coronado Island in San Diego, CA. BUD/S has changed very little since it was first created in 1943 when the first students trained in Fort

Pierce, FL. Many studies and thousands of man hours have been spent trying to figure out what makes the men who succeed in this program different from those who fail, get injured and never recover and continue to train, and the ones who quit… My personal opinion is that either a man has got what it takes and makes it or thinks only of his own personal pain and cannot look past it, so quits.

The weeding out process starts the day you show up to BUD/S. When checking in you must be in your Dress Blue Uniform. You are immediately assigned a person who walks you around to the different parts of the base to get you officially checked in as a student. You are walked around in a group in your uniform carrying a large manila-colored envelope. In that envelope are your orders to BUD/S, medical records, dental records, chest x-rays, and service record. You have to check in with Medical, Dental, Personnel and Administration, and finally Supply to be issued your training gear so you can start pre-training.

The basic issue of gear consists of a couple of sets of Battle Dress Uniforms (BDUs), knife with sheath (usually it is a used one and it is better to go out into town and buy a new one), dive socks, sea bag, Underwater Demolitions Teams (UDT) life jacket, gear belt, boots, a couple of covers, helmet, white t-shirts, and a small piece of rope that is tied to your pants that you use for underwater knot tying, a mask, wetsuit top, wetsuit hood, wetsuit booties and fins. I am still amazed that so much pain can be brought on by so few items.

Pre-training can last up to four or five weeks depending on when your class is scheduled to start the First Phase of training. During this time you wear a white T-shirt under your uniform. This tells everyone that you have not made it through Hell Week. You also wear a standard eight-point uniform cover instead of a helmet. This lets everyone know that you are not in a class. Being in BUD/S is bad enough but not being in a class is the worst. While a student is in pre-training you are assigned to PTRR or Physical Training Rest and Recuperation. PTRR is also where all students injured during training are assigned and is more commonly referred to as "Pathetic Trainee Requests Relaxation."

The daily routine for a student in pre-training is very simple. You muster in the morning and do a roll call, and uniform inspection. Your uniform from head to toe must be squared away. Most of the students fail and hit the surf. Hitting the surf is when you run with a swim buddy out to the beach, jump into the water then run back. Or when the instructors want to take it to the next level you will be told to get wet and sandy. After getting wet you roll in the sand and cover yourself in beach sand. Somehow after the first time, you will continue to find sand in places you did not know even existed on your body, in your gear or barracks room for the next year.

After inspection, the class leaders, the officer in charge of the class (OIC), and the leading petty officer (LPO) meet with the proctor who has been assigned to that particular class. The daily schedule is given to them and the class meets in the pit. The pit is the area behind the PTRR barracks and medical department. A quick meeting is held and the class gets ready for its first evolution of the day. It is changed depending on the training schedules,

Picture of the larger classroom used for First Phase before Hell Week. After Hell Week, the classes switch to the smaller rooms next to the First Phase office. This is on the first floor of SEAL Team 7's original building. (Authors' collections)

but on any given day as a PTRR student you will run, do physical training (PT), and swim at the Combat Training Tank (CTT). In between you will eat chow three times a day which is mandatory, no meals can be missed. You will also be in the pit taking power naps and stretching between evolutions.

You will do this all day everyday until it is time for you to class up. Classing up is when your group is assigned a date to begin First Phase of BUD/S training.

First Phase is the official beginning of a student's journey through 26 weeks of fun, sun, cold, and misery. There is no short supply of the last two. The weekend before First Phase begins the class has a class up and helmet painting party. This will be the last time that all of the people who began together will ever be together as a whole group again. Everyone shaves their head down to the scalp, and shows up with their newly painted green helmet and shows it to the LPO and OIC. They look at everyone's helmet. If any are screwed up there is a little time to fix it before Monday's first inspection. There is definitely excitement in the air as the wives and girlfriends are at the party and it is always an informal gathering.

First Phase has a very strict schedule. When I went through BUD/S in 1997 we mustered as a class at 0430 everyday. The class OIC and LPO get with the boat crew leaders (other officers and petty officers in charge of seven men who make a boat crew). Head counts are given and if a student has quit or one is injured the OIC and LPO must know before seeing any instructors. After muster the class will run to the grinder for Physical Training or as I like to call it Personal Torture. The classes will PT for an hour then run to chow. The chow hall for BUD/S is across the street on the other side of the base one mile from the grinder. Because of this at a minimum a student will run six miles a day just to eat. The running is on the asphalt street and a lot of lower body injuries start to form. The most common are stress fractures in your shins.

After chow the class will run to the next evolution of the day. Usually it is swimming at the CTT to do underwater knot tying, life-saving skills, and drown-proofing. After that the class will run to chow for lunch.

Immediately after chow the class runs back to the BUD/S side of the base and gets ready for another evolution. Depending on the class schedule you will do Inflatable Boat Small training on the beach and in the surf. The small boat drills are designed for one thing and that is team work. There is no way in hell to make it through the surf and back without it. It is also a time for the instructors to quickly see who has a difficult time communicating under pressure. The students who do not perform get singled out but the whole boat crew pays for an individual's mistake.

The class will also do conditioning runs, run the obstacle course, log PT, timed swims, timed runs, and swimmer rescues in the surf. Usually after the beach evolution is over the class will change in the pit and run to the First Phase classroom for classes on surf observations, tide calculations, and core values. During the classes chances of the class getting beat are about 100 percent. "Getting beat" is a slang term used by all students. The instructors do not literally beat on you. It is similar to the Army's term of "getting smoked," which describes the toll taken on the body by the intense physical difficulty of the training or punishment meted out by the instructors.

Everyone is beat down and tired, so staying awake is hard as hell. Everyday someone will fall asleep in class. It happens so fast that you do not even know you fell asleep. The class the instructor is giving comes to a grinding halt and the whole class gets beat.

After the classes you will run to chow and then come back for the class proctor's meeting. After that the class is secured for the night. During the night all students will clean gear, iron uniforms, sharpen knives, clean the UDT life jacket, clean the barracks, study and do homework, as well as stand duty. Even though you are not in class there is very little time for rest. For nine weeks you are always wet, there is not a time you are dry, you are always tired, and no matter how many sweatshirts you wear at night you are always cold. This schedule is the same all way up to the weekend before Hell Week.

After you are secured from Hell Week you go through medical for a final inspection before you are given your brown T-shirt. That dry brown shirt has made grown men cry and to this day is the warmest thing I have ever put on my body.

You are given a brief about sleeping and eating over the weekend. All students are escorted to their room and are under 24-hour watch and surveillance. If you need to get up to use the rest room someone has to walk you to the bathroom and back. The reason is that your body is in a state of shock and recovery from Hell Week. I personally slept for roughly 18 hours before waking up. Now the pain really starts. After shutting down and sleeping for

Dip bars and pull-up bars out on the beach just outside the BUD/S compound. (Authors' collections)

so long your body now has time to tell you just how bad it hurts. Sunday you are allowed to leave the base. Even in bed and bone dry I would still shake and be freezing my ass off.

Following Hell Week is Walk Week. You have the option of wearing running shoes or boots for the week. There is no running and all the PT sessions are for stretching only. It is also the time the class gets into hydrographic reconnaissance classes. This training goes all the way back to World War II and is still used to do underwater mapping before an amphibious assault on an enemy beach. Two weeks of hydro recons and written tests bring First Phase to a close.

Hydro sucks because it involves long hours in the water, and more specifically it is right after Hell Week. All of the students are "hydrophobic" and get cold just smelling the salt in the air from the ocean.

After First Phase is Second Phase. It is commonly referred to as Dive Phase. It is eight weeks in length and focuses on dive medicine, dive physics, open-circuit diving, and closed-circuit diving. The time between the phases is one weekend off after leaving First Phase on a Friday. Over the weekend the students get their uniforms ready for inspection and prep all gear before the start of the next week. The class also paints their helmets blue. Going into Dive Phase is very exciting. For one you are no longer in First Phase, but also this is the phase where a student begins to learn the basic tactics and techniques to become a combat swimmer.

The days are not as difficult physically as in First Phase. The class musters in the morning for PT and runs to chow. When the class gets back it goes straight into the classroom, that is, after hitting the surf or hitting the dip tank. The dip tank is a small tank filled with water that is used to check your diving rig for leaks and bubbles. Because the Dräger, a German made re-breather, is 100 percent closed-circuit the rig cannot have any leaks in the pre-dive before getting in the water.

Classes are all day long with a lot of studying at night. The tests are all written in the classroom and are no joke. A ton of information is given to the students in a short amount of time. The first week is all dive medicine. This focuses on what happens to the body while it is under pressure, the effects of atmospheric pressures on your body and different things that can and do happen under water. Each student is pressed to 140ft in the hyperbaric chamber to see if they can medically handle the effects of that pressure.

Medical training also consists of breathing 100 percent CO_2 gas and slowly going unconscious. This effect causes hypercapnia (a condition where CO_2 builds up in your system) and it is the build up of CO_2 in your blood stream while diving with the Dräger that could happen and the diver must understand the effects. It can be caused by a few things, but the most important lesson is that the students know what it feels like and can recognize the early warning signs. The first week ends with the dive medicine test. It must be passed with a minimum of 70 percent for enlisted and 80 percent for officers.

The second week is dive physics. Dive physics is nothing more than solving physics problems as they apply to atmosphere and pressure. It is taught in the same shotgun manner and must be learned very quickly. Classes begin on Monday of Week 2 and the written test is on Friday. No calculators are used and all of the problems must be solved using long-

Picture of the rope-climb platform for BUD/S PT. The platform is on the beach right next to the dip and pull-up bars. The ropes are approximately 30ft long. (Authors' collections)

THE UNITED STATES NAVY SEAL CREED

In times of war or uncertainty there is a special breed of warrior ready to answer our Nation's call. A common man with an uncommon desire to succeed. Forged by adversity, he stands alongside America's finest special operations forces to serve his country, the American people, and protect their way of life. I am that man.

My Trident is a symbol of honor and heritage. Bestowed upon me by the heroes that have gone before, it embodies the trust of those I have sworn to protect. By wearing the Trident I accept the responsibility of my chosen profession and way of life. It is a privilege that I must earn every day.

My loyalty to Country and Team is beyond reproach. I humbly serve as a guardian to my fellow Americans always ready to defend those who are unable to defend themselves. I do not advertise the nature of my work, nor seek recognition for my actions. I voluntarily accept the inherent hazards of my profession, placing the welfare and security of others before my own.

I serve with honor on and off the battlefield. The ability to control my emotions and my actions, regardless of circumstance, sets me apart from other men. Uncompromising integrity is my standard. My character and honor are steadfast. My word is my bond.

We expect to lead and be led. In the absence of orders I will take charge, lead my teammates and accomplish the mission. I lead by example in all situations.

I will never quit. I persevere and thrive on adversity. My Nation expects me to be physically harder and mentally stronger than my enemies. If knocked down, I will get back up, every time. I will draw on every remaining ounce of strength to protect my teammates and to accomplish our mission. I am never out of the fight.

We demand discipline. We expect innovation. The lives of my teammates and the success of our mission depend on me — my technical skill, tactical proficiency, and attention to detail. My training is never complete.

We train for war and fight to win. I stand ready to bring the full spectrum of combat power to bear in order to achieve my mission and the goals established by my country. The execution of my duties will be swift and violent when required yet guided by the very principles that I serve to defend.

Brave men have fought and died building the proud tradition and feared reputation that I am bound to uphold. In the worst of conditions, the legacy of my teammates steadies my resolve and silently guides my every deed. I will not fail.

(Source: http://www.sealchallenge.navy.mil/seal/images/sealcreed.jpg)

hand written math. There is also a chart that is used to figure out the problems. A chart is needed when converting atmospheric pressure and pounds per square inch as it relates to bar or millibar (millibars are units of pressure and on the Dräger the gauge is measured in bar or millibar instead of pounds per square inch). This chart is on the board for four days and must be memorized because it is erased during the test.

Those who have passed both tests move on to the third week. Pool Week is the start of underwater hell. It starts out with the entire class on open-circuit (compressed air, bubbles escape to surface unlike closed-circuit which is pure oxygen). Basic skills are performed and skills tests are done throughout the week, such as ditch and don. During this test you must remove all of your gear underwater and put it all back on and perform your own underwater diving supervisor check. Once you signal to an instructor that you are done you are inspected. If even one strap is twisted you will be failed. Attention to detail and patience is the name of the game. This same drill must be performed in the dark as well as with a buddy. Doing it with a buddy requires the pair to switch gear under water while breathing off the same regulator and set of tanks.

After all of the training is done for the day the class gets in the water with their tanks, 12lb-weight belt, horse collar life jacket, mask and fins. The class must tread water for five minutes with their hands out of the water. If your hands touch the water you fail and will be pulled out of the water. Those who pass will only do it once. Those who fail will do it everyday until they do it or be failed from the phase.

The fourth week is Pool Competency Week. Pool Comp, as it is known in BUD/S, is when all of the skills you have been working on are put to the test. The final two days are the worst for the students and the most dreaded. While on open-circuit students have to demonstrate their ability to be comfortable under the water. This is done by completing four simple tests.

The students enter the water and are taken to the bottom by an instructor. The student crawls on his hands and knees back and forth along a black tile line at the bottom of the pool. While crawling back and forth the student is put through a simulated surf hit. Your mask is ripped off your face, fins ripped off your feet, regulator ripped out of your mouth and you are tumbled to simulate being hit and tumbled by a wave. You must right yourself and regain your composure. The fins and mask are now gone for the rest of the test.

The next part of the test is a series of interruptions in your breathing apparatus called first, second, and third stage interruptions. First a simple knot is tied into the exhalation hose so you can still inhale air but you cannot blow it out. You must exhale through your nose. The difficulty is not choking and panicking on the bottom. Because your head is pulled to the side by your hose wrapped around your tank valve the mouth piece is not all the way in your mouth. Every time you inhale water floods into your mouth. So you must inhale and drink the water underwater in order to continue to breathe. If you cannot get the knot undone you will need to take off your equipment, untie it and put it back on.

The next test is the same as above except it is with your inhalation hose. So now you can breathe out but not in. Usually this is a simple knot and can be undone while the tanks are on your back. If you cannot get it undone while holding your breath you will have to ditch your tanks and fix it quickly before you run out of air.

The fourth and final test is designed to see all students ditch their gear and calmly perform simple tasks while underwater. This test is commonly referred to as a "Whammy Knot." The instructor will place his hand in front of your face, you will get one deep breath, and the mouth piece is tied into a knot over your valves. The student is then to make every effort to undo the disruption. Only once all possible attempts have been made to undo the knot can you drop the weight belt to the back of your calves, undo the waist and chest strap of your tanks and pull them over your head. After trying in vain to fix it you have to signal to the instructor that you are ready to perform an FSA or Free Swimmer's Assent. After getting a signal from the instructor you must lay your tanks down on the pool bottom, stow all of the straps, stow your mouth piece, shut the air off the tanks, and lay your weight belt on top of the tanks, and give a thumbs up to the instructor. The instructor will bring you to the surface while you exhale all of the air in your lungs. Once on the surface you yell out "I FEEL FINE." You are brought over to the side of the pool and your gear is recovered by an instructor. If you have passed everything you will be passed. If not you will be given three more attempts before being failed from Dive Phase. My class lost 22 people in Dive Phase.

The rest of Second Phase is diving every day with the Dräger re-breather. During the entire phase you must still do PT once a day, and once a week do a timed 2-mile ocean swim, timed obstacle course, and timed 4-mile run. While diving with the Dräger the class is taught how to use the attack board and navigate under water at night. You also learn how to find your way around the bottom of a ship or boat in a harbor at night. The phase is brought to a close with the class doing a ship attack and planting simulated explosives on the ship.

THE SEAL TRIDENT "BUDWEISER"

The SEAL Trident is the most coveted warfare pin in the US Navy. About 15,189 men since 1943 have earned the right to wear one. The Trident is a symbol that is recognized by all military personnel throughout the world. It is representative of all the elements in which the SEAL teams operate: sea, air, and land. The Trident signifies the maritime experience and the SEAL reputation as masters of the sea. The Eagle signifies the ability to strike from the air and watch over America's security. The Flintlock pistol signifies elite land warfare skills and fire power carried into combat. The Anchor signifies the proud heritage of the US Navy and the teamwork with other forces. The Bald Eagle on the Trident is the only symbol or device in the US that portrays the Eagle with its head down. This signifies the Eagle's respect for the fallen who have sacrificed their lives for America's freedom.

(Source: US Navy/Chris Osman)

Third Phase is the longest phase. Third Phase concentrates on land warfare skills and tactics. Again you will have the weekend off as a class to get your gear squared away and paint your helmet red. Going into Third Phase, you start to see the light at the end of the BUD/S tunnel. The light is quickly extinguished the first time you are introduced to the instructors. Third Phase teaches patrolling, hand and arm signals, communications, land navigation, weapons handling, shooting, ambush tactics, counter-ambush tactics, sentry removal, underwater demolitions and obstacle removal, over the beach insertion and extraction, more hydro reconnaissance, rappelling, and explosives, both electric and non electric.

Because of the subjects covered there is a lot of classroom time and a lot of field time. The instructors cut no quarter and if anything are even harder on the students because now, if you make a mistake you could kill someone else. If someone is unsafe doing anything they are taken out of the training immediately.

Some of the training in Third Phase is done locally. The final phase of Third Phase is done out on San Clemente Island. San Clemente Island has been owned by the United States Navy since 1934. It is 55 nautical miles (nm) south of Long Beach. The island is 21nm long and 4½nm wide. When I went through training the class spent four weeks on the island. After returning from the island the class spends one week preparing for graduation. This includes the Command Master Chief's PT which by then is the easiest PT in BUD/S – Hooyah PT – where all graduates are highly motivated. All instructors and students also

This is a picture on the front of one of the BUD/S IBSs. It belongs to the "Smurf Crew": the shortest guys in BUD/S, who are all in the same boat crew. The picture was painted on by a BUD/S class. (Authors' collections)

BUD/S (BASIC UNDERWATER DEMOLITION/SEAL) 2007/8

SEAL training is extremely demanding, both mentally and physically, and produces the world's best maritime warriors. The focus during this training is based on three core pillars:

- Men of Character: The nature of our mission requires men who will uphold the Navy Core Values – Honor, Courage, and Commitment.
- Physical: The nature of our mission also requires men who are physically fit and capable in every environment, especially the water.
- Technical: Finally, maritime special operations require SEALS who are intelligent and can quickly learn new tasks.

Following basic training at Recruit Training Command, Great Lakes, IL, and basic rating training, you will begin Basic Underwater Demolition/SEAL (BUD/S) Training in Coronado, CA. This six-month course of instruction will focus on physical conditioning, small boat handling, diving physics, basic diving techniques, land warfare, weapons, demolitions, communications, and reconnaissance.

First Phase (Basic Conditioning) – 7 weeks – First Phase trains, develops, and assesses SEAL candidates in physical conditioning, water competency, teamwork, and mental tenacity. This phase is eight weeks long. Physical conditioning with running, swimming, and calisthenics grows harder and harder as the weeks progress. You will participate in weekly four mile timed runs in boots, timed obstacle courses, swim distances up to two miles wearing fins in the ocean, and learn small boat seamanship.

The first three weeks of First Phase will prepare you for the fourth week, better known as "Hell Week." During this week, you will participate in five and one half days of continuous training, with a maximum of four hours sleep total. This week is designed as the ultimate test of one's physical and mental motivation while in First Phase. Hell Week proves to those who make it that the human body can do ten times the amount of work the average man thinks possible. During Hell Week, you will learn the value of cool headedness, perseverance, and above all, TEAMWORK. The remaining four weeks are devoted to teaching various methods of conducting hydrographic surveys and how to create a hydrographic chart.

Second Phase (Diving) – 8 weeks – Diving Phase trains, develops, and qualifies SEAL candidates as competent basic combat swimmers. This phase is eight weeks long. During this period, physical training continues and becomes even more intensive. Second Phase concentrates on combat SCUBA. You will learn two types of SCUBA: open-circuit (compressed air) and closed-circuit (100% oxygen). Emphasis is placed on long distance underwater dives with the goal of training students to become basic combat divers, using swimming and diving techniques as a means of transportation from their launch point to their combat objective. This is a skill that separates SEALs from all other Special Operations forces.

Third Phase (Land Warfare) – 9 weeks – Third Phase trains, develops, and qualifies SEAL candidates in basic weapons, demolition, and small unit tactics. This phase of training is nine weeks in length. Physical training continues to become more strenuous as the run distance increases and the minimum passing times are lowered for the runs, swims, and obstacle course. Third Phase concentrates on teaching land navigation, small-unit tactics, patrolling techniques, rappelling, marksmanship, and military explosives. The final three and a half weeks of Third Phase are spent on San Clemente Island, where students apply all the techniques they have acquired during training.

(Source: Naval Special Warfare Center 2008, http://www.sealchallenge.navy.mil/seal/buds.aspx)

participate in the Commanding Officer's run which is typically a four-mile beach run with instructors and students at a nice and easy pace run to cadence. These are the first times either one of the senior SEALs PT with the graduating students. Later uniform preparations, gear turn in and just a little bit of drinking complete the school.

After BUD/S each student is given ten days to report to Army Airborne School at Fort Benning, GA. The school is three weeks long, broken into Ground Week, Tower Week, and Jump Week. After graduation the class says its goodbyes. Now the class will be broken up because the men are all going to different commands.

Once you check into a team you are assigned to a department. I was assigned to a training cell at ST-3 in Coronado. I was placed on mandatory six-month probation and given an initial gear issue and waited for 6 weeks before beginning SEAL Tactical Training (STT). STT was 14 weeks and built on all of the basic skills learned at BUD/S. After STT I was assigned to Echo Platoon. I trained with the platoon until my probation was over and then had to pass the senior enlisted review board. After that board was over I waited about two or three days before being awarded my Trident. I received my Trident on October 23, 1998.

BUD/S has not changed very much since Chris Osman attended. [See opposite.] Today BUD/S is an "A" (advanced) school and the SEALs have their own rate. Since 1943 all SEALs had a regular rate or job description from the traditional Navy. Now one can join the Navy and go through BUD/S in hopes to get the rate of SO or SEAL Operator. All enlisted SEALs now wear this designation. This means that in tests for promotion SEALs are competing against other SEALs rather than any other people in the fleet doing the same rate.

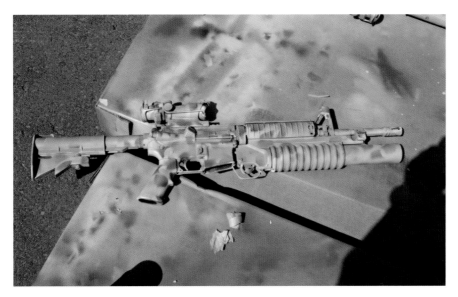

The M4 is the most commonly used weapon in use by the teams today. This one has a 14in. barrel and a Trijicon ACOG sight. The newest versions of this weapon also have a 10in. barrel used for urban warfare. The weapon comes complete with a SOPMOD kit that gives the operator the ability to add different combat optics to the weapon. Aimpoint red dot sights, EOTECH holographic sights, and Advanced Combat Optical Gun sights (ACOG) are the three most commonly used today. In addition to the sights each operator also gets a visible and infared laser, forward mounted assault grip, a weapon mountable light, and a suppressor. This weapon system has replaced the HK MP5 and MP5SD which are no longer in use. (Authors' collections)

Graduating BUD/S does not mean a sailor is an SO. After graduation, all students go to static line and freefall training in San Diego, CA, at Skydive San Diego, a local drop zone about 20 minutes from the team area. After jump training all students go through SEAL Qualification Training (SQT). This training is the same as STT but it also includes cold weather training in Alaska and lasts 16 weeks instead of 14 weeks. After SQT the students are awarded their tridents and assigned to a SEAL team.

The amount of training done before assignment to a team means that SEALs must be considered some of the best-trained and qualified operators in the world. Every new operator checking into his team is qualified in demolitions, both on land and underwater; open- and closed-circuit diving; static line and freefall jumps; as well as cold weather trained. The SEALs are unique in the level of training they receive before they reach the first day of training with their unit or team. After all of the basic training SOs are then assigned to a platoon and attached to a task unit to begin work-up for 12 months before their first six-month deployment.

Some SEALs will also attend inter-service schools, such as US Army Ranger school. The corpsmen at the team must continue their training and go on to Fort Bragg and attend the 18 Delta medical courses for Army special forces personnel. These are six months in length and must be completed before they

Sniping weapons used by US military personnel. (Authors' collections)

Weapons used in sniper training. (Authors' collections)

are assigned to operate in a platoon. It takes a year and a half for corpsmen to complete training from the time they begin BUD/S until they are awarded their Trident and are operational.

A SNIPER IN TRAINING

Sniping created a new paradigm in SEAL tactics, most notably during combat operations in the urban environment in Iraq in 2003. Navy SEAL Kyle from ST-3 provides an account of his enlistment and training experiences from boot camp, to advanced school and finally to sniper school. Kyle joined the Navy in 1999 at the age of 24. He had decided he wanted to be a SEAL after finding out about an uncle who had died in Vietnam:

> I come to find out I had an uncle. It was a little shady, don't know if he was actually a team guy in Vietnam or if he was a riverboat driver, but he died out there and they were telling me all these stories about how Navy SEALs were the greatest thing ever and all this. I thought all right and so I bought into the whole myth that we were the greatest ever, but actually I'm biased and believe it. I decided I wanted to be a SEAL.[24]

Kyle went through boot camp, of which he said, "I thought it was lame. I was prepared to get my ass beat and actually I got more out of shape in boot camp

Picture of an operator's M4 with 10in. barrel, suppressor, PEQ2, IR laser aiming device, ACOG, fixed blade knife, weapons light, SIG P226 9mm w/ Surefire weapon light. (Authors' collections)

than I was when I went in." While in boot camp he took the screening to go to BUD/S. Following boot camp, he went to A-School:

I went to intelligence specialist school 'cause I thought after I joined the Navy that I wanted to do something cool and the Navy doesn't have a lot that's cool to offer. So I thought you know, intelligence specialist, like kind of be a half-assed spy maybe. I didn't know anything about it so that's what I went to do and came to find out that's one of the longer fucking A-schools. Four months, it was right there at Dam Neck [Virginia]. So being up there I got to see DevGru running around with all sorts of cool toys. There I actually got into better shape.

However, frustratingly for Kyle, "they didn't have enough instructors so they had to limit the guys coming into BUD/S." So to fill the time he had to do scruff duty:

Basically you're going to BUD/S but they don't have room for you yet in the class. So you have to go somewhere and they just PT or whatever. And there are three main locations where you go to: BUD/S and just sit there, or Little Creek or back to boot [camp]. They sent me to Tennessee. And then when I got there I was working for the detailers and I actually got screwed 'cause you're a bitch boy for them and you answer the phones, and do all the paperwork and stuff and they didn't want to let me go so I ended up staying there for eight months. But then finally I got to go, the good thing was the detailer said he'll write in my orders that I can go to any team I wanted to go to. So I told him I said I want to go to SOCOM. It was right before Farce 21 [NSW21]. I want Team 3, they're the Middle East platoon.

Kyle finally joined BUD/S Class 231, but he perforated an eardrum and graduated with Class 233. After BUD/S he went through jump school at Benning, then to four months of SQT, just after they changed from STT to SQT: "I was actually in the second class of SQT. Second or third class." Kyle received his Trident at the Team after doing an "oral board":

> Had to go to each department, had a little sign-off list. Had to talk to each department head and once they felt they were comfortable they would sign it off and then once you had them all signed off you go to the Chief's Board and then they drill the shit out of you.

Kyle then joined Charlie Platoon. After his first deployment to the Middle East he went through SEAL Team Sniper School during post-deployment leave. The school was arranged in three sections:

> You got your PIC which is all the camera and computer shit, and then the next one is Scout, which is basically your stalking, your field craft, your hide sites – everything. Then the last sequence is called the Sniper portion and basically you're shooting, you still have

Sniper training in Indiana. The student is trying to get used to taking shots from uncomfortable positions. (Authors' collections)

some stalks in there and field craft, but it's not as intensive, it's mainly just you shooting. And it's about a three-month-long school.

The West Coast Sniper School at Coalinga, CA, was closed because of valley fever (a fungal infection of the lungs), so Kyle's training took place at several locations:

… the PIC was all done at the Stick, the Elephant Cages, which is the NSW training facility, formerly owned by NASA. Then the Scout portion was at Pendleton, and it was right after the fire so it sucked [in terms of camouflage]. You had to crawl around and get pissed off at all these instructors who were like "Oh yeah, you're not going to see where I'm coming from." Pendleton was also where we did our shooting too. But now we've combined the Sniper portion of it with the East Coast and it's in Indiana. We got a brand new .300 now too, or a new model, it's got an AI (Accuracy International) with a folding stock. It's still a 26in. barrel but the next mod that comes out is going to be a 24in. barrel with threaded suppressor. SOCOM right now is working on a new .338 round and it's going to take place of the .300. It was going to be the .408 CheyTac [Cheyenne Tactical] cartridge but the CheyTac is made for a specific round and they cannot mass-produce that round so we can't go with them. I shot that gun and it is outstanding. You can shoot it at 2,500yds, and it outshoots the .50. The .338, it'll shoot about 2,200[yds].

VISIT BOARD SEARCH AND SEIZURE TRAINING

Changes in warfare in the late 20th and early 21st centuries have meant that the SEALs have had to train for new types of missions, such as Visit Board Search and Seizure (VBSS). When taking over a ship the objective of the initial assault is to gain control of the ship, and secure the unknowns (the ship's crew). After the ship's crew is secured the platoon does a methodical search throughout the ship. Once the ship is secured and all personnel are accounted for with the ship's captain, the MIF (Maritime Interdiction Force) team is called up to take the ship and ship's personnel to a holding area. The MIF team is usually from a smaller ship like a destroyer or fast frigate. The MIF teams are the ones used for the compliant ships. A compliant ship will stop, drop anchor and allow the Navy to search it for any contraband.

Chris explains the different techniques available to the SEAL platoon in a takedown of a non-compliant vessel:

Doing ship takedowns is a mission that the SEAL teams are tailored for. It is a maritime target, and they can be assaulted from air and by sea. When I was doing these types of missions my platoon would either be on a ship, or we would sit on the Mark Vs in a small

flotilla of boats. If we were on a ship we would be on stand-by 24-7 for weeks at a time. All of our gear was staged and we could jock-up [gear-up] in less than ten minutes and ready to board a helicopter to fast-rope onto the ship. The helicopters and crews were on stand-by as well so all of the ropes are rigged to the helicopter and checked everyday to ensure they are ready to go. A brief is held daily to give the platoon call signs and frequencies for the helicopters and other assets in the area.

VBSS training gone horribly wrong. (US Navy)

Another way of taking a ship down is by doing what is called a hook and climb. The hook and climb is done by racing up to the target vessel in a RHIB [Rigid Hull Inflatable Boat] driven by the SBT [Special Boat Team] detachment. The detachment or DET is the same DET that a platoon works with during the work up cycle before deployment.

The Platoon will usually be in a Mark V with all of the platoon gear secured to the back deck. The 2 RHIBs will be in between two Mark Vs.[25]

Sometimes the Arabian [Persian] Gulf has very rough water and it is very cold in the winter. The guys in the RHIBs take a beating and they would go out night after night for eight to ten hours getting their asses beat and soaked from head to toe. They never complained and were very dedicated to keeping those boats working. They were an extension of our platoon and there is no way the VBSS mission could have been performed without them.

Chris Osman recalls a tragic incident during VBSS training:

On December 19, 1999, while my platoon was training with a Force Reconnaissance [United States Marine Corps] platoon off the coast of San Diego, the SBT guys saved the Marines' lives after their helicopter crashed into the water. Our platoons were doing joint exercises for the up-coming deployment. Our target vessel was the re-supply ship the USS *Pecos*. It was a simulated nighttime hit in broad daylight. We had to do the hit during the day because the Marine helicopter pilots were not qualified to insert an assault team onto a moving ship at night. My platoon was to do a hook and climb to secure the flight deck and hold security outside while the Marines fast-roped onto the back deck of the ship. Once on the back deck the Marines would assault the ship. We did one run the day before and the helicopter was only about 10ft off the deck while the

Marines fast-roped in. Because of this the next day our platoon OIC told me and the two other guys on the flight deck to move toward the superstructure when we saw the helicopter coming in. I looked and saw the helicopter approaching, and moved. As I watched the helicopter approach it flared and it hit the back of the ship. It actually landed on the ship but its rear wheel was stuck in the metal safety net at the end of the flight deck. The pilot powered up and because the wheel was stuck the helicopter flipped over and hit the water on its side. As the helicopter was falling, the Marine in the hell-hole (the hole in the bottom that you fast-rope out of) dove out before the helicopter hit the water. The helicopter immediately flipped over. It was on the surface upside down for about 20 seconds before it sank. While it was sinking the two RHIBs that had just inserted my platoon raced up and the guys from the DET put their fins on and jumped in and saved a couple of the Marines from drowning. Unfortunately six Marines and one Navy corpsman died that day. The helicopter was a CH-46 Sea Knight. The platoon commander of the Force Reconnaissance Platoon was Capt. Erik Kapitulik. Killed in the accident were: Gunnery Sgt. James Paige Jr., Staff Sgt. William C. Dame, Petty Officer 1st Class Jay J. Asis, Staff Sgt. David E. Galloway, Staff Sgt. Vincent A. Sebasteanski, Staff Sgt. Jeffrey R. Starling, Cpl. Mark M. Baca.

On April 5, 2000 Echo platoon from ST-3 took down the largest ship since these types of missions started in 1991. The name of the ship was the *Akedemik*. It was a Russian flagged vessel and was smuggling over 90,000 metric tons of Iraqi oil. Chris Osman recalls:

My platoon was on a fast frigate that was patrolling in the Arabian Gulf at the time. During the day (the platoon's down time), intel was passed that this ship was meeting up with another vessel to do a transfer of oil at sea. The Navy monitored the transaction from a far distance. At night the ship traveled into international waters. My platoon was put on alert that day. As darkness fell my platoon was told we were going to take the ship down. The platoon loaded into a helicopter and flew to the target. The flight was about six to seven minutes. As we approached the target the fast rope was kicked out the door. I was a communicator for the platoon and I was the number 6 man on the rope. As I grabbed the rope and went out the door I looked at the ship for the first time. It was absolutely massive. It had an eight-story superstructure and it even had a swimming pool outside on the back deck of the superstructure. I hit the deck and joined the platoon on the port side of the ship as we made our way up the superstructure. Once we made it to the bridge we assaulted the bridge, taking control of the ship's wheel (helm) and powered it down. One of the platoon members turned the ship to course 180 degrees to keep it in international waters. A tactic used by some smugglers once they know an assault force has boarded the vessel is to lock the wheel, turning the ship out of international waters. What they are basically doing is trying to cause an international incident for the United States. The rest of the platoon hit the engine room and aft steering. Once those spaces were secured we mustered the crew for a head count. The crew was checked against the ship's manifest as well as their personal documents. One of the ship's crew was a little belligerent and was trying to take pictures of the platoon. He was detained and his pictures were erased. The ship was taken down without incident. The ship and its oil were later sold at an auction.

Another real-world VBSS mission was conducted by Navy SEAL Tom and his teammates from ST-8 in February 2002. From Bahrain the SEALs were transported in a US Navy C-2 twin-engine cargo plane to the USS *Roosevelt* aircraft carrier, from where they would conduct VBSS missions in the Persian Gulf. During their time on the carrier, ST-8 executed five ship takedowns.

One night, the platoon was on stand-by when intelligence came down and informed them that a ship was coming from India and was headed north through the Persian Gulf. The key information regarding the ship was that it carried a person who was somehow linked to al-Qaeda. The platoon was told to prepare. The plan called for Tom's SEAL platoon to leave the carrier and link up with another ST-8 platoon on the USS *Shreveport*, an amphibious dry dock ship. The operations order directed one platoon to be the Boat Assault Force (BAF) while the other platoon was the Helicopter Assault Force (HAF). At approximately 0200 hours the two platoons staged.

As the boats were moving in toward the target during darkness, the HAF loitered far enough away not to give away its position and alert the targeted ship. The SEALs from the BAF hooked onto the side of the ship to begin the assault and the two helicopters descended from their altitude, allowing the second platoon to fast-rope onto the aft of the ship. Because of the height of the antennas and booms on the vessel, the SEALs fast-roped from 90 to 100ft.

The BAF platoon was designated to take down the captain's bridge of the ship, while the HAF was designated to take down the lower half of the superstructure and secure the engine room and aft steering. The BAF platoon made their way to the target area. They set up on the port side and made entry after sliding the door open and throwing flashbangs into the bridge to temporarily stun any crew members in there. The helmsman on watch was zip-cuffed and the platoon moved into the skin of the ship. After the bridge, aft steering, and the engine room were secured, the two platoons started clearing and searching the remaining rooms and spaces of the ship. The two platoons breached more than 50 doors and captured more than 20 personnel. The high value target (HVT) was not among them. He was not on board.

The Maritime Interdiction Force (MIF) team was called in from the USS *Shreveport* and the SEAL platoons left before sunrise. Both platoons were picked up by the ship's RHIBs and taken back.

TOM'S VBSS MISSION *(Authors' collections)*

GOPLATS

Gas and Oil Platforms or GOPLATs perform a valuable function for the US economy by providing natural gas and oil from deep wells beneath the ocean floor. They are all located offshore, so the responsibility for protecting this national interest lies with Naval Special Warfare. The GOPLATs are only accessible from the air and from the sea, and only the Navy SEALs have the capability to assault them from both.

GOPLATs are easily accessible and rarely defended, which makes them a target for terrorists. The platforms are staffed by civilians working for a gas and oil supplier, who are usually no match for terrorists. Once a platform has been secured, it can be used as a means for the terrorists to get media exposure for their cause; the workers may be used as hostages, to try to extort money from the oil companies; or anti-aircraft munitions may be launched from the platforms. The first mission of Operation *Iraqi Freedom* was for the SEALs to capture two GOPLATs (see Part IV).

All SEAL platoons practice retaking a GOPLAT with an assault force, and destroying an enemy GOPLAT to deny the enemy vital resources. The retaking of the GOPLAT starts by first getting to the target as a platoon. There are four ways of reaching the target.

First is an assault by air. The platoon or task unit will simply fly in under the cover of darkness, fast-rope onto the target, and begin the assault. This is the least preferred method because a helicopter has to hover for the unit to fast-rope in. The helicopter can easily be shot down with machine-gun fire and RPGs. Adding to the danger is the water. If the helicopter goes down it will almost certainly go into the ocean with everyone on board.

The platoons may also assault the GOPLAT via surface craft. This was the method used for the assaults during Operation *Iraqi Freedom* in 2003. The SBT will insert the task unit as well as provide heavy machine-gun support, and security around the target. The boats will simply pull up to the platform and the assault force will get on the GOPLAT and begin the assault.

Platoons can also insert via surface swimming. The platoon is dropped off by SBT away from the GOPLAT. The platoon swims to the target with all of its gear, on the surface. As the platoon passes under the GOPLAT a ladder will be rigged to the platform and the team will climb on board. Once all operators are out of the water the assault will begin.

The last way to get to the target is by diving to the target on Dräger. The platoon will again wear all of its gear for the assault, including body armor. The platoon will have one man on the attack board who will lead the entire platoon to the target. When the platoon reaches the target all the operators will hold on to the legs and cross members (support structures underneath the GOPLATs) that hold the structure up. All members will start to de-rig their Dräger. Once everyone has sent the signal that they are ready to surface the platoon will all surface together. Once on the surface the Dräger is let go. It is tied to the platform so it will not sink to the bottom of the ocean. A ladder is rigged up and the platoon climbs up. Once on board the platoon will begin the assault.

PART II

SMALL WARS 1989–2003

THE INVASION OF PANAMA 1989

First Blood for SOCOM

OPERATION *JUST CAUSE*

The US military had not been involved in combat since the invasion of the small Caribbean island of Grenada in 1983, and the SEALs were keen to participate in the operation in Panama in 1989. The restlessness among troops who languished in peacetime caused some men to look for action elsewhere in such diverse fields as law enforcement and mercenary work worldwide. But the invasion of Panama foretold a resurgence of American foreign policy reliant on its military strength.

The US invaded Panama on December 20, 1989, following a year of diplomatic tension between the US and Panama, including charges by the US that the dictator General Manuel Noriega was complicit with money launderers and drug traffickers. Noriega had been in power since 1983. A national election was held in 1989, in which Noriega's candidates were defeated, yet were then declared victorious with Noriega's support. One of the rightfully elected vice presidents-elect also underwent a highly publicized beating.

In a statement issued by President George H. W. Bush hours after the invasion started, the reasons cited for the invasion were: the need to safeguard the lives of US citizens in Panama; the defense of democracy and human rights in Panama; to combat drug trafficking; and to protect the integrity of the treaties that governed the neutrality of the Panama Canal. In his statement, Bush claimed that Noriega had declared that a state of war existed between the US and Panama in mid-December, and had threatened the lives of all Americans living in Panama.[26]

SEAL Team 2 during Operation *Just Cause*. In the far distance smoke tendrils can be seen rising from the Commandancia – the headquarters of the Panamanian defense offices. (Chris Dye)

The following day, a Marine lieutenant, Robert Paz, was killed, and a US Navy SEAL lieutenant, Adam Curtis, and his wife were assaulted.

The United States Navy's special warfare component for the invasion of Panama consisted of Naval Special Warfare Group 2 (NSWG-2), headquartered at Little Creek, VA. It was part of the Navy's Task Force White that not only included SEAL platoons of NSWG-2 but also sailors from special boat and countermine units. In total some 707 sailors constituted Task Force White.[27]

One SEAL platoon from ST-4 under Commander Tom McGrath was already on rotation in Panama. An additional four platoons were requested for this invasion and flew in along with other special operations forces (SOF) under the leadership of USSOCOM commander General Wayne A. Downing on December 18, 1989.

The primary missions for the naval special warfare forces were threefold: deny the Panamanian Defense Forces (PDF) the use of their patrol boats in Balboa Harbor; deny Noriega the use of his personal jet at Paitilla Airport; and isolate the PDF at Flamenco Island.[28]

One additional mission was tailor-made for the US Navy's combat swimmers. This operation called for the destruction of Manuel Noriega's other possible means

Map of military operations during Operation *Just Cause*. (DOD)

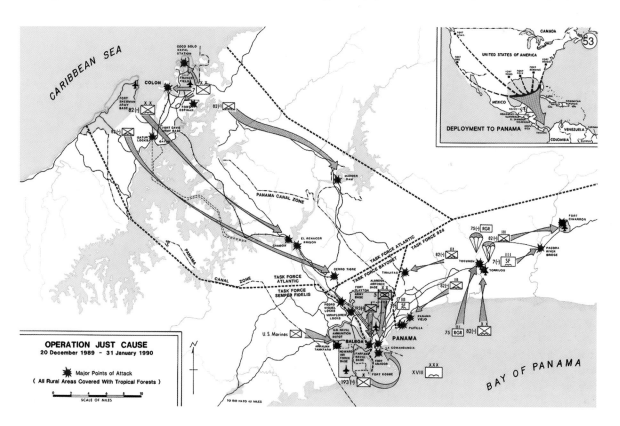

of escape, his boats. The *Presidente Porras* was then berthed at Balboa Harbor and another vessel was anchored at Colon. Balboa Harbor also docked numerous civilian vessels alongside PDF patrol boats. Task Unit Whiskey (TUW), responsible for these operations, was to execute the two missions simultaneously just after midnight on December 20, 1989.[29]

For the mission at Balboa Harbor, the first real combat swimmer mission since World War II, TUW was commanded by Cdr Norman J. Carley. There were two dive pairs. No.1 comprised Lt Edward L. Coughlin and EN-3 (Engineman 3rd Class) Timothy K. Eppley and No.2 comprised ET-I (Electronics Technician 1st Class) Randy L. Beausoleil and PH-2 (Photographer's Mate 2nd Class) Chris Dye. The equipment for each dive pair included an MK-138 Mod 1 haversack armed with an MCS-1 clock and an MK-39 safety and arming device with a MK-96 detonator. In support at Rodman Naval Station was a four-man fire support team, armed with .50-cal. machine guns, 60mm mortars, and an MK19 40mm grenade launcher. Finally, a group of six SEALs in two patrol boats, led by Lt j.g. (Junior Grade) Martin L. Strong, stood by as a quick reaction force in case the dive pairs were compromised.[30]

An SDV clock, top secret at the time this picture was taken, which was used to trigger the explosive attached to General Noriega's boat at H-hour during Operation *Just Cause*. (Chris Dye)

THE BEGINNING

Navy SEAL Chris Dye was an E-5 at the time of Operation *Just Cause*. A short, highly confident man, clearly supremely capable and to the point, he had served in the Navy for three years prior to being accepted into BUD/S Class 129 in 1984. He was dismissed from the class after being involved in a brawl and spent the next two years on a carrier. In 1986, he joined BUD/S Class 142 and upon graduation he joined ST-2, H Platoon in 1987. Like most commandos he suffered through peacetime training and seemingly endless diving. "That is what ST-2 did – dive."[31]

As the political situation grew more intense in Panama and the likelihood of an invasion increased, Special Operations Command stepped up its planning and rehearsal phases. ST-2 deployed to Florida in December 1989, along with other SOF units, to prepare for possible missions. US Army Rangers rehearsed their combat parachute assaults, other SOF units conducted their tasks, and ST-2 continued to dive.

ST-2 re-deployed home to Little Creek, VA, after the training exercise, to enjoy the upcoming Christmas holidays. A handful of SEALs stayed behind that weekend for a training course slated to start the following Monday at Hurlburt Airfield, the home of special operations aviation.[32]

Sometime that weekend the few SEALs remaining in Florida heard that Operation *Just Cause* was good to go. Chris Dye did not believe his swim buddy who told him "To pack up his shit." He was doing laundry and he wasn't going to fall for some trick just to amuse his fellow SEALs. Finally, he relented, packed up, rented a car and "… hauled ass to Atlanta to catch a flight back to Virginia because nobody wanted to miss the flight from Norfolk to Panama." War was calling.

When the combat swimmers arrived at their base in Little Creek they discovered that ST-2 was in isolation, locked down and without communication to the outside world. The SEALs packed up and loaded massive pallets in the icy cold winter weather. Dye's hands were frozen solid after he finished the pallets. Unfortunately, the gear for a SEAL who was not going on the mission was already packed and loaded and it fell to Dye to undo all of his hard work. Three unpacked pallets later Dye found what was needed, removed it, and then repacked the pallets. His hands were even number than before. It was a good thing a combat mission was afoot.

Late that evening the SEALs boarded a packed C-141 for their flight to Panama. The aircrew informed the naval commandos that upon landing they might be engaged by the PDF, because operational security might have been breached. Since the C-141 had nothing but ammunition crates on board, the SEALs packed themselves up with more so as to be prepared for whatever circumstances lay ahead of them.

Black humor is common within the special operations forces. Men face danger together and humor can be a defense mechanism for the impending trials of combat and the possibility of losing one's life and comrades. Chris Dye recalled during the flight to Panama, a SEAL master chief asking a young ensign if he owed him 20 dollars. The inexperienced ensign replied in the affirmative. "Well then," said the master chief, "get over here and give me another blowjob so I can owe you forty."

At 0800 hours, December 19, 1989, the C-141 landed in Panama. The special forces operators were geared up and ready but all they found was a sleeping bus driver, waiting for their arrival to transport them to Rodman Air Station, their operating base.

The platoons off-loaded from the bus and were immediately ordered to monitor their intended prey: the boat in Balboa Harbor, Pier 17, located directly across from their base. ST-2's frogmen used a scope to keep a close watch. Without Noriega's boat at the floating dock, ST-2's mission would have been aborted, so the commandos were keen to know where their target vessel was at all times. The other SEAL divers departed for Colon on a similar mission. All in all, two groups of four divers each were assigned respectively to the two boats. Two dive teams per target would ensure that at least one team would successfully execute the assigned operations.

Unbeknown to the team assigned to the destruction of the *Presidente Porras*, the other targeted boat at Colon became engaged in a firefight and was ultimately destroyed by a Little Bird, a small well-armed helicopter, of the newly founded Task Force 160, the aviation arm of the Special Operations Command.

Toward the late afternoon the teams were briefed again. It included information about the boat's positioning, length, and type of engine. The *Presidente Porras* was anchored "bow out." Other elements of the brief included the "Reset Point." A Reset Point is a known underwater object where the diver can reorient himself should he lose direction. For example, if the target is in a harbor, the piers have a known distance from one another. From a pier or a quay wall, it may be a three-minute swim to a known point, where the diver would know to turn on a particular azimuth using his compass, and swim in that direction for a predetermined length of time to the location of the target.

Another issue raised at the briefing involved the actual means required to destroy the vessel. The *Presidente Porras* had an aluminum hull to which limpet mines could not be attached (limpets are normally attached magnetically and triggered with a timer). The SEAL dive teams had to come up with another manner of securing the explosives. The four SEALs decided to build the charges from scratch. The idea was to create a "Safe and Arming Device" (S&A) using C-4 explosives. To trigger the device, a classified brand new SDV (SEAL Delivery

Vehicle) digital clock was used. The mission also required a simultaneous explosion with H-Hour, the commencement of Operation *Just Cause*, at 0100 hours on December 20, 1989.

The carrying devices were World War II-era haversacks with steel plates. Twenty pounds' worth of C-4 was jammed into each of the two haversacks with a 2lb C-4 block intended to set off the larger explosive. The divers knew that a 22lb charge could be far more than actually required for the mission and certainly 44lb of C-4 would be extremely destructive. Ultimately they agreed it was worth the risk of a super-explosion, for if only one team was able to execute the mission, that single charge would have to do the job. There would be no opportunity to correct any mistakes.

At long last the dive teams donned their gear: a flight suit worn over a rubber suit, a 686 Smith & Wesson revolver with two speed loaders, a knife, a couple of canteens of water, the bubble-free Dräger diving rig and, of course, money, vital in case the mission went wrong and the SEALs needed to escape and either evade trouble or bribe themselves out of it.

Chris Dye poses with his 22lb WWII-era haversack filled with the explosives used to blow up Noriega's boat. (Chris Dye)

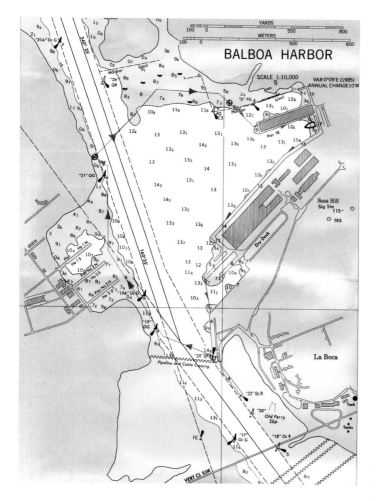

BALBOA HARBOR

The actual mission map used by combat swimmers targeting the *Presidente Porras* in Balboa Harbor, Panama. The X on the left is the departure point for the mission. The top X is the second point where the SEALs were inserted for the mission. On the right can be seen Pier 17, with a small black boat drawn on, indicating the position of Noriega's boat. The X at the bottom marks the exfiltration point where the dive pairs were met by the exfil boat teams. (Chris Dye)

As the combat swimmers loaded onto their Zodiacs they spotted ST-4 departing for their mission. Operational security was so good that none of the SEALs knew what the other teams were doing. Members of ST-2 made fun of their comrades in ST-4 as some of the SEALS had cut off their BDU sleeves, mimicking the actors who played hardened commandos in the popular movie *Predator*. ST-4 was loaded into Zodiacs, and towed by a US Navy patrol boat to a release point. It all looked "very comical" to the other SEALs.

The two dive pairs, Edward L. Coughlin and Timothy K. Eppley, and Randy L. Beausoleil and Chris Dye, loaded into their combat rubber raiding craft (CRRCs). Commander Carley supervised the operation from the first boat. Each Zodiac was manned by a boat driver and an M60 gunner. Their task was to suppress any enemy fire across the harbor from the SEALs' departure pier at Rodman. Other SEALs helped form a defensive perimeter around the base.

The two boats departed toward their insertion points. The second Zodiac was experiencing engine troubles, forcing Commander Carley to return after successfully inserting the first dive pair. CRRC 1 then towed the other boat to a closer insertion point to make up for the lost time.

Combat swimmer Chris Dye hit the water and went down like a rock. He had not accounted for the added 22lb of explosive. "What the fuck am I gonna do?" Dye did not panic but instead thought quickly and inflated his life jacket. He achieved almost neutral buoyancy and was able to control his underwater movement. The divers also had to make sure that they did not go below the depth of 20ft at which their Dräger re-breathers operated safely.

The divers were moving well just a few feet below the surface of the murky water. The protective cloak of the dark water was intermittently penetrated by phosphorescence, illuminating their trail. All of a sudden, they were caught by something. It seemed as though an ancient monstrous Kraken had reached out with her tentacles and ensnared the intruders: in reality, however, the combat swimmers had become ensnared in the branches of a submerged tree. Panic did not sink in, and after a brief struggle, they managed to free themselves. They continued underwater to their target until they reached the floating pier where the *Presidente Porras* was anchored. The phosphorescence sporadically betrayed their location. The SEALs swam the pier's entirety without surfacing, instead "staying on bag" by breathing almost 100 percent pure aviator's oxygen. Other boats, mostly whalers, were tied up throughout the harbor area. Counting each, the divers finally located Noriega's boat. Dye thought they must have passed the other dive pair as he and Beausoleil had been dropped off closer to the target and they had not encountered the other SEALs so far. He thought they had been compromised or had encountered other unforeseen obstacles.

While Dye remained underneath the boat, Beausoleil took measures to identify the vessel. He stayed between 8 and 5 feet below the surface, allowing him to use the "shallow water peak," or the depth of the water where he could use

Chris Dye shows off the Captain's wheel in 2007, which he recovered in Balboa Harbor from Noriega's private boat, *Presidente Porras*. (Authors' collections)

the reverse reflection to read the boat's name or see other identifying marks. This procedure requires the diver to come up from the depths of the water in a controlled ascent, never breaking the surface. Vision was rather good that night, as the harbor was well lit and Beausoleil noticed crew and PDF movement on the boat, and it appeared that some were loading cargo onboard. This was indeed their target.

Upon determination of the correct boat the plan was to jam the explosive against the hull and allow the other dive team to attach its haversack to the lead of the one already in place. Chris Dye attached the haversack to the port propeller shaft, set the charge and double-checked it and its timer. The other team was supposed to attach the haversack to the starboard propeller shaft, arm their system, and then tie the detonating cord leads between the charges to ensure dual priming.[33] Total time for attaching the haversack was a minute or less. With the sudden reduction in weight, Dye quickly found that he was being pushed toward the surface by his inflated flotation device. He motioned to his swim buddy to push him back down. They dove toward the floating dock where Chris released the air undetected below the surface. "Where was the other team?" he wondered. Dye and Beausoleil did not see the other divers and Dye was sure that they had been killed or died during the infiltration.

While the SEALs were below the floating dock, a firefight broke out around the harbor. H-Hour had been moved up by 15 minutes and the US Army had engaged PDF forces in Balboa Harbor, but it had not been possible for TUW to move up H-Hour. The divers had long departed on their infiltration routes and there was no way for the unit's commander to notify the pairs of combat divers.

Unbeknown to Dye and Beausoleil, the other dive pair of Coughlin and Eppley set their charge during the skirmish. Subsequent debriefings revealed that Coughlin's team thought the firefight was triggered by the discovery of the other SEAL pair.

Dye and Beausoleil began their exfiltration route dive as soon as Dye had managed to deflate his Secumar life jacket. They knew that Balboa Harbor anchored civilian boats as well as a Russian intelligence-gathering vessel, which they swam beneath en route to their pick-up point at Pier 5. They were to reunite with CRRC 1 and CRRC 2, which in the meantime had had the sputtering motor replaced at Rodman.

Beausoleil and Dye surfaced en route, prior to crossing a danger area, the dry dock between Pier 17 and Pier 5. They tried their radios to give their unit commander the pro-word (a secret word that indicated that a particular sequence or task of the mission had been accomplished) to indicate that they had successfully attached and armed the explosive device. Neither MX300 radio worked. The radios were wrapped in waterproof bags and the radios had always worked during rehearsals. This time, however, the bags had not protected the radios from the water. Although neither man had felt the explosion, subsequent discussions centered on the possibility that the underwater detonation ruined the waterproofing and radios.

Finally they decided to "haul ass crossing the dry dock area" to their pick-up point. Both swimmers were overheating, as they were dressed for cold-water diving as they had done on the East Coast for years and they had little warm-water experience. They tried to cool off by taking repeated breaks during their swim. While dealing with that, an ocean-bound tanker suddenly passed directly over them in the narrow canal, and the divers were forced to go as deep as

ORDER OF BATTLE FOR THE INVASION OF PANAMA: JOINT SPECIAL OPERATIONS TASK FORCE

Task Force Red (Headquarters, 75th Ranger Regiment)
1st Battalion, 75th Ranger Regiment, Hunter AAF, GA
2d Battalion, 75th Ranger Regiment, Fort Lewis, WA
3d Battalion, 75th Ranger Regiment, Fort Benning, GA

Task Force Black (Headquarters, 3d Battalion, 7th Special Forces Group)
3d Battalion, 7th Special Forces Group Panama
Company A, 1st Battalion, 7th Special Forces Group, Fort Bragg, NC

Task Force White (Headquarters, Naval Special Warfare Group Two)
SEAL Teams 2 and 4, Naval Special Warfare Group Two, Little Creek, VA
Naval Special Warfare Unit 8, Panama
Special Boat Unit 26, Panama

Task Force Green
1st Special Forces Operational Detachment - Delta, Fort Bragg, NC

Task Force Blue
SEAL DevGru, Dam Neck, VA
7th Special Forces Group (-) Fort Bragg, NC
1st Battalion, 7th Special Forces Group, Fort Bragg, NC
2d Battalion, 7th Special Forces Group, Fort Bragg, NC
Support Company, 7th Special Forces Group, Fort Bragg, NC
112th Signal Battalion (-), Fort Bragg, NC
528th Support Battalion, Fort Bragg, NC
160th Aviation Group (-), Fort Campbell, KY
617th Aviation Detachment, Panama

possible to avoid being killed. The water became so turbulent it felt like being in a "washing machine" and only a few straps kept them from losing their life-saving equipment. Many SEALs cut the strap of the mouth piece off their Dräger re-breathers, finding them unnecessary, but Dye and Beausoleil had both kept theirs intact. That decision saved their lives as they tumbled violently beneath the tanker. They had to break all the rules of diving and dove well below 40ft, much lower than the Dräger re-breather allowed. "After ten minutes at that depth, they swam up to their normal operating depth of 20ft and headed for Pier 5, their preplanned extraction point."[34]

> At 0045, Commander Carley led the two CRRCs from Rodman and headed for Pier 6 [5]. They arrived at the seaward end of the pier fifteen minutes later and floated quietly under the pier. While waiting for the dive teams, Carley and his CRRC crews heard firefights overhead near the pier and saw tracer rounds flash overhead. Nonetheless, they stayed in place. Because the swim teams were late, Carley began to worry about them and sent CRRC 2 to the next pier down current to see if the divers had missed the first extraction point. CRRC 2 returned without the divers. At 0200, Coughlin and Eppley arrived at Pier 6 [5].[35]

Dye remembered that "there was no genuine plan in place for the SEALs to give a far recognition signal to the pick-up crews." Ever the joker, he dove right up to the rubber boat and instead of tapping on the boat, he grabbed the gunner on board, no doubt startling the poor man. Had he known that on the pier PDF forces were engaged in combat he would never have just "yanked on the dude's pants." Once onboard they were filled in on what had really had happened while they were underwater. The others had seen the firefight and the explosion of the *Presidente Porras* and surrounding vessels from the Zodiacs.

ST-4 patch. (Authors' collections)

Commander Carley used an infrared strobe light to alert the Americans at Rodman of their arrival. "At 0220 – three hours, twenty minutes after they had left Rodman – the teams beached their boats back at Rodman, their mission accomplished."[36]

Everyone was pleased. The divers could not believe "how cool it was. It made their night." Noriega's boat was "ass-end destroyed, the engine vaporized as it went straight up and then straight down into the harbor." The explosion was so powerful that it destroyed several boats and blew out a number of windows in the buildings surrounding the immediate area. Some of the pieces of the *Presidente Porras* landed on other SEALs and SOF personnel, who were then engaged in a hot fight for the Commandancia, the headquarters of

Paitilla Airport, ST-4's objective.
(Tony Duchi)

the PDF. The pieces of the boat that landed there were returned to ST-2 later. Subsequent to the mission, Chris Dye dove to the wreckage and recovered the captain's wheel.

There was no time for celebrations, however, as their skipper returned from the Tactical Operations Center (TOC). They were told that ST-4 at Paitilla Airport had encountered a problem.

PLANES, BOATS, AND LIZARD-LINES

Tony Duchi is a slender fit-looking man with a ramrod-straight back. He has an earnest demeanor and was candid in his observations on the role he played during Operation *Just Cause*. He reflected on his experiences with a smile or maybe an ironic chuckle. As was typical of most special operations personnel, the 1980s had not been kind for anyone seeking combat action. Tony was bored by the lack of it and his SEAL buddy Rick Asherman was thinking of joining the Israel Defense Forces.

Tony was in great spirits about the upcoming combat mission.[37] All those long months of peacetime training were about to be put to the test of real combat. Rick, the M60 machine gunner, had linked over a thousand 7.62mm rounds together, inspired by the film *Predator*. A belt normally held 100 rounds, linked together by small black metal clasps. One hundred rounds would last about ten solid bursts, each burst consisting of six to nine bullets, or it could last one long one, eating up the entire belt in a few short seconds. Putting a bunch of links together, though, could cause the gun to jam as the belt-fed M60 was a bit finicky and needed ammunition fed as neatly as possible. Asherman was going to have a lot of rounds to use on this mission. A 60-gunner was the most important member of his team as he was in possession of one of the best weapons carried by Navy SEALs. Lt John Connors, Duchi and Asherman, and the rest of Bravo Platoon, SEAL Team 4 were ready for their mission.

Tony remembered vividly the recall notice to go to war. He hadn't believed it. Another recall? He had just received a speeding ticket for an earlier one that had turned out to be a practice alert. "Is this for real?" he asked, "'cause I don't want to get another ticket." This time, December 1989, it was for real. A recall has a very specific sequence of events, brilliant in its simplicity. The SEAL receives a call, then he calls the next man on the list, and then he drives as fast as possible to the team area to muster. Tony rang the next SEAL on the list, then drove to the base. This time the SEALs did muster, but they were not all happy. Many older SEALs, who already felt that they had missed out on the Vietnam War and the invasion of Grenada, were not included in this mission. For Tony, however, the opportunity to see real combat had finally arisen.

In mid-December 1989, along with several thousand other commandos, ST-4 rehearsed its particular mission at Hurlburt Field, FL: the destruction of Manuel Noriega's private Learjet. The rehearsals in general went well even though few SEALs were impressed with their commanding officer (CO), Cdr Tom McGrath. Crossing the beaches en route to their target, a senior SEAL saw one of his comrades sprawled on the sand, barely crawling forward underneath the weight of a PRC-77 (radio). He stopped yelling at the man upon realizing that it was SEAL officer Tom McGrath. Word quickly spread through the ranks. The CO eventually ended up commanding from the patrol boats while the Executive Officer (XO), who had served with ST-6 in Operation *Urgent Fury*, took charge of the rehearsal.

The operation called not only for the destruction of the airplane but also for the SEALs to push other lightweight aircraft onto the tarmac once the primary target had been destroyed in order to prevent the use of the airport in general.

Paitilla Airport is located at the very edge of the Pacific Ocean in the southwestern part of Panama City. Several tall apartment complexes oversee the far end of the tarmac and a pier juts out just a few hundred feet away from the runway.

After debarkation, Golf Platoon was to rush straight up to the hangar housing Noriega's jet with Bravo Platoon acting as a blocking force. Delta Platoon's primary target was the air traffic control tower. The command and control element included Air Force combat controllers who were responsible for communicating with an aerial weapons platform in the form of a highly destructive AC-130 gunship, nicknamed Spectre. The SEALs wore Glint tape (tape that can only be seen through infrared night vision goggles), which helped pilots identify friendly from enemy forces.

PAITILLA AIRFIELD ASSAULT, OPERATION *JUST CAUSE*
December 19, 1989

THE MISSION:
- Secure Paitilla Airfield
- Deny access

CONCEPT OF OPERATIONS:
- CRRC launch from Howard AFB
- Patrol boat tows CRRCs to insertion point off Punta Paitilla
- CRRC mass insertion
- Debark at north end of runway
- Golf Platoon moves to Noriega's hangar, secures Learjet
- Bravo Platoon acts as blocking force covering main road ingress
- Delta Platoon to secure air traffic control tower on opposite side of runway
- C2 element provides 60mm fire support and communications
- Move aircraft to middle of runway, disable with minimum damage
- Wait for relief

EXECUTION:
- Full rehearsal at Hurlburt Field
- Final mission planning/deployment to NSWU-8 Rodman
- Insert via CRRC at 0045 local, 15 min prior to H-Hour
- Three platoons and C2 element move into positions
- Golf takes fire
- Bravo moves to support
- Fire suppressed 2–3 times
- Hangar catches fire
- Platoons consolidate in perimeter
- Call for medevac
- Relieved 36 hours later

CASUALTIES
KIA
- LTJG John Connors
- ENC Don McFaul
- BM1 Chris Tilghman
- TM2 Ike Rodriguez

WIA
- 13 others

(Source: Interview with Tony Duchi, 2007, Bahmanyar/Osman)

A number of SEALs questioned their mission. Airfield seizures were generally considered the Rangers' domain, since they had the manpower and relevant expertise. Nonetheless, senior Navy personnel dismissed out of hand any concerns that the mission might either be better handled by a different unit or handled with greater stealth. Arguments that several well-placed sniper teams might be more appropriate or that a small raiding team would be better were ignored. The middle ground was taken in the form of a unit too large for a clandestine strike, but not large enough to handle a straightforward direct action mission.

The SEALs were not impressed with their mission, yet still were anxious to participate in a real action after years of frustrating peacetime service. They may also have known that SEAL officer Adam Curtis was held prisoner by the Panamanians and that wasn't good. Adam Curtis would eventually become a controversial SEAL team commander during the Global War on Terrorism, post September 11, 2001.

ST-4 arrived at Rodman for more briefings and preparation. Buses transported the eager SEALs to Howard Air Force Base from where they would inflate and launch their CRRCs, and be towed via a lizard-line (a 1in. tubular nylon rope) by a large, powerful patrol boat to their line of departure. Fifteen or so Zodiacs each carrying four men made for a rather comical non-tactical towing method. Just outside of Punta Paitilla Airport the boats stayed out in the bay waiting for the commencement of H-Hour, all the while encountering a number

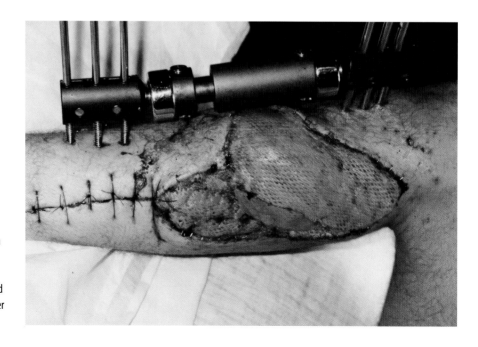

Left and right:
Tony Duchi was badly wounded during the attack on Paitilla Airport, and he needed surgery and skin grafts on his leg. While he was in hospital recuperating, he was visited by President Bush and the First Lady. Unbelievably after receiving this wound, Tony went back into active service and served his country on many other missions. (Tony Duchi)

of fishing boats and other civilian vessels; so much for operational security. H-Hour had been moved up by 15 minutes because everyone in Panama seemed to know of the mission.

Duchi was troubled by the mission's loss of the element of surprise. At the same time the SEALs were young, arrogant, and convinced of their invincibility – who really cared if the PDF knew they were coming? Yet there was also the troubling news in the final brief that an Armored Personnel Carrier (APC) factory was near the airport, so now B Platoon had also to contend with light armored vehicles. However, the SEALs were carrying some 60mm, light anti-tank weapons that should counter the APCs but it meant that B Platoon would have to block the tarmac as well as keep an eye out for APCs.

Golf Platoon would make all haste moving straight up to Noriega's hangar. "Boy scouts can do this job," Tony remembers the SEAL CO saying. "Old men with rusty rifles who'll run away at the first sight of the SEALs were guarding the airport." Delta Platoon was to seize control of the towers. Tony and all the SEALs knew the intimate details of the mission.

A two-man recon team in an indigenous canoe infiltrated the beach area and flashed the awaiting SEAL raiders the Red Lens Morse Code letter alpha, the pro-word for the insertion to go ahead: "At 0045, the new H-hour, Task Unit Papa, three SEAL platoons, a total of ninety-two men led by Cdr Tom McGrath, landed from rubber raiding boats along the beach at Paitilla."[38]

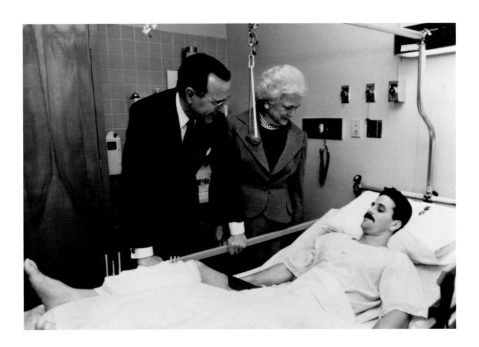

This boat was used to tow ST-4's rubber raiding crafts to their departure points in the assault on Punta Paitilla Airport. (Tony Duchi)

The SEALs were running up the beaches of Panama when Duchi spotted Asherman falling down and all his beautifully linked M60 ammunition slinking out of the ruck onto the ground. Upward and onward B Platoon went. They reached a chain link fence with a hole in it. The SEALs mustered on the other side of it as US stealth bombers and anti-aircraft fire painted the sky a multi-colored canvas.

Duchi's platoon leader placed his men in a ditch, but the ditch was too far away for them even to see the road they were supposed to block. Arguments went back and forth as gunfire and the sounds of war pierced the air. Then the argument to move into a better position became null and void – Golf Platoon had been engaged and the priority now was to support them. Something was wrong. Tony's buddy was the radioman and Tony could catch snippets of urgent communications.

Command and control elements, including the Air Force combat controllers, were in the rear of the various platoons. The XO ordered 2nd Squad of B Platoon forward. "Go, go, go…"

Duchi spotted SEALs from Golf Platoon firing into a hangar. He moved forward with his M203 in hand and ready to pop the enemy, yelling all the while at the other SEALs that he was friendly and moving into their area. The remnants of Golf Platoon were at almost a 90-degree angle to Bravo Platoon's line of march.

Tony's squad filled in the depleted ranks. Six or seven wounded comrades were to their front and the enemy-held hangar was in an open, exposed danger area. On his left he saw a burning Cessna but it was not the intended target. His immediate thought was "What the fuck am I doing here?" He found no target to fire at. Instead he grabbed the nearest wounded SEAL to his front and pulled him by his web gear back toward friendly lines. The wounded man was actually dead. As Duchi pulled the man desperately back, his legs were shot out from underneath him. Thirty minutes after the beach insertion Tony Duchi lay seriously wounded on the ground at Paitilla Airport without having fired a single shot. He aimed his M203 at the hangar to his front and squeezed the trigger, only to miss the target with his 40mm grenade that floated harmlessly over the building. His contribution to Operation *Just Cause* had ended.

The SEALs engaged the enemy forces two or three times to suppress their fire while rescuing some of their comrades and consolidating their positions. Duchi's buddy pulled him back toward the rear where the SEALs had gathered the wounded. Parts of the airport were on fire, the shooting had stopped and Noriega's Learjet had been destroyed. First aid was being administered and Tony began to realize that some of his friends had died, including his platoon leader John Connors and his BUD/S classmate Ike Rodriguez. It was ultimately discovered, despite his silence, that Asherman had been shot in the inner thigh with a large exit wound in his buttocks. Fun eventually would be had at Asherman's expense, but that would come later… Tony Duchi remembered clearly being loaded into a C-141 with litters stacked four high. Panama had not been so easy for some.

COUNTER-DRUG OPERATIONS IN BOLIVIA 1991

Ghostly SEALs

DAZED AND CONFUSED

One of the Navy SEALs' primary tasks is that of training foreign troops. This process is called FID and stands for Foreign Internal Defense. Essentially, this is a training task where American troops go overseas to train local military and law enforcement officials in small-unit tactics. This task in general used to be the exclusive domain of the United States Army special forces commonly known as the Green Berets. But with the creation of USSOCOM many traditional tasks were reorganized. The Navy SEALs then became the task force unit for all maritime and riverine tactics. Most SEALs deplore this training task as they consider themselves primarily a direct action strike force. SEALs have, however, historically trained foreign counterparts since their creation in 1962. In Vietnam for example, Navy SEALs trained and advised Vietnamese naval commandos.

Launched in 1987 by the Drug Enforcement Agency (DEA) and Department of State's Bureau of International Narcotics Matters, Operation *Snowcap* was intended to disrupt the cultivation, manufacture, and distribution of cocaine in several South American countries. Bolivia was one of the major contributors to the cocaine influx into the US and was targeted as such.

According to the DEA, Operation *Snowcap* had six general objectives:

1. To encourage, through diplomatic efforts, coca source countries to participate in crop eradication.

Special operations forces in Guatamala. (Tony Duchi)

2. To suppress cocaine production through the destruction of clandestine cocaine laboratories and the seizure of precursor chemicals, coca paste, cocaine base, and cocaine hydrochloride.

3. To investigate and prosecute major cocaine-trafficking organizations and to seize their assets.

4. To support enforcement efforts against cocaine trafficking by providing timely intelligence.

5. To increase personnel and financial and technical assistance dedicated to foreign cocaine enforcement programs.

6. To improve domestic and foreign drug law enforcement officers' skills through training.[39]

DEA special agents were sent to Bolivia to team up with the newly formed UMOPAR (Unidad Móvil de Patrullaje Rural – Mobile Rural Patrol Unit), Bolivia's counter-narcotics police force. Together they gathered intelligence and conducted raids on known processing facilities, but met with little success as the local population was quick to tip off drug lords. When Operation *Snowcap* began, the economy of Bolivia was dependent on the coca leaf trade. The Bolivian people were reluctant to give up their main source of income to foreign agents.

Another successful mission for UMOPAR and their American advisors. (Tony Duchi)

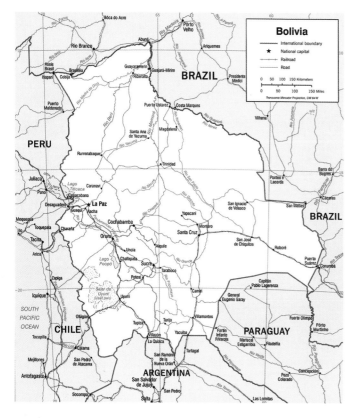

Map of Bolivia. (CIA)

US special forces were brought in to train UMOPAR and the DEA. They were not permitted, by Operation *Snowcap*'s rules of engagement, to participate in any anti-narcotics operations. ST-4 sent men to help in this FID mission. Reporter James L. Pate noted the "good wishes from three US Navy SEAL advisers, who grumbled good naturedly" while they watched "the last-minute preparations for the dawn helicopter raid" conducted by UMOPAR and the DEA in 1991.[40] Although the SEALs were not officially present and were not officially participating in the operation, they were relied upon for rescue or support in emergency situations. In March 1988, Frank E. White, then a DEA chief, wrote a memo in which he requested more special forces participation:

Recommend that the Special Forces attend all enforcement briefings, from the issuance of the Warning Order, to the Five Paragraph Field Order. Now we don't even issue orders. Possibly our ineptness in planning, briefing, and conducting operations has been pointed out to us, resulting in a schism developing between units. If anything goes wrong, while the *Snowcap* and UMOPAR are in the field, the only force capable of immediate reaction is the Special Forces. As they are wont to say, they can't help if they don't know the plan and radio frequencies. On one operation, we provided the Special Forces with the wrong frequency, which they monitored. We then couldn't even summon help, which to me is bordering on suicide. We have a long way to go. We need a joint command center which should be in the Special Forces compound, covering all field operations, to include naval riverine program.[41]

His answer came from President George H. W. Bush in August, 1989, where in National Security Directive 18 he agreed "to expand DOD support of US counter-narcotics efforts and to permit DOD personnel to conduct training for host government personnel and operational support activities."[42]

Tony Duchi, who speaks Spanish fluently, nonchalantly commented that they were only training the rural police forces in Bolivia at the time, and that, in effect, this deployment was an FID mission and not a direct action mission. The SEALs

like to joke that FID missions are "training tomorrow's enemies today."[43] Small-unit tactics and boat tactics as well as riverine operations were taught to the Bolivians in conjunction with the Federal Bureau of Investigation, the Drug Enforcement Agency and the US Coast Guard. The SEALs spent three and a half months in South America. Tony also mentioned that Denzel Washington's character, Creasy, in *Man on Fire*, the Hollywood movie, was part of Operation *Snowcap*.[44] Hollywood films like to make their heroes tough and mysterious and the SEALs' missions in Bolivia were certainly the latter.

Navy SEALs were instrumental in training local law-enforcement officials in riverine operations and tactics. (Tony Duchi)

YUGOSLAVIA 1999
AND BOSNIA 2003

Navy SEALs – European Style

THE DAWNING OF A NEW ERA

The year was 1996 and the big firefight in Mogadishu, Somalia, had happened three years earlier where a number of American special forces soldiers were killed while hunting for a local Somali warlord.[45] The Navy SEALs' contribution to this operation was limited to a handful of members from DevGru. Peace "sucked" for all adventurous men but joining the military was still something.[46] In 1996, two weeks after he graduated high school, Tom enlisted as an Undesignated E-2 (no rate) for BUD/S. Navy boot camp was easy. Right after Tom finished BUD/S he was sent to the US Army's Airborne School at Fort Benning, GA. The Navy's plans for Tom saw him as a corpsman and subsequently, his orders sent him to the top medical training program the US military has to offer, the 18D Special Forces medical course at Fort Bragg, NC. At long last Tom was assigned to ST-8 in April of 1998. While at ST-8 Tom prepared for the SEAL Tactical Training (STT) course, but was yanked out of it to become the corpsman for the actual training class, a blow to any man's morale. However, as luck would have it, Tom was sent to a SEAL platoon to occupy the vacant slot as the platoon's secondary corpsman. He was the only member without STT training and the requisite Trident. Nonetheless, he participated in the pre-deployment work-up when NSW 21 took effect and all SEAL units were being slowly realigned. For the SEALs of ST-8 that shift in organization required an additional eight months of training for a European deployment.

US Navy SEAL conducting a special reconnaissance mission in Kosovo, in support of KFOR operations. (Authors' collections)

YUGOSLAVIA

The genocide that occurred in Yugoslavia from 1991 to 2001 involved Serbs, Croats, Bosnians, Albanians, and Macedonians. During that ten-year span the vicious fighting and ethnic cleansing killed well over 100,000 men, women, and children, with nearly two million people displaced. The vast majority of the victims were Bosnian Muslims.[47] Mercenaries flocked to the support of various ethnic and religious militias and armies. Nationalism, the pursuit of nationhood, and abiding racial and religious tensions all contributed to Yugoslavia's implosion. The international community was slow to react. In the post-Cold War era, intervention had taken the form of peace-keeping, but events in Mogadishu in 1993 had forced a re-evaluation of that term. Both the European Community and the US first acceded to the independence of the former Yugoslav slates, and then initially focused their efforts on trying to "manage the crisis on the ground… alongside on-going international diplomacy." But when presented with the reality of genocide, they "refused to fully commit to the force option to decisively resolve the problem on the ground."[48]

SEAL Team 8's primary mission was to conduct special reconnaissance operations and report the intelligence to their higher command located at Camp Bondsteel, the main base of the US Army under NATO's Kosovo Force (KFOR) in the UN-administered Serbian province of Kosovo.[49] KFOR had deployed in the aftermath of a 78-day air campaign launched by the alliance in March 1999 to halt and reverse the humanitarian catastrophe that had unfolded.[50] Tom's platoon stayed in country for three months, conducting a number of reconnaissance

Camp Bondsteel, Kosovo. (DOD)

missions, until it was pulled out and rotated with a different SEAL platoon that was in Germany at the time.

Upon returning to the US Tom was given four days of leave. After time off, he attended High Altitude, Low Opening (HALO), the military freefall school, Range Safety Officer and Riggers (a person trained to pack, maintain and repair parachutes) Training as part of his professional development (ProDev). After ProDev he went straight into another work-up for a SEAL strike platoon.

BOSNIA REVISITED 2003

Tom and his platoon had just returned from conducting special operations missions in the Persian Gulf in 2003 and he already had orders to form a new SEAL team. He had been back only nine days when he attended the commissioning ceremony and became a plankowner [founding member] of ST-10. Team 10 was located inside the quarters of ST-2 because its building was not yet ready.

Once at ST-10, Tom went through ProDev again for Dive Supervisor as well as static line and freefall jump master schools. During the work-up the platoon was assigned to EUCOM (US European Command). The SEALs were already six months into their new work-up training when the platoon was told that they would be going into Bosnia to capture personnel indicted for war crimes (PIFWC). Hence, the final six months of the work-up were designed to prepare the platoon for that particular prisoner snatch mission in Europe. One such target was Radovan Karadzic, who had many supporters in the region: "President of Bosnia during the war there from 1992–95. During his years in power (according to the indictment by the Hague) he was complicit in the rape and murder of thousands of innocent Muslims. He is accused of acts of genocide as part of a campaign to terrorize the population."[51]

The safe house in Bosnia that the SEALs operated out of. (Authors' collections)

Along with several others, Karadzic had been found guilty and was a war criminal on the run. NATO countries sent special forces operatives to apprehend the guilty parties and among these operatives were Navy SEALs.

In October 2003 the platoon left Virginia for Germany, then proceeded on to Bosnia via a civilian rotator flight. The platoon was split into several small groups to avoid raising any suspicions upon their arrival. The SEALs were camouflaged as ordinary civilians, and even their gear was shuttled in at a later time. At the airport a liaison had arranged for the commandos to receive their vehicles. The hunters smoothly transitioned from the airport to a safe house in the devastated town of Sarajevo.

EXTRACTS FROM THE INDICTMENT OF RADOVAN KARADZIC AND RATKO MLADIC BY THE INTERNATIONAL TRIBUNAL FOR THE FORMER YUGOSLAVIA (CASE NO. IT-95-5-1)

Part I of the indictment, Counts 1 to 9, charges a crime of genocide, crimes against humanity and crimes that were perpetrated against the civilian population and against places of worship throughout the territory of the Republic of Bosnia and Herzegovina.

Bosnian Muslim and Bosnian Croat civilians were persecuted on national, political and religious grounds throughout the Republic of Bosnia and Herzegovina. Thousands of them were interned in detention facilities where they were subjected to widespread acts of physical and psychological abuse and to inhumane conditions. Detention facility personnel… intended to destroy Bosnian Muslim and Bosnian Croat people as national, ethnic, or religious groups and killed, seriously injured and deliberately inflicted upon them conditions intended to bring about their physical destruction…

Radovan Karadzic and Ratko Mladic, between April 1992 and July 1995, in the territory of the Republic of Bosnia and Herzegovina, by their acts and omissions, and in concert with others, committed a crime against humanity by persecuting Bosnian Muslim and Bosnian Croat civilians on national, political and religious grounds. As set forth below, they are criminally responsible for the unlawful confinement, murder, rape, sexual assault, torture, beating, robbery and inhumane treatment of civilians; the targeting of political leaders, intellectuals and professionals; the unlawful deportation and transfer of civilians; the unlawful shelling of civilians; the unlawful appropriation and plunder of real and personal property; the destruction of homes and businesses; and the destruction of places of worship.

(Source: http://www.un.org/icty/indictment/english/kar-ii950724e.htm)

Target folders were handed to the platoon members. Within two weeks, and with the help of one of their operators who spoke fluent Serb and Croat, one of the targets was located. The man was vacationing with his wife and two children in a pleasant ski chalet. Once the information had been processed and with very little notice, the SEALs planned the prisoner snatch. The only valuable information other than the location of their target was his name and the type of vehicle he was driving, but there was no time to wait for further intelligence.

The 14-man platoon disguised itself as a group of ordinary civilians and made its way through Sarajevo en route to the chalet. Once near the target Tom and his buddies stayed in their vehicles and rotated watches, keeping their eyes on the resort hotel for 12–14 hours at a time. The SEALs had hoped that the PIFWC would emerge from the chalet and their plan was to seize him when he entered his parked vehicle. Time went by and nothing happened. Time was of the essence. How long could the American operators disguise themselves sitting in cars?

The importance of their task in Bosnia was brought home to SEALs by artwork seen painted on walls reminding viewers not to forget the genocide. Within Karadzic's safe house the SEALs found a portrait of Radovan Karadzic, the man they were hunting. (Authors' collections)

Opposite:
A valley in Afghanistan that a SEAL platoon was watching during an SR mission in 2005. The picture was taken from the SEALs' hide site. (Authors' collections)

The platoon decided to send one of their language-fluent operators into the chalet to see if he could somehow locate the target or persuade him to leave his room with the help of the concierge. While that operator was on his way inside, another SEAL walked over to the target's car and slashed one of the tires. Within a few short moments one of the rotating chalet security guards noticed the flat tire. The language-fluent commando noticed the alert guard's reaction and decided not to enter the chalet to engage the concierge. Instead he waited in the chalet's coffee shop to see what would happen next. Over the hotel's intercom system he heard the guard announce that the owner of the vehicle with a flat tire should come and fix it. Upon hearing that and seeing a man answer the announcement, the operator signaled his team, alerting them of their prey.

As the target changed the tire the platoon surrounded him. One of the platoon members tapped the target on his shoulder and asked him what his name was. Once he said his name, the platoon took him into custody for interrogation. He was the bodyguard of Radovan Karadzic.

The platoon received intelligence analysis from that particular capture that led them to Karadzic's house, which the same platoon raided. They received an intel brief that Karadzic had just had surgery and was going to his house to meet someone. Again there was very little time to operate. The platoon jocked-up at their safe house, and waited until 2200 hours to move out towards the target's house. They pulled up, and assaulted the home without any information regarding the layout of the target building. Unfortunately, Karadzic was not there. The house was empty but there was warm bread and half-finished drinks on the table. Obviously he had just managed to escape. In fact, the platoon found his crutches. While the platoon was in Karadzic's house his caretaker arrived only to be captured and interrogated. To this day Karadzic remains free.

PART III

GLOBAL WAR ON TERRORISM: AFGHANISTAN 2001–07

AFGHANISTAN

The Men Who Would be Kings

SOMETHING WICKED THIS WAY COMES

On September 11, 2001, two airplanes attacked the World Trade Center in New York City; another airplane was targeted at the Pentagon; a fourth missed its target and crash-landed when its civilian passengers overpowered the terrorists and went to their deaths. No one can forget the horrifying images of skyscrapers on fire and people jumping off the high rises, choosing a cruel conscious death over an equally cruel death by fire or smoke, fire and smoke created by aircraft fuel, burning ever so powerfully, melting steel, concrete and flesh alike.

New York City was permanently marked. It is a city that symbolizes America's freedom and diversity over the past three centuries, a symbol of America's financial and political power, a symbol of everything American – now its arteries were laid open through two surgical strikes by members of al-Qaeda, a religious/political sect bent on destroying Western influences in Muslim countries, most notably in Saudi Arabia and Iraq.

Al-Qaeda (The Base) was founded around 1988 and was rooted in an organization that had recruited and trained Mujahideen warriors to fight the Soviets in Afghanistan from 1979 to 1989. That organization was the Maktab Khadamāt al-Mujāhidīn al-'Arab (MAK) or Services Office and was supposedly headed by Saudi Arab Osama bin Laden and Palestinian religious scholar Abdullah Azzam.[52] Abdullah Azzam and his two sons were assassinated when a remote-detonated 20kg TNT device was triggered as they were on their way to

SEAL in Afghanistan practicing with a .50 cal. (Authors' collections)

Friday prayers in Pakistan in 1989.[53] With the death of Azzam the opportunity arose for bin Laden to assume sole leadership of al-Qaeda.

Almost 3,000 people died in the attack on the World Trade Center. In the aftermath of the assault, American citizens were shocked, paranoid, and vengeful. Amongst the US military, "bugger-eaters," "savages," "ragheads," "Islamofascists." and "Hadjis" were the new catch phrases for the enemy.[54] One ST-3 patch reads: "Embrace the Hate."

Former CIA senior intelligence analyst Michael Scheuer was responsible for all CIA operations involving al-Qaeda's founding father Osama bin Laden and believed that the US was "being attacked for what we do in the Islamic world, not for who we are or what we believe in or how we live."[55] He continues:

This patch was carried by some SEALs to honor the fallen firefighters of 9/11. (Authors' collections)

> There's our military presence in Islamic countries, the perception that we control the Muslim world's oil production, our support for Israel and for countries that oppress Muslims such as China, Russia, and India, and our own support for Arab tyrannies. Publicly promoting democracy while supporting tyranny may be the most damaging thing we do. From the standpoint of democracy, Saudi Arabia looks much worse than Iran. We use the term "Islamofascism"– but we're supporting it in Saudi Arabia, with Mubarak in Egypt, and even Jordan is a police state. We don't have a strategy because we don't have a clue about what motivates our enemies. What benefit do we get by letting China commit genocide by inundation by moving thousands and thousands of Han Chinese to overcome the dominance of Muslim Uighurs? What do we get out of supporting Putin [Russia] in Chechnya? He may need to do it to maintain his country, but we don't need to support what looks like a rape, pillage, and kill campaign against Muslims. The other area is Israel and Palestine. We're not going to abandon the Israelis but we need to re-establish the relationship so it looks like we're the great power and they're our ally, and not the other way around. We need to create a situation where moderate Muslims can express support for the United States without being laughed off the block.[56]

In 2006, Niall Ferguson explained his view of 9/11 and the events following it:

> What we see at the moment is an attempt to interpret our present predicament in a rather caricatured World War II idiom. I mean, "Islamofascism" illustrates the point well, because it's a completely misleading concept. In fact, there's virtually no overlap between the ideology of al-Qaeda and fascism. It's just a way of making us feel that we're the "greatest generation" fighting another World War, like the war our fathers and grandfathers fought.

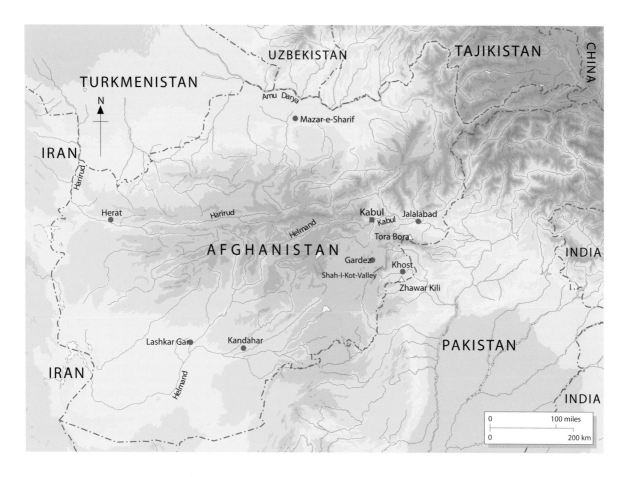

Map of Afghanistan. (Osprey Publishing)

You're translating a crisis symbolized by 9/11 into a sort of pseudo World War II. So, 9/11 becomes Pearl Harbor and then you go after the bad guys who are the fascists, and if you don't support us, then you must be an appeaser.[57]

The SEALs were active in operations immediately following 9/11, and Chris Osman recalls his experiences right after the attacks:

I was a member of ST-3 based in Coronado, CA. I was in Marine Corps Scout Sniper School Class 4-01 on 9/11. The course was over and the class was going to graduate in three days. I came in to the schoolhouse when the Chief Scout Sniper Instructor asked, "Have you heard the news about the planes being hijacked?" I said no and went into the class to hear what was happening. About an hour later I was told that I had a phone call in the office. When I answered I was told that my platoon had been recalled and I was to get to the base as quickly as possible. I, along with a platoon mate also in the school, gathered all of our gear and left. When we got to the team about an hour later I went to the platoon space and talked with my OIC. He said we were loading out and to take everything. I was the ordnance rep for the platoon so I went down to the armory and started to pack all of the platoon weapons and associated equipment. Once that was done and staged to be put on an aircraft loading pallet, our platoon was called into a briefing room for a meeting with the CO of Team 3. Commander Adam Curtis told both Echo and Hotel platoons that we were staying in isolation and that only one platoon was going to go forward. My platoon was going first, with Hotel platoon to follow into country 30 days behind us.

Six days later we loaded all of our gear onto a C-5 cargo plane and took off from North Island Naval Air Station in Coronado, CA. We flew straight to Washington State and picked up some Army Rangers. They flew with us to Iceland for refueling and then onto Rota, Spain. We stayed the night in Spain and left the next morning. We flew into Kuwait, and from there we were taken to Camp Doha. My platoon was given an in-brief as to the layout of the base and the dos and don'ts because it is an Army-run base. We relieved a platoon from Team 3 and immediately took over their job of doing VBSS missions.

The platoon was bummed out because we all thought we were going in right away to get some payback. The other platoon was moving forward to Oman to stage for missions in Afghanistan. Morale was not the highest because again we thought that we were missing

The Afghanistan landscape held many new challenges for the US Navy SEALs deployed to support Operation *Enduring Freedom*. (DOD)

out on the war. A few months before, the platoon was excited about doing VBSS missions since at that time it was the only real mission the West Coast teams were doing. About three weeks later while out on a patrol with the MK Vs and RHIB flotilla we were called by Commander Mann on the boat's radio. He told the OIC to get everyone into the cab so all of us could hear his brief. We were told that a High Value Target (HVT) was spotted and we were going to take it down in about five minutes. He briefed us on the background of the vessel. *A117* was the name of the ship. It was the ship used by al-Qaeda to smuggle explosives into Africa. Those explosives were then made into the two bombs that were used to blow up the two US embassies in Tanzania and Nairobi. The explosions had killed hundreds and wounded many more.

The platoon was then told that no matter what we had to do, to get on board and use whatever means necessary to take control of the ship. All of a sudden the platoon was going into the fight before any of our friends from the other platoons and by luck we were given this target. The platoon quickly jocked-up on the back of the MK V and crossed over to a RHIB so we could begin the assault. A pro-word was passed giving us the green light to insert and start the mission. It took less than three minutes for us to come alongside the vessel. A ladder was hooked to the side and we climbed up a small caving ladder to the back deck of the ship. The platoon boarded the ship quickly and as I was holding security outside a hatch opened up. One of the platoon mates shouted out "Open door!" and before

A vehicle used by a SEAL platoon in Afghanistan in 2005. The hood was painted by a SEAL, with an M2 .50 cal mounted in the truck bed. (Authors' collections)

everyone was over the rail I, along with seven or eight other operators, began the assault. The guy in the doorway was hit in the face and I zip-cuffed him on the port side walkway of the ship. After that I joined my four-man element and we went straight down to the engine room. We breached the aft steering and control room; once inside we saw four men at the controls and in less than 20 seconds had them off the control panel and zip-tied. They were searched and we took them out to the back deck so they could be photographed. After the ship was secured the platoon mustered together to begin the long methodical search of all of the spaces. The initial assault took less than three minutes before our comm guy passed the pro-word letting our task unit commander know that we had control of the ship. We spent another hour or so searching the vessel. It was loaded with cigarettes. Later the MIF [Maritime Interdiction Force] team came over from another ship that was patrolling in the area and relieved the platoon so we could go back to the MK Vs. This is the one mission that I personally thought was the best one I had ever done. It was specifically a SEAL mission and no other unit outside of the teams was capable of doing it. I was also lucky that I was with a platoon that got to strike back four weeks after 9/11 and take down a ship that was not just another oil smuggler.

This is a picture of a local Afghani truck; trucks are typically rigged up with chimes or bells and were nicknamed "jingle trucks." (Authors' collections)

DEPLOYMENT TO AFGHANISTAN

The Taleban, a militant religious sect, had ruled Afghanistan with an iron fist since 1996. They provided a safe operating haven for al-Qaeda and refused to hand over or oust members of bin Laden's fighters despite an American ultimatum handed to them post-9/11. Once the ultimatum expired, the US launched a full-scale invasion. The mission for the coalition of forces invading Afghanistan was, as President George W. Bush put it in December 2001: "Taleban gone, the country secure, the country stable, that al-Qaeda cells be rounded up, Taleban fighters brought to justice. The over 6,000 troops, prisoners being held – prisoners of war being held by our allies interrogated, finger-printing. I mean, there's a lot to do. And the American people just must understand when I said that we need to be patient, that I meant it. And I don't know the exact moment when we leave, but it's not until this mission is complete."[58]

Helicopter picking up someone after a mission in Afghanistan. In the foreground is a female FBI agent. (Authors' collections)

SEAL in Afghanistan practicing with a .50 cal. This is done to ensure weapons proficiency at all times. Mounted to the weapon is an IR laser designator for nighttime engagements. (Authors' collections)

Chris Osman's comments show some of the problems that the SEALs had in deploying to the challenging, and land-locked, country of Afghanistan. After their successful VBSS missions in the Persian Gulf, in November 2001, the platoon:

… flew to Misera Island off the coast of Oman to begin staging to go into Afghanistan. Once we were in Oman we did daily briefs and were given all of the maps the intel people had of the area. Basically they did not have any and we had to use our EVAC charts used for escape and evasion to try and figure out the lay of the land. It was hot as hell during the day so the platoon worked at night. At night it was around 92 to 95 degrees. The platoon hooked up with some of the guys that had just returned from the recon of Camp Rhino. They worked with us modifying the vehicles the Army was ordered to hand over to us. We spent almost two weeks trying to set the vehicles up for our platoon's gear. During this time we were assigned two Air Force combat controllers, who were later shit-canned by our OIC and chief, before we went into Afghanistan. We flew into Qandahar International Airport in the second week of December 2001. I was cold as fuck. We were in 100-degree heat and three hours later we were in

SEALs standing next to a Humvee, Afghanistan, 2001. (Authors' collections)

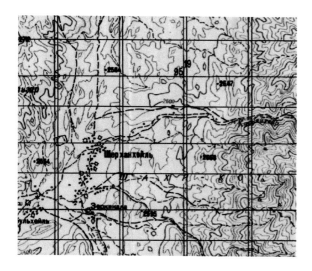

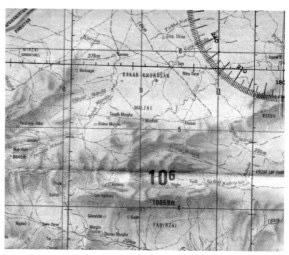

Left:
Soviet-era map of Afghanistan which proved to be worthless due to its lack of detail. (Authors' collections)

Right:
Escape and evasion map manufactured for American forces. This map was used by Navy SEALs, when it became available, for land navigation purposes. (Authors' collections)

23-degree weather. Going from one extreme like that to the other without time to acclimate to the change sucked ass. We met up with Delta Platoon from ST-3 which was already there after making the trip from Camp Rhino.[59]

Other SEALs recalled their impressions of Afghanistan. The climate, the landscape, the available intelligence and lack of maps exercised the capabilities of the SEALs, and a lack of suitable equipment not only limited the SEALs' ability to effectively carry out missions, but endangered SEAL lives. Navy SEAL Darrick remembers clearly the stripped-down Humvees that Alpha Platoon of ST-3 acquired from the Rangers in Oman prior to providing SR (Special Reconnaissance) intelligence for the Camp Rhino invasion in November 2001. The vehicles' seats were "shitty office chairs" and the SEALs had almost no mobility training at all.[60]

Marcus Luttrell feels that one cannot really train for the rugged mountains of Afghanistan. One of the major adjustments the SEALs also made in-country was to the weight of their rucksacks. Their gear was dropped down to around 30–40lb and personal body armor was left at base. He spent three and a half months in-country and executed 30 patrols before his last one during Operation *Redwing*. When he talks about the beauty of the country there is real affection present in his voice. "In many ways the country is the Wild West."[61] His recon skills were put to the test and "if you can recon there, you can recon anywhere." The Taleban always had the advantage of being on their own turf. "The landscape," he says, "is surprising. Trees, grass, green pastures, not to mention the amazing skies and the horse-shoe-shaped mountains with banks of haze on the top. The caves are pretty nuts as they go from some small spaces into huge ones."[62]

TASK FORCE K-BAR

The early portion of Operation *Enduring Freedom* (OEF), the invasion of Afghanistan which began officially on October 7, 2001, was commanded by Navy SEAL Rear Admiral Albert M. Calland III. The operation saw the theater of operation divided into two primary areas, each with its own mission, tailor-made for the diverse multi-national special operations forces that would participate in the assault. "The northern command, code named Task Force Dagger, focused on fighting with the Afghan resistance to defeat the Taleban government while the Combined Joint Special Operations Task Force South, code named Task Force K-Bar, focused on the destruction of al-Qaeda's ability to conduct operations in Afghanistan."[63] SEAL Captain Robert S. Harward was the commander of TF K-Bar until April 2002, and his forces included 2,700 personnel from Naval Special Warfare, Army Special Forces, Air Force special operations aircraft and special tactics personnel as well as special operations forces from Germany, Australia, New Zealand, Canada, Denmark, Norway,

Inside shot of the modified Humvees that the SEALs inherited in Oman from the US Army. The office chairs serving as seats were taken from the Tactical Operations Center on Masirah Island, Oman. The legs were taken off the chairs, and then they were bolted into the wheel well. Cargo straps hold down ammunition cans, water bottles, and 5gal. gasoline cans. (Authors' collections)

TASK FORCE K-BAR STANDARD OPERATING PROCEDURES

The combined and joint nature of Task Force K-BAR meant that it was imperative to outline Standard Operating Procedures (SOPs) to be used by all task force personnel in order to avoid confusion and to facilitate command and control. Below is the SOP for Combat Search and Rescue (CSAR) missions.

1. General

CSAR missions are designed to recover isolated persons (ISOPERS) by the most effective means possible from an area of operations (AO). A CSAR element has designated aircraft with dedicated ground force elements attached for dismounted recovery by force in a hostile environment.

2. Operation *Enduring Freedom*

OPERATION *ENDURING FREEDOM* (OEF) CSAR is provided by the Joint Services Operational Air Command (JSOAC). VBJSOAC CSAR forces are currently based out of Jacobabab, Pakistan located approximately 250nm south east of Qandahar airport and comprises the following assets:

    a. 2 x CH53's
    b. 2 x Para Rescue Teams
    c. SEAL PL Quick Reaction Force (QRF) and
    d. 1 x Combat Control Team

3. Response Times

JSOAC CSAR assets are maintained on 24 and 7 standby at 30-min notice to move (NTM). Flight time to the K-Bar AO is approximately 2.5 hours.

CSAR Phases CSAR operations are conducted in 5 phases as follows:

    a. CSAR Mission Alert Phase:
    b. Ingress Phase;
    c. Terminal Area Phase;
    d. Egress Phase; and
    e. Recovery Phase.

(Source: Task Force K-Bar, Standard Operating Procedure Manual, December 2001)

and Turkey.[64] He directed special reconnaissance and direct action missions throughout the country.

TF K-Bar was also supported by other aircraft from a carrier group and included F/A-18 Hornets and F-14 Tomcats for close air support. General James N. Mattis' Marine Corps Task Force 58 added some conventional infantry punch if and when needed.[65]

SEAL practicing firing a LAW rocket in Afghanistan. (Authors' collections)

One of the challenges presented to the commander of TF K-Bar was the multi-national component of the coalition special operations forces. In order to effectively execute their missions and in order to be able to work coherently together new standard operating procedures were put in place. The 50-page classified document was created in December 2001 and was distributed to all coalition SOF units.

CAMP RHINO

Tom and his fellow SEALs from ST-8 flew from Virginia through Germany to Bahrain, landing finally on Masirah Island off the coast of Oman. The platoon was in Oman for a week alongside a platoon from ST-3. Unfortunately, the SEALs did not have any vehicles in their Table of Organization and Equipment (TOE) and both platoons had to modify four Humvees that were donated by the US Army. Once the vehicles had been overhauled to meet their specific needs, the commandos practiced driving in their new beasts. Night vision goggles were used for nighttime driving and in all mobility training; the SEALs rehearsed contact drills as well. The ST-3 platoon lacked training in vehicle off-road driving so two members from ST-8 were asked to become ST-3's primary drivers. One of those drivers was Jeff Taylor, who was killed four years later while conducting rescue operations during Operation *Redwing*, in Afghanistan.

In November 2001, Tom and his SEALs' first top-secret mission during OEF was to conduct a special reconnaissance of a group of buildings in south central Afghanistan that was intended to become the forward operating base (FOB) of Camp Rhino. The previous month 199 soldiers of 3rd Battalion (-), 75th Ranger Regiment, had conducted a combat parachute assault on the same compound, Objective Rhino, to seize a remote desert landing strip, gather intelligence, establish a forward arming and refueling point for rotary-wing aircraft, and assess the capabilities of the airstrip for future operations.[66]

The intelligence gathered from the SEALs' mission would be critical to the TF K-Bar commander who needed as much information as possible to conduct a risk assessment prior to inserting the Marines, whose primary mission was to secure the buildings and surrounding area. The targeted building was a hunting lodge, and that fact comprised the total information available prior to the mission. The maps of Afghanistan in the military's possession were old Soviet ones with Cyrillic

ST-3 operators from Delta Platoon inside a CH-47, flown by Army TF-160 Pilots. Photograph taken in 2001. (Authors' collections)

writing and to a scale not suitable for US forces. It was up to the SEALs to bring some light to bear on the situation.

The SEAL insertion via special operations aircraft went fairly smoothly. Tom and his fellow SEALs were in-country alone for four days, because their vehicular reconnaissance missions took a little longer than anticipated. Staying clear of hostilities was, of course, a concern, but executing the mission at hand was of far greater significance. It did not help that Afghanistan was a cold place in October. Nonetheless, the SEALs transmitted the key intelligence back to higher command, where Captain Harward made the decision to proceed with the operation.

Four days after the SEALs began their reconnaissance, two members of US Air Force special operation combat control teams freefell into the black night near the target location. Their mission was to mark the drop/landing zone for the oncoming aircraft carrying the Marines. Once on the ground the CCT contacted the waiting SEALs, who drove to the air commandos' location, rendezvoused and enabled the CCT to mark the landing zone for the incoming Marines and to execute their mission successfully. The SEALs from ST-8 and ST-3 provided security as the aircraft and helicopters arrived and performed a smooth insertion. General Mattis and his Marines and SOF personnel cleared the structure and surrounding area. Tom's ST-8 platoon stayed at Camp Rhino for 45 days. The SEALs from ST-3 departed Camp Rhino for Oman the same day.

During the 45 days they spent at Camp Rhino, ST-8 conducted numerous Rat Patrols (vehicular desert patrols) in their vehicles around Camp Rhino's area of operation (AO) for General Mattis. The Rat Patrols lasted two to four days and their primary mission was to conduct special reconnaissance. The standing orders

US Navy SEALs pose in front of the site that later became Camp Rhino. The battle damage to the building is probably from the first raid conducted by Army Rangers the month prior. (Authors' collections)

Tail ramp of an Air Force Pave-Low helicopter rigged with a fast rope. Hanging off the end of the weapon can be seen hoses, fitted so that when the weapon is fired the brass and links fall out of the back of the helicopter. The grey matting on the floor is Kevlar lining. (Authors' collections)

(SO) given to Tom and his comrades by Camp Rhino's commander were simple: kill anyone (hostile). During one of their missions the team was soft compromised by two local Afghans with a single camel.[67] The SEALs quickly captured and detained them. Their mission compromised, the SOP called for immediate extraction or exfiltration, but the SEALs had permission to kill any armed combatant and that might have allowed them to continue. The SEALs decided to break down their vehicle hide-site and extract. They did not kill the two men only because they were not armed. Once the SEALs were ready to depart, they cut the restraints off the locals and drove off. Tom's platoon took pride that this was the only time they were compromised in 45 days of reconnaissance patrolling. Ultimately, other SOF teams were discovered, at times with disastrous results such as Operations *Anaconda* and *Redwing*.

In mid-November Delta Platoon from ST-3 relieved ST-8. ST-3's mission changed from reconnaissance to supporting the push north toward Qandahar Airport. From Camp Rhino ST-8 deployed to Bahrain via Oman, preparatory to deployment elsewhere in the Global War on Terrorism.

In 2007, Navy SEAL Darrick looked comfortable in his flight suit. He looked like a typical California beach boy with blond hair, and a ton of ink. Darrick had tattoos like a number of other new school SEALs. He is happily married and has a pretty exciting civilian job now.

One of the most fascinating stories came from his participation in an alert that actually dealt with the possibility of an attack on the US mainland pre-9/11. Like all SEALs, Darrick and his platoon participated in work-up deployments as well as actual overseas deployments. Rehearsals to take down GOPLATs were practiced at Point Hueneme, off the coast of southern California. The GOPLATs were taken down by inserting via fast-roping off aerial platforms or by swimming to the target once the Zodiacs brought the combat swimmers close enough to the site. The swimmers then used a hook and ladders to storm the gas and oil platforms. They had passed all their requirements with flying colors and had returned to Coronado. One afternoon, word came down that a cargo ship captained by an eastern European man was going to ram the vessel into the submarines at submarine base Point Loma. Once a vessel of that size entered a channel there was no way to stop it. Delta Platoon spun up, put on flight suits and balaclavas, and had weapons at the ready. The SEALs were ready to go. Then they were stood down. The platoon stood by for six hours when another intelligence briefing revealed that the sought-after captain had disembarked from the ship in Mexico. The situation resolved itself and San Diego was left in its slumber.

By the time the second tower collapsed in New York City on 9/11, Darrick and his teammates had gone into lock-down aboard a US Navy vessel. Once the

USO Show with Drew Carey, Wayne Newton, Neal McCoy, and Dallas Cowboys Cheerleaders in Qandahar Airport, Christmas 2001. The United Service Organizations is a congressionally chartered, private, nonprofit organization which has been supporting the US military since before World War II, through morale-boosting programs and recreational services at 130 locations around the world including centers in Kuwait, Qatar and Afghanistan. The USO organizes celebrity entertainment tours which bring volunteer celebrities to entertain, lift morale, and express the gratitude and support of the American people. (Authors' collections)

A group of SEALs was soft compromised by local Afghans after the seizure of Camp Rhino. The Afghani men were captured and held until the SEALs broke up their hide-site. They were then released without incident. (Authors' collections)

second plane hit the sky-scrapers, they all knew it was indeed an attack and not just a tragic accident. Their chief told them that they would be going to war and the SEALs watched the first salvo of Tomahawk missiles launched from the USS *Peleliu* with grim determination. CNN covered the opening shots. The SEALs were going to stage out of Pakistan along with some Marines.

Jacobobad Airbase in Pakistan was the base for SOF personnel to stage CSAR missions for special operations forces in Afghanistan. Seventeen SEALs with a mobile communications team (MCT) stayed inside a hangar but did not deploy during the opening phases. Special forces operational detachments (Green Berets) fought alongside anti-Taleban forces, sometimes on horseback.

Darrick and his platoon executed several missions in support in CSAR. On one flight their helicopters were shot at. Darrick could feel the rounds ripping into the helicopter. Kevlar blankets covered the floors of the aircraft, but one tactical officer was hit. Tracers dotted the dark night as American .50 cal. armor-piercing rounds struck back at the Taleban/al-Qaeda fighters (TAQ).

The SEALs, however, also pulled personal security detachment duty for General Tommy Franks, Commander in Chief, Central Command. They flew into Uzbekistan and Bagram Airport in a C-130 and bumped into a SEAL from ST-2 who had, along with six British Special Boat Service commandos, taken the prison where Mike Spann of the CIA was killed and John Walker Lindh, the American Taleban, was captured. Darrick recalled that the SEAL looked like a native Pashtun instead of a clean-shaven American sailor. ST-3 also provided SR intelligence for the Camp Rhino invasion in November 2001.

On one particular mission during ST-8's later deployment to Afghanistan, a Marine helicopter gunner incurred the SEALs' wrath as he lit up their Rat Patrol while they were traveling at night in the desert. Golf Platoon was in four Humvees tricked out with IR strobe lights and Glint tape to help identify them as a friendly force. Yet somehow the Marine gunner mistook them for the enemy and started spraying them with his machine gun. Frantically the SEALs' accompanying CCT contacted the helicopters and the Marine sergeant ceased firing. Once back at Camp Rhino the SEALs updated their list of the Most Wanted; 1) bin Laden, 2) the Marine Corps sergeant. The sergeant left Camp Rhino shortly thereafter.

The early nights at Camp Rhino were tense. Marines were told to shoot at anything on two feet and weapons were constantly discharged at both real and imaginary enemies, including, one night, an innocent camel. Other nights, American 81mm mortars and air assets were all over the place.

One day a particularly grizly scenario developed at Camp Rhino. The Chief told his SEALs that a B-52 bomber had dropped a JDAM (Joint Direct Attack Munition) on an ODA team (a US special forces operational detachment Alpha team). A 12ft bomb had landed within 100ft of the special forces Green Berets who also operated out of Jacobobad. The rescue helicopters returned to camp and both SEAL platoons were needed to unload the mangled bodies of their comrades. Some of the wounded were missing parts of their skulls, arms, and other body parts. It was an ugly mess. Air Force para-rescue jumpers trained as medics attached to the SEALs were the first ones to help the wounded. Darrick and his fellow commandos carried them away from the helicopters' rotor wash. Four

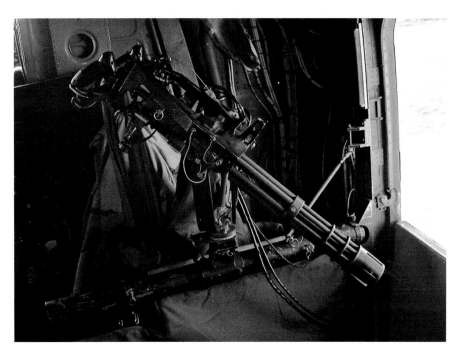

A minigun on the starboard side of a TF-160 helicopter. (Authors' collections)

helicopters carried about 21 wounded men. Some were placed into body bags. One soldier's arm was only attached by his skin. The scene was so horrible that the "head medical officer had a one-thousand-yard-stare and became more or less useless."[68] The SEALs helped him sit down as the other medical personnel continued to assist the wounded ODA personnel. Camp Rhino had a resident news team who wanted to videotape the scene but they were told to stay indoors or they would be arrested.

WAGONS EAST

JSOTF (Joint Special Operations Task Force) South Commander Harward wanted to be part of the convoy tasked with traveling to Qandahar as that city was about to become the new staging area for special operations missions. The 14-vehicle convoy of Humvees and trucks carried SEALs, ODA guys and MCT personnel on the 60nm trip from Rhino. It was bitterly cold but Harward managed to stand, Patton-like, in one of the vehicles. As the lead navigator, Darrick needed a map but none was immediately available. The Marines only had large-scale maps that were useless for normal military operations. Darrick had no real idea of the terrain or of the locations of the minefields en route to Qandahar.

The trip was filled with strange incidents. One time they drove into this "huge fucking town and the convoy arrived at a dead-end." Darrick yelled back for the other vehicles to back up as local villagers came out of the buildings. It was "shit eerie" as the Americans had no clue who these people were. For all they knew these were hardened Taleban supporters. Darrick worried about grenades landing on the convoy as the locals came closer but Commander Harward wanted a local guide. So, Darrick pointed to a local and his map and hand-and-arm signaled for

CONVOY FROM CAMP RHINO TO QANDAHAR INTERNATIONAL AIRPORT, 2001

The convoy being briefed at Camp Rhino; ST-3, Delta Platoon before leaving Camp Rhino; and shots of the convoy en route.

(Authors' collections)

directions. The local pointed in a specific direction and ended up traveling, by no choice of his own, ten miles with the convoy. He was "dumped" on the side of the road later.[69]

Another unnerving factor was that the convoy was required to drive with their headlights on as ordered by Commander Harward. Coalition air assets had orders to fire on all vehicles that traveled at night without lights on. Many SOF personnel believed that Glint tape and IR strobe lights should have been enough as target identifiers. Now, with their lights on, some of special operations commandos believed the Taleban forces could ambush the convoy more easily. Driving the vehicles without lights would have been manageable as NODs (Night Observation Devices) were capable of illuminating the dark roads. But with the vehicles' lights on, the Americans' advantage of nighttime vision was canceled out and they were left vulnerable to attack.

The road near Lashkar Gar turns into a small channel and the locals had set up a checkpoint, with AKs (Avtomat Kalashnikova) and RPGs (rocket-propelled grenades) ever present. As the convoy approached the check-point, one sailor from Dam Neck recommended staggering the vehicles so as to present a less

SEAL team posing in front of Qandahar International Airport. (Authors' collections)

Sunset shot of the tent city outside of the terminal at Qandahar International Airport. (Authors' collections)

uniform target. That suggestion was immediately countermanded by Commander Harward and the convoy proceeded in a straight, single file, a perfect target for an ambush. Darrick was convinced he was going to get hit. He prepared to rush out of the lead vehicle and engage anyone in the nearby buildings. Fortunately, the convoy moved forward unmolested and hit a hard-ball highway to Qandahar. They "hauled ass" and hit the city.

One last interesting point made by Darrick regarding Afghanistan concerns an incident that took place after the Taleban had been crushed. The SEALs were near bin Laden's former training location at Tarnak Farms when one of them took a step forward. Had it not been for one Mujahideen sniper who pulled him back, he would have stepped on an undetected mine and blown them all to smithereens. Afghanistan is one of the most mine-ridden countries in the world and one other Navy SEAL was subsequently killed in this area from exactly the fate that Darrick had narrowly escaped.

For Darrick the war soon ended. There simply was too much bureaucracy and micro-management, especially during times of war, for him to tolerate staying in any longer. It was time to go home and spend time with his family.

TASK FORCE K-BAR MISSIONS

ZHAWAR KILI

Michael, a Navy SEAL officer, recalled how ideal Afghanistan was for special operations teams executing their missions. When the SEALs from ST-3 arrived they were given a target list specifying 96 HVTs and these targets were divided among all the special operations units present. The list was fought over quite a bit. DevGru, in particular, hunted HVTs such as bin Laden and Mullah Omar. Competition was intense.[70]

Zhawar Kili was not their original target. SEAL Team 3 was originally allocated a smaller compound that 20 men easily could have taken down. The Zhawar Kili complex was large and the special forces ODA teams had the manpower to hit it: "We were not originally assigned this target but the ODA team from 5th Group that was going to do it had to leave the country after they hit a target and killed members of the Anti-Taleban Force. They were still in Oman when [our] platoon returned to palletize all the gear to come home months later."[71] The SEALs were thus tasked with the Zhawar Kili cave terrorist complex near Khowst instead. But they needed help and to that end the Marine Corps provided a 50-man security element for the mission into the sensitive site.

BRIEFING AND PREPARATION

The SEALs received several intelligence briefs on the history and make-up of the base camp and the tunnel complex above, accompanied by maps and photographs prior to their mission. The briefs were based on information reports rather than finally evaluated intelligence, and the information "regarding the physical description of the Zhawar facility dates back to the period between 1987 and 1989," although the information regarding bin Laden's association with the caves was current.[72]

Task Force K-BAR, the special operations task force composed of coalition SOF personnel commanded by US Navy SEAL commander Robert Harward. (Authors' collections)

The brief told the SEALs that the Zhawar Kili cave complex had been established in the early 1980s "as an eastern Afghanistan resistance base prior to the Soviet occupation."[73] The commander appointed at that time was still in charge of the complex. Prior to a US military strike on August 20, 1998, the base camp facility had been used "as a safesite and meeting location by Usama (Bin Ladin), a terrorist training facility, and assembly or meeting area for personnel associated with Bin Ladin."[74] The camp facility was said to be mainly populated by Arabs (al-Qaeda) and Taleban personnel. The base camp facility was described as consisting of "at least three large tunnels and three to four small caves. In addition, the Zhawar complex contains sleeping quarters, a kitchen, a mosque, and a training area."[75]

The base camp complex was spread out over at least 500m along a dry stream bed; some of the distances between elements of the complex were unknown, and other details were lacking. It was estimated there were three large tunnels, but "the exact number of tunnels/caves is unknown, source can only remember details about the main area."[76] There was a description of the insides of the caves, tunnels, and associated room structures, and the security measures in place between 1987 and 1989.

Above the base camp was a large cave complex built into a ridge of the Sodyaki Ghar mountain by the Mujahideen during the Soviet–Afghan War, 1979–89. It was a logistics base, with 11 tunnels reaching 500m into the mountain. "In 1986 the complex contained a hotel, a mosque, several arms depots and repair shops, a garage, a medical point, a communications center and a kitchen."[77] At that time it garrisoned a 500-man regiment, and although not fully equipped for combat, it was considered invincible. An Afghan government attack on the base in 1985 was unsuccessful, a second attack the following year was slightly more successful, and following 57 days of bombing and fighting the Soviets were able

Task Force K-Bar target lists. (Authors' collections)

AQ008: ZHAWAR KILI COMPLEX, JANUARY 6–14, 2002

Post-deployment briefing. *(Authors' collections)*

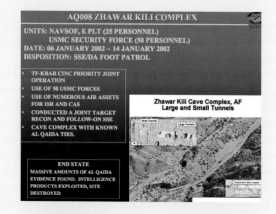

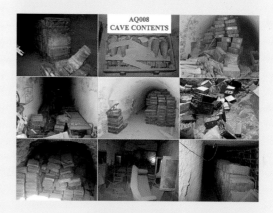

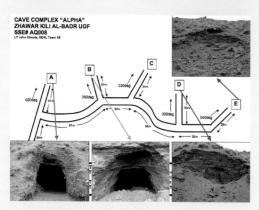

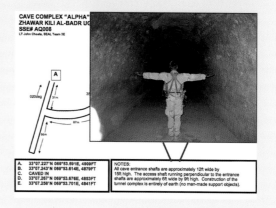

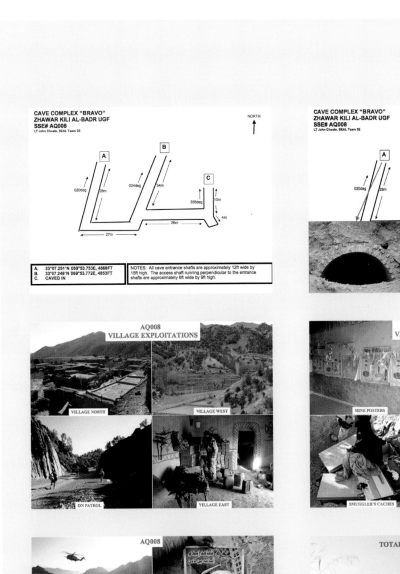

CAVE COMPLEX "BRAVO"
ZHAWAR KILI AL-BADR UGF
SSE# AQ008
LT John Choate, SEAL Team 3E

NORTH

A. 33°07.251'N 069°53.753E, 4868FT
B. 33°07.248'N 069°53.772E, 4853FT
C. CAVED IN

NOTES: All cave entrance shafts are approximately 12ft wide by 15ft high. The access shaft running perpendicular to the entrance shafts are approximately 6ft wide by 9ft high.

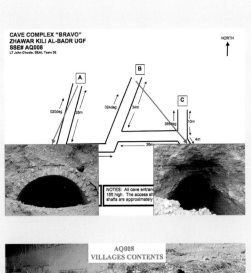

CAVE COMPLEX "BRAVO"
ZHAWAR KILI AL-BADR UGF
SSE# AQ008
LT John Choate, SEAL Team 3E

NORTH

NOTES: All cave entrance shafts are approximately 15ft high. The access shafts are approximately

AQ008
VILLAGES CONTENTS

MINE POSTERS

HIDDEN FIGHTING HOLE

SMUGGLER'S CACHES

ROOFTOP DECORATION

AQ008
VILLAGE EXPLOITATIONS

VILLAGE NORTH

VILLAGE WEST

ON PATROL

VILLAGE EAST

AQ008

RESUPPLY

AL QAIDA PROPAGANDA FROM AQ008

GRAVE DIGGING

"JDAM " & "CAS" – AFGHAN REFUGEES

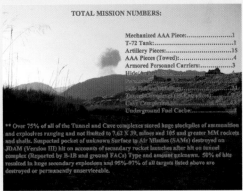

TOTAL MISSION NUMBERS:

Mechanized AAA Piece:	1
T-72 Tank:	1
Artillery Pieces:	15
AAA Pieces (Towed):	4
Armored Personnel Carriers:	3
Hide/Am...	
Personnel ...	
Safe Hou...	
Tunnel Complexes (Destroyed):	
Cave Complexes ...	
Underground Fuel Cache:	

** Over 75% of all of the Tunnel and Cave complexes stored huge stockpiles of ammunition and explosives ranging and not limited to 7.62 X 39, mines and 105 and greater MM rockets and shells. Suspected pocket of unknown Surface to Air Missiles (SAMs) destroyed on JDAM (Version III) hit on accounts of secondary rocket launches after hit on tunnel complex (Reported by B-1B and ground FACs) Type and amount unknown. 50% of hits resulted in huge secondary explosions and 95%-97% of all targets listed above are destroyed or permanently unserviceable.

to rout the Mujahideen from the facility for a few hours, which they then aimed to destroy before the Mujahideen counterattacked. A description of the facility came from a magazine article published in Russian in the 1990s by the colonel tasked with the destruction. The colonel was "amazed that caves and the buildings within the caves were still in perfect condition even after the amount of bombs and precision munitions that had been dropped on them."[78] In the four hours they had before withdrawal, they could not destroy the caves, despite laying 200 anti-tank mines in the primary caves. The facility was operational again with three weeks, and the caves were improved and lengthened.

Chris thought that the caves were nowhere near as numerous and deep as the briefings had led his team to believe. He felt that "there was not much information on [the complex] other than we were told that it had been getting bombed for the last couple of days."[79] He recalls:

> We were briefed by the commanding officer of Task Force K-Bar, Commander Harward. He really did not have that much information to pass because there was really none available at the time. Our mission was to go in and patrol the area and take pictures of the damage. We were told that a Marine security element of 50 men would provide perimeter security while we were in the middle searching the area. The platoon was briefed that we were going in for 12 hours only. Because the vehicles we had did not fit into the helicopters we went in on foot. Each man wore his land warfare gear with a drop leg holster. The holster was to do a transition from our M4 to our handgun like we do in CQB (Close-Quarters Battle) because of the caves. In tight quarters like a cave or a house you do not have time to fix a jam or reload if your primary weapon goes down so you must quickly pull out your handgun to finish the fight.
>
> Harward did platoon rehearsals with the Marines and did a practice dirt dive patrol around the airport. The platoon met up with the pilots that were flying us into the area.

One of the problems for the SEALs during preparation was that the Zhawar Kili complex was about two kilometers away from the Pakistani border: "approximately three kilometers north and four kilometers west of the Afghanistan and Pakistan border."[80] Strategically and tactically, this proximity allowed enemy personnel to flee across the mountain ranges into Pakistan where American troops were prohibited from entering. Any close air support, or any useful air strikes had to enter Pakistani air space and that, of course, was prohibited.

"We were at this point assigned a chemical weapons super freak from the Army, two FBI agents, along with the two combat controllers and two Navy EOD operators, both of whom were already part of the platoon."[81] The SEAL platoon's AOIC carried video and camera equipment for intelligence-gathering purposes.

The team also carried DNA kits as a back-up to the FBI agents to gather samples from dead bodies, finger-prints, hair samples and so on. Photos of the killed were to be used to identify key enemy personnel.

It was planned that air strikes would obliterate any personnel inside the caves and the area in general before the SEALs inserted in what was arguably the most high-profile mission of the war thus far. The mission lasted much longer than

---

Below is an outline for mission planning which details the pertinent information necessary to execute the mission properly and notifying all involved Joint (J) sections.

SENSITIVE SITE EXPLOITATION (SSE)

REF: JSOTF-S MISSION FOLDER

1. JSOTF-S mission folder must be completed with the exception of :

    a. Fragorder

    b. Comm request (Comms will be generic IAW standing AOR *ICEOI*)

    c. Execution checklist (generic execution checklist will be provided)

    d. Air support request (operations will facilitate this, as this is a 6-hour readiness state)

2. J-CODE support plan:

    a. J-1

        1). Submit a completed manifest to operations of all personnel conducting mission.

    b. J-2

        1). Ensure unit conducting mission will provide all target information.

        2). Give complete route analysis to and from target.

        3). Give all navigation aids/maps/charts to unit conducting target.

        4). Review all ISOPREP information and issue blood chits for unit conducting exercise.

    c. J-3

        1). Provide asset requests (i.e. air request, surf ace support, etc.)

        2). Provide fire support coordination.

    d. J-3.5

        1). Assign lead mission planner to coordinate mission folder and permission checklist.

    e. J-4

        1). Have ordnance rep standing by for ammo/ord draw.

        2). Coordinate unit short term sustenance (96 hour supply of food/water)

        3). Pre-stage any resupply requested.

        4). Pre-stage any on/off-load requirements (truck, fork lift etc…)

    f. J-6

        1). Make comms "smart-packs" up and distribute accordingly (J-3, lead mission tracker, unit conducting mission, FOB, and watch-standers).

        2). Draw and have available all crypto requirements.

        3). Have J-6 rep to coordinate supporting arms comms issues.

        4). Update execution checklist with pertinent unit information.

planned; the air strikes did nothing to help, but the information gathered was a public relations dream-come-true for the American president.

THE MISSION

The SEALs and Marines flew in CH-53s to Zhawar Kili near Khwost, which was about 180 km from Qandahar. "We inserted via CH-53E helicopters. The flight was long – almost three hours. The helicopters did a mid-air refueling and we continued on."

The operations order called for the insertion to take place on a higher elevation than the complex so the Americans could more or less walk down toward their target. The elevation difference to the target was approximately 700ft but as they approached their landing zone a small village was spotted that was not on the Soviet maps. A quick decision saw them insert southeast of a flat area forcing them on a 3,000–4,000m hump so that they could enter the area from the southern end of the valley.

The Marine Corps security element covered the left and right flank of the SEAL platoon as they maneuvered toward their objective. Their formation was staggered and it reminded Chris and Michael of their training during pre-deployments in the US. Communication was constant among the officers but conversations were short. The SEALs were deep in enemy territory. The American troops stripped off their outer cold weather gear at the security halt because the weather was good and humping across the country heats up the body and can cause heat stroke.

The unit humped seven miles and executed many cave assaults. The travel and the assaults took much longer than expected and it was tough, hot work. The SEALs also found more intelligence than anticipated: tanks, BMPs (Boyevaya Mashina Pekhoty – Combat Vehicle of Infantry), stingers, bio/chemical suits, PRC-77 radios, cryptology tapes as well as the high-speed PRC-177 Deltas. CCT (Air Force combat controllers) operators marked the numerous cave entrances with their GPS for future CAS (close air support) missions. The FBI examined gravesites that were much larger than previously thought. The team dug up all the bodies for identification purposes.

Once we inserted all of us stopped and during the initial security halt stripped off our jackets we were wearing during

Chris Osman standing next to a poster of Osama bin Laden after his platoon raided a terrorist training camp adjacent to the Zhawar Kili cave complex in January 2002. The post-9/11 posters show bin Laden in front of cartoon-type planes crashing into the World Trade Center. The posters were taken off the wall and sent to the National Security Agency to be analyzed. (Authors' collections)

the flight in. We started to patrol and quickly realized that the bombs did not do shit and had missed about 90 percent of their intended targets. The platoon patrolled up to where the caves began and started entering the caves just like we would a house or a ship. I was nervous as hell because the caves were so deep that the light on our weapons just faded away into the dark. It was very difficult to see in some of the caves, added to that was the ever-present possibility of stepping on landmines and/or booby traps. We searched the caves for hours and found a huge stockpile of weapons, ammunition, BMPs, a couple of tanks, and stolen US PRC-117 radios. There were chemical suits, Stinger missile boxes, pretty much everything you would need to start a war. It was painstaking, very hot work. The sun had come out and because of the time constraints of 12 hours we did not have time to take off our cold weather underclothing and it was hotter than a fox in a forest fire. As we continued to clear the caves the combat controllers and our AOIC were marking the entrances of the caves with GPS as well as other larger targets like the tanks and BMPs. The info was then going to be disseminated once we were back at the airport for follow-on strikes. The platoon cleared the last cave and took a short break to drink some water and get a quick bite of an MRE [Meals Ready to Eat – dehydrated food]. After that we got up and patrolled to our extract point and waited to be picked up by the Marines. Little did we know what was about to happen.

The SEALs kept their chain of command informed, but were directed in minute detail by Commander Harward, who sought much more information. Pictures

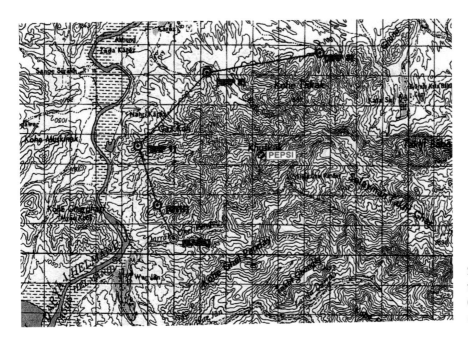

Sample evasion route map taken from Task Force K-Bar's Standard Operating Procedures manual. (Authors' collections)

An MK12 SEAL Sniper Rifle. Picture taken by operators on an SR in Afghanistan in 2005. The operator who took the photo was later killed in a rescue mission during Operation *Redwing*. (Authors' collections)

were sent back electronically to him. After ten hours they were told to stay in place and to expect a re-supply drop. The Marines continued to perform their security mission.

An impromptu meeting between the leadership of the SEALs and Marines was set up to discuss the situation and address the questions of where to spend the night and how to organize their defenses. They decided to take over a small farm area they had passed earlier in their mission. It had also been marked as the extraction point. A three-man SEAL element moved toward the village to secure it. Chris recalls:

The FBI agents who were with us were supposed to be working on DNA samples on any dead people and were supposed to dig up any graves that were found. The enemy was known for burying their dead within 24 hours so part of their mission was to bring back DNA to be analyzed to find out if any of the bombs dropped before we got there killed anyone of significance. A few of the pictures were sent back via SATCOM (Satellite Communication) to Commander Harward to look at while we waited to be picked up. He asked to speak with the FBI agents to see if they had dug up any of the graves. When they told him no he had the extract cancelled and the helicopters turned around about 10 minutes before our scheduled pick up. Commander Harward told my OIC that we were not leaving and we had to go back to dig up the bodies. This presented a couple of issues. One was that we had not brought any overnight gear to brave the elements with, and neither had the Marines. We were told no matter what we were coming out in 12 hours so we packed for a 24-hour op. I had my gear set up so I would never drink the two quarts of water on my belt. It was strictly for Escape and Evasion. I had water but most of the guys drank theirs. And we all brought one MRE so we were fucked in the food department. Another issue was a base camp to hole up in so we could stage our gear and lighten the load a bit because we all had on packs with rockets, body armor and ballistic helmets. The Marines were in a similar situation as well. So the top four leaders in the platoon had a quick pow wow with the Marine leaders and it was decided that we would patrol back to the caves and take over a small village that was up on one of the hills.

It was dark out and myself and two other guys dropped all of our armor and hauled ass up the hill on the back side of the village. We moved in just with our H-gear and weapons. We didn't come in from the front but maneuvered to the rear of the village. We then sat and listened for about five minutes. We entered the courtyard and as one guy held security we went room to room doing two-man entries and cleared the village. Most of the doors had been locked so we kicked them in. There were some small chains with locks on them. Not much of an obstacle though. I seem to remember six doors and remember the villages were really like one or two big buildings that looked like a mini fortress. We cleared the rooms with two men, the others pulled rear security. Once we did our job we contacted the leader's element. Two of us stayed to keep the village secure and I moved toward my platoon and the Marines where I contacted them at the bottom of the hill. We grabbed our gear

A copy of the Koran taken from the rubble from bin Laden's headquarters building at Tarnac Farms by a SEAL operator. Photograph taken in 2001. (Authors' collections)

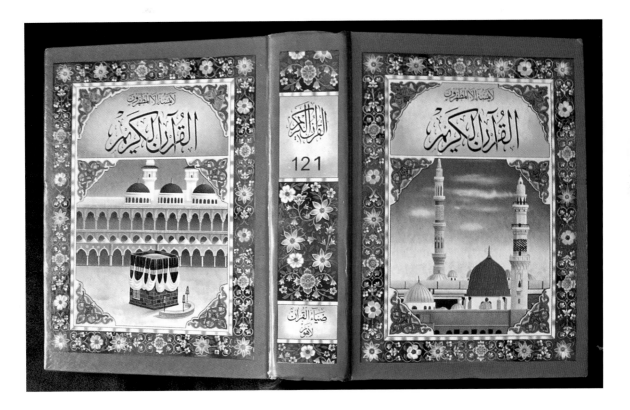

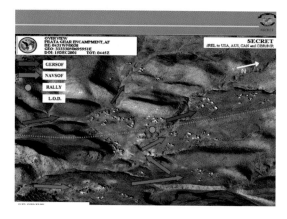

AQ036: Prata Ghar Village, January 23–24, 2002. Post-deployment briefing. (Authors' collections)

and moved to our new camp. CCT set up in a small room for their comms shit. They cut holes in the roof for their coaxial cables and Sat stuff. You know they still had to support the mission and call in all those coordinates.

Immediately the Marines set up a four-corner security watch, while we hunkered down to get some sleep. The room the platoon was in had a small cooking stove so we lit a fire in it to keep warm and everyone crashed out in seconds. "Holy Shit, what the fuck is up with all the smoke?" That was my OIC when he walked into the room at about 3am. We were so tired that no one woke up when burning embers caught one of the bedrolls on fire. We were snoring logs while the room was filling with smoke. After we figured out what the hell was going on he called out names of some of the guys in the platoon to go out on a foot patrol to locate some dead people an AC-130 gunship had just engaged. We were to go find them and do DNA samples on them. I was one of the guys picked to go out on the patrol while the other guys went with the FBI agents to dig up gravesites. The SEAL/Marine element split in half that morning with one half of the SEAL platoon with CCT sent to locate the enemy killed during the previous night, while the other half with the FBI continued with the original mission.

Chris patrolled toward the last known location of the Taleban forces, but it required a P-3 Orion aircraft to vector them in. The Spectre gunship had left as soon as it lost the protective cloak of the dark. The gunships are "slow as shit" and provide an inviting target to the enemy, hence their night deployment only. It was morning nautical twilight (defined as the time when the center of the sun is more than six degrees below the horizon but less than 12 degrees) when the SEALs were supposed to be standing on top of the dead bodies from the previous night's kill. But within 30 seconds they heard voices behind them and the SEALs went prone, low to the ground, when they spotted locals coming out of the cave entrances that littered the general area. The OIC called for air strikes and after some time and communication and GPS issues, the CCT got a bird on station. Two F-18s missed their target, unsurprising given that their speed makes it difficult for them to hit specific areas. They were also hampered by the proximity to Pakistan, and the fact that the map grid coordinates were based on the unreliable old Soviet maps. The SEALs engaged the three hostiles but eventually a B-52 slammed the area with JDAMs. After the strike the SEALs found some burnt clothing. A P-3 Orion claimed that 12–15 enemy were killed and must have been vaporized by the massive payload dropped on them. The mountain was smoldering.

On the way to the bomb craters the SEALs came upon a small house, which they quickly cleared. Here they found caches of suitcases filled with passports, money, and clothing. They assumed this was a safe house. After having taken a GPS coordinate the team departed. A subsequent air strike reduced the building to rubble.

Chris and his platoon patrolled back to their village. There they linked up with the other half of the platoon, which had finished its sensitive site exploitation and graveside DNA mission. A short 12-hour mission had entered its second full day. The combined American force was to stay there for an additional eight and a half days.

Echo Platoon from SEAL Team 3 being briefed on the hood of a Humvee at Qandahar International Airport. A SIGINT (signals intelligence) hit came up from a known terrorist's cell phone and the platoon was tasked with a vehicle ambush mission. The platoon is being shown the road the vehicle would be travelling. (Authors' collections)

131

THE VILLAGE OF THE DAMNED

The task force finally killed some animals to eat. Although at first the Marines refused to do so, hunger eventually forced them to join in. The days passed filled with a variety of missions and tasks.

Day 3 brought a much-needed aerial re-supply as well as two desert patrol vehicles (DPVs) and much-desired sniping rifles. Day 4 saw a four-man element carrying out reconnaissance on another valley to put eyes on yet another compound. After they monitored the compound for two hours they radioed their platoon, which then patrolled up and assaulted it to no avail.

In the meanwhile the Marines had pulled over an indigenous vehicle with a passenger who had a hand-held GPS system. The vehicle was kept and the prisoner, deemed unfriendly, was sent back with helicopters a little bit later during that day. The SEALs used the indigenous vehicle and took an additional six-man team and their DPVs to check on the grids that were discovered on the hand-held GPS. As was to be expected, the DPVs got stuck in the soft sand. It was considered a "shit vehicle without armor, just speed with a single rear wheel drive." To top it off it was a four-cylinder vehicle and it used regular fuel, which, unlike diesel, does not start well in higher elevation, thus rendering the vehicles almost useless.

At long last one DPV, alongside the indigenous vehicle, managed to take off toward a terrorist training camp nicknamed T2 – the Tarnak Farms Two. Several

Picture of a JDAM hitting the front entrance of a cave in the Zhawar Kili cave complex, January 2002. Air strike called in by Air Force combat controller attached to SEAL Team 3, Echo Platoon. (Authors' collections)

years earlier, this site had been targeted by the Clinton Administration with a rather impotent missile strike, which was in response to the bombings on US embassies in Tanzania and Kenya. It was a massive complex and the 11–12 men cleared the buildings and the surrounding area. Of course, they used a sniper overwatch position to give them an edge in case of contact. The snipers spotted an individual moving in a nearby lower dry riverbed less than 30ft away. The SEALs did not see him because there was a 10–15ft drop to the creek. The OIC ordered them to capture him alive if at all possible. Chris moved up quietly from behind and slammed the unsuspecting victim straight into the ground. It had been a scary moment for Chris but he had stuck to his task well. Chris and his buddy noticed other tracks, which the platoon soon followed for about 1–2km. There they located another village, cleared it, and found landmines and small arms. They bumped into some friendly civilians, who made it known that bin Laden was in the hills of Pakistan. The SEALs departed and marked this village with a GPS coordinate as well. T2 and the village were later leveled by B-52 strikes. More CAS was dumped in the Zhawar Kili area in nine days than would be later dropped during the entirety of Operation *Anaconda* (which involved thousands of coalition and anti-Taleban forces, and is considered one of the largest military operations since the Gulf War of 1991).

The DPV patrol had also managed to capture two prisoners in another vehicle and, once consolidated, the three enemy prisoners of war (EPWs) were airlifted out to Qandahar for interrogation. The whole platoon now had access to one DPV and two local vehicles for their mobility operations.

During that night all the previously marked 60-plus cave entrances were bombed. The CCT continuously received new coordinates for more and more CAS runs. The SEALs also provided detailed information about the configuration and layout of the caves. They even provided pace counts and sketches. The CCT became so worn out from calling in CAS that they asked the SEALs to help them out. It was a non-stop bombing campaign and the CCT needed to eat and sleep.

Day 5 was the day the three EPWs were picked up following another helicopter re-supply run. A four-man team was inserted in the early hours of the next day to observe a trail suspected to be used by TAQ fighters infiltrating from Pakistan. If they encountered anyone at all their orders were to kill them. They joined another team composed of six Marines and two snipers at a location that was an enemy ambush site. Here they found a hot tea pot, six Chinese grenades, six RPGs, and an SKS rifle. One of the RPGs now decorates a hall at NAVSPECWARGROUP 1. Chris believes that their insertion scared the enemy, who then left the area. And like all other locations, this one too was bombed by air assets later.

After a day off, Day 7 of a seemingly never-ending operation saw two snipers on overwatch as the platoon with the Marines swept through a valley toward Pakistan. Chris and his sniping partner discovered a trail as the platoons started to bound back toward their Afghan village. They received permission to follow the trail. The two SEALs were patrolling the area and discovered a small sleeping area. They kept going when Chris heard a soft alert from his team-mate. Chris had walked right by a small cave entrance without noticing. Chris' heart almost stopped. Luckily it was empty, and they cleared the small cave/hardened log bunker without incident. Here they found blankets, sleeping bags, plates, cooking pots, an area for a small cooking fire. The ashes were probably a couple of days old. Coordinates were taken so that the cave could later be destroyed.

Day 8 saw the men prepare to depart the area, at long last. But CAS missions continued non-stop. Day 9 was the extraction day. They all humped back down the hill for their pick-up after successfully completing their simple, 12-hour mission. Back at Qandahar TF-K Bar Commander Harward demanded the SEALs shave before granting them a debriefing.

Below and opposite:
The inside of the compound of a target site. SEAL Team 3 and German KSK commandos performed a pre-dawn assault on this target, Prata Ghar, in 2002. Units captured a weapons cache with automatic weapons, grenades, mortar tubes and rounds. All munitions were blown in place before the team extracted from the target. (Authors' collections)

PRATA GHAR

One of Germany's most significant joint special operations missions occurred with the SEALS. For the first time since World War II, the Germans were conducting operations outside Germany. The German government's commitment to the US after 9/11 was so strong that special legislation was passed for their deployment.

The Kommando Spezialkräfte (KSK) provided a large contingent to Task Force K-Bar. Chris recalls the number was between 60 and 65 members present in Qandahar. Their small arms were all manufactured by the German company of Heckler & Koch (HK). Their hand guns were all HK USPs and their assault rifles had E.O. Tech Holographic Weapons Systems sights. The Germans, like all the other coalition special operations forces, arrived after the American SOF. The KSK unit discipline, cohesiveness, and equipment were impressive. Although the quality of all the foreign SOF was very good, one could tell the Germans had a lot of money compared to other forces such as the New Zealand Special Air Service whose equipment was not nearly as well funded. Chris Osman notes:

I thought we were very high-speed and had the best personal equipment but the Germans were far superior in that aspect. We lived out of parachute bags and they had metal lockers and stackable containers. Their cold weather gear was made up of matching white Gortex and the Germans were the only force that exclusively used their own nation's manufactured weapons systems. All the other spec ops units used American-manufactured small arms. One interesting thing was that only the West Germans spoke English and they had to translate for their comrades from the east. The Germans also had their own doctor on missions while the SEALs, for example, had to rely on corpsmen only. You could really tell their government supported them unconditionally.

This particular operation was a joint sensitive site exploitation and direct action mission involving 15 US Navy SEALs who had been at Zhawar Kili, two Air Force Special Tactics Squadron members, two explosive ordnance disposal personnel, two FBI agents, one other special ops member, and 40 hard-core KSK.

The SOF personnel involved in the operation took one C-17 to Bagram. There they stayed for two days until they received their final go-ahead for the mission. At Bagram they prepped the details. Maps indicated the layout of the target: one four-story central building and 13 smaller ones. The Germans were to hit the big building and the SEALs were to clear the remaining 13 structures. No vehicles were to be involved. Task Force 160 provided two CH-47s for the pre-dawn assault. The SOF element had only seen one photograph of the buildings in their target folders and they were told that some Predator footage indicated the set of buildings was occupied. The SOF unit never got to see any of those video images.

The wheels of the helicopters went up at 0400 hours and the flight lasted about 45 minutes in the cold winter night. Snivel (cold weather) gear was comprised of uniforms, long johns, gloves, hats, boots, gaiters, and anything else that was available and might keep the men warm.

It was pitch black inside the transport helicopter and any information had to be passed by the tail gunner or crew chief, who controlled the ramp, with a small board that had a tiny green light as illumination. If the information was crucial the little board was passed to every member on the aircraft.

Some time before 0500 hours, the tail ramp dropped as the SEALs stood up at the one-minute mark from insertion. In less than 60 seconds the commandos hit their landing zone (LZ). The white lights on their M4s were to be used in building clearing and those structures were only 35yds away from them. Each one of the houses had a unique American city as a code name or pro-word. So whenever an SOF team

Patch of Echo Platoon, ST-3. (Authors' collections)

cleared a building they radioed to their OIC with the appropriate pro-word such as "going to NY City" or "cleared Washington D.C." Each message that indicated their progress was sent to Bagram.

The SEALs also carried more than they needed in their rucksacks as the experience of the nine-day mission in Zhawar Kili was still fresh in their minds. Extra food, overnight gear, more ammunition, and LAW rockets added pounds to their already heavy rucksacks.

As the helicopters landed on their pre-designated LZs, the SEALs exited and moved 20ft or so to the rear of the helicopters. The SEAL platoon formed a half-moon-shaped line, facing the target buildings. Once in that formation they took a knee as their heavily laden rucksacks pushed them into the snow. Unbeknown

ENDURING FREEDOM MISSIONS EXECUTED BY ECHO PLATOON, SEAL TEAM 3

- AQ032 – Landi Karez compound
    Mounted SSE (combined operation)
    15 x SEALs, 2 x STS, 2 x EOD, 2 x FBI, 1 x CTIC
    50 ATF security force

- AQ008* – Zhawar Kili cave complex
    SSE/DA for nine days (combined/joint operation)
    17 x SEALs, 2 x STS, 2 x EOD, 2 x FBI, 1 x CTIC, 1 x CRD

- AQ036 – Prata Ghar village
    SSE/DA for 15 hours (combined operation)
    15 x SEALs, 2 x STS, 2 x EOD, 2 x FBI, 1 x CTIC
    40 x German SOF

- AQ049D* - Ali Kheyl Taghowstay compound
    SSE/DA for 15 hours (combined operation)
    17 x SEALs, 2 x STS, 2 x EOD, 2 x CTIC, 2 x Army PSYOPS
    24 x German SOF

- AQ050A – Ahmed Kheyl cave complex
    SSE/DA for 15 hours (combined operation)
    17 x SEALs, 2 x STS, 2 x EOD, 2 x CTIC
    24 x German SOF

- Operation *Anaconda* QRF
    16 x SEALs, 1 x STS, 2 x EOD, 1 x CTIC
    5 x Norway SOF
    15 x Danish SOF

- AQ058 – How-e Madad compound
    Mounted SSE/DA for 4 hours (combined operation)
    16 x SEALs, 2 x STS, 2 x EOD, 2 x CTIC
    6 x desert patrol operators
    15 x Danish SOF
    10 x Afghan military forces
    4 x US Army special forces

*Denotes CINC priority targets

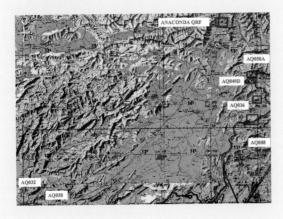

Map of the area of operations for Echo Platoon, ST-3. (Authors' collections)

to the SEALs, as they spilled out of their helicopter, the accompanying "EOD guy sunk into very deep snow where his foot got stuck, tearing his calf muscle and rendering him useless. He just laid there."

Once organized, they moved toward a set-point to link up with the German SOF who were in the second TF-160 helicopter and landed 15 seconds later. Chris remembers taking off his rucksack as the second helicopter flared in and the rotor wash created a little storm in their midst. As the helicopter flared, one of its door mini-guns roared. Tension or a jolt as the plane landed caused the Army aircrew member to depress the trigger. The accidental discharge was alarming as the SEALs thought he was engaging enemy personnel. However, soon they linked up with the Germans. Since their surprise landing had been compromised by the accidental gunfire, the coalition SOF executed their mission without noise discipline. Doors were kicked in as the various teams split into well-rehearsed maneuvering and covering elements. The SEALs cleared buildings to the left and right as the German KSK went between and headed straight for their target – the biggest building.

Chris and his team-mates thought they had taken fire and had a man down. After they had cleared their second target building aggressively they discovered that the man down was the injured EOD operator who had fallen, not wounded by enemy fire. The unfortunate injured man was taken out of the target area by the second helicopter. Their platoon chief told them to take it down a notch and to stop shooting off doors. One room, Chris remembers, had a chain and he called and motioned for the SEAL who was the breacher to blow off a door. Three shotgun rounds later, the breacher kicked in the door only to discover a small group of women and children. Chris and his breacher proceeded to clear the room, leaving the women and children unharmed and without a door to the room. The SEALs moved on to the next house.

Left:
Operation *Anaconda* Quick Reaction Force, February 26–March 10, 2002. Post-deployment briefing.

Right:
SEALs sitting on tarmac 20 minutes after they were bumped off the QRF helicopters by the Rangers during Operation *Anaconda* and the rescue mission of Neil Roberts. (Authors' collections)

LESSONS LEARNED

- Units must have the ability to conduct immediate planning and rapid execution. Flexibility was our biggest asset.
- The importance of good fire discipline and PID cannot be overstated.
- NSW units should all have mobility training prior to coming to this AO.
- Missions are largely asset driven. The ground scheme of maneuver was dictated by rotary wing load limitations, which in turn was driven by terrain and elevation. Mission analysis was often fruitless without prior knowledge of which assets would be available for mission execution.
- JDAMs are extremely effective, especially when the ground unit has a means of determining the precise geographic target coordinates.
- Units must avoid the temptation to place more troops to task than required. Risk mitigation is a balance of a force large enough to deal with the expected enemy threat, yet not so large as to put an unnecessary number of soldiers in harm's way.
- When forward staging to an FOB, units should bring as much gear as possible to allow for execution of any type of mission. The idea, for example, of "We are only on QRF" may lead to equipment shortfalls in other mission areas.

(Source: ST-3 debriefing notes, 2002)

Both SEALs and KSK finished their mission and consolidated their forces. As usual in Afghanistan, weapons and small arms were found throughout their target area. The mission was executed in less than 25 minutes.

The coalition forces met with the village elders. They were offered tea or "chai" while an eight-man platoon patrolled an area near a road thought to have had a number of caves that had been pointed out in their target picture. The suspected caves turned out to be simply shadows, since no caves were discovered. However the alert SEALs spotted smoke tendrils rising from a wooded area. Chris and another SEAL cautiously ascended the hill for about 30yds and pushed carefully through a tree line, where they encountered a single-family structure where a mother and her two children lived. She spotted Chris with his raised M4, although her back had been turned to him, and began to scream "Spetznas" repeatedly. In her terror and unaware of the current political situation, she had mistaken the SEALs for Soviet special forces, who had fought in Afghanistan from 1979 to 1989. She grabbed the closest child and ran off along with another woman and three other children. Chris noted that the women were unveiled and that he had never seen anyone react and flee that fast before. The ghosts of wars past were still haunting this picturesque mountain area. The SEALs cleared the building, re-linked with their platoon, then returned to the village and blew up all of the weapons and ammunition. There was nothing left to do but get out of there and defrost.

A funeral ceremony took place the day after the battle of Takur Ghar took place. Neil Roberts's gear is on the far right. The rest of the gear belongs to the other special operations personnel killed during the rescue operations. The ceremony was held inside Task Force 11's (DevGru/Army Delta) compound. The large green GP (general purpose) tents in the background belonged to the Rangers who were called to go in as the quick reaction force. Photo taken March 2002. (Authors' collections)

Back at Qandahar the SEAL Commodore threw a party for the German KSK and their SEAL brothers, celebrating their first joint operation, and the Germans' first combat operation since 1945.

OPERATION *ANACONDA*

Operation *Anaconda* took place in Afghanistan in March 2002 and was intended to clear an area of TAQ fighters by means of a hammer and anvil maneuver. The hammer was comprised of anti-Taleban forces led by US special forces who were to force the Taleban forward toward the anvil of American troops already set up at strategic locations to block the Taleban's retreat. Numerous SOF reconnaissance elements dotted the valleys, providing valuable intelligence and CAS support to the American and anti-Taleban forces.

Unfortunately, one SEAL, Neil Roberts from DevGru, fell out of a helicopter when it took some fire as they were about to insert in a hostile LZ. A rescue attempt by his team-mates resulted in the death of another special operator from the AF STS (Air Force Special Tactics Squadron). Subsequently, a Ranger QRF (Quick Reaction Force) was shot down as well and split from its secondary support helicopter. The Rangers from the second helicopter climbed to the top of the mountain where they, with the help of CAS and coalition SOF reconnaissance elements, managed to hang on until rescued in the evening. This incident resulted in the death of a total of seven SOF personnel, and Operation *Anaconda* proved unsuccessful in its primary mission – the destruction of al-Qaeda and Taleban forces.[82]

OPERATION *REDWING*

Operation *Redwing* was a large-scale operation which took place in Afghanistan on June 28, 2005. As with all operations, special reconnaissance teams deployed to provide valuable intelligence, or to call in CAS or, at times, to interdict high value targets. One four-man SDV team conducting a reconnaissance mission was compromised and all but Marcus Luttrell were killed by TAQ fighters in a desperate firefight.

The official US Navy report states the following, based on Marcus Luttrell's debriefing and other investigations after the rescue: "On June 28, 2005, deep behind enemy lines east of Asadabad in the Hindu Kush of Afghanistan, a very committed four-man Navy SEAL team was conducting a reconnaissance mission at the unforgiving altitude of approximately 10,000ft."[83] Marcus Luttrell commented that "conducting SR missions is all about stealth – it's a very cool aspect."[84] Sometimes for SR missions they would be dropped off on mountain peaks with 12 guys, then they would spread out. Operation *Redwing* was a large multi-branch operation where the SEALs provided sniper overwatch and DA mission support. The report continues:

> The SEALs, Lt Michael Murphy, Gunner's Mate 2nd Class (SEAL) Danny Dietz, Sonar Technician 2nd Class (SEAL) Matthew Axelson and Hospital Corpsman 2nd Class (SEAL) Marcus Luttrell had a vital task. The four SEALs were scouting for Ahmad Shah, a terrorist in his mid-30s who grew up in the adjacent mountains just to the south.
>
> Under the assumed name Muhammad Ismail, Shah led a guerrilla group known to locals as the "Mountain Tigers," who had aligned with the Taliban and other militant groups close to the Pakistani border. The SEAL mission was compromised when the team was spotted by local nationals [shepherds], who presumably reported its presence and location to the Taliban.

One of the perks of deployment in Afghanistan – the best seat in the house. (Authors' collections)

A fierce firefight erupted between the four SEALs and a much larger enemy force of more than 50 anti-coalition militia. The enemy had the SEALs outnumbered.

They also had terrain advantage. They launched a well-organized, three-sided attack on the SEALs. The firefight continued relentlessly as the overwhelming militia forced the team deeper into a ravine.

Trying to reach safety, the four men, each now wounded, began bounding down the mountain's steep sides, making leaps of 20 to 30ft. Approximately 45 minutes into the fight, pinned down by overwhelming forces, Dietz, the communications petty officer, sought open air to place a distress call back to the base. But before he could do so, he was shot in the hand, the blast shattering his thumb.

Despite the intensity of the firefight and suffering grave gunshot wounds himself, Murphy is credited with risking his own life to save the lives of his teammates. Murphy, intent on making contact with headquarters, but realizing this would be impossible in the extreme terrain where they were fighting, unhesitatingly and with complete disregard for his own life moved into the open, where he could gain a better position to transmit a call to get help for his men.

Detailed hand-drawn map by an unknown operator before Operation *Redwing*. (Marcus Luttrell)

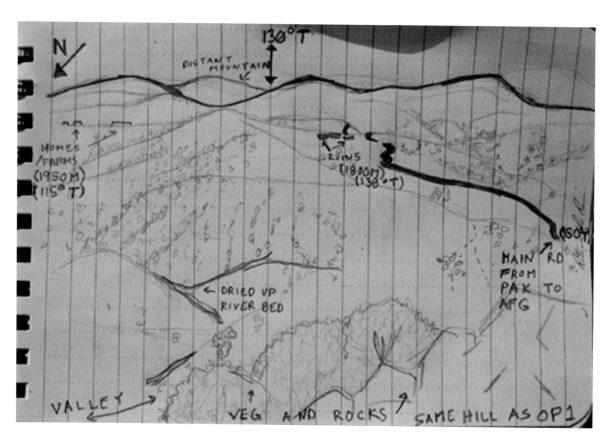

Moving away from the protective mountain rocks, he knowingly exposed himself to increased enemy gunfire. This deliberate act deprived him of cover and made him a target for the enemy. While continuing to be fired upon, Murphy made contact with the SOF Quick Reaction Force at Bagram Air Base and requested assistance. He calmly provided his unit's location and the size of the enemy force while requesting immediate support for his team. At one point he was shot in the back causing him to drop the transmitter. Murphy picked it back up, completed the call and continued firing at the enemy who was closing in. Severely wounded, Lt Murphy returned to his cover position with his men and continued the battle.

An MH-47 Chinook helicopter, with eight additional SEALs and eight Army Night Stalkers aboard, was sent in as part of an extraction mission to pull out the four embattled SEALs. The MH-47 was escorted by heavily-armored, Army attack helicopters. Entering a hot combat zone, attack helicopters are used initially to neutralize the enemy and make it safer for the lightly-armored, personnel-transport helicopter to insert.

Marcus Luttrell and Chris Osman at Luttrell's house near Houston, TX, in 2007. (Authors' collections)

The heavy weight of the attack helicopters slowed the formation's advance, prompting the MH-47 to outrun their armored escort. They knew the tremendous risk of going into an active enemy area in daylight, without their attack support, and without the cover of night. Risk would, of course, be minimized if they put the helicopter down in a safe zone. But knowing that their comrades were shot, surrounded and severely wounded, the rescue team opted directly to enter the oncoming battle in hopes of landing on the brutally hazardous terrain.

As the Chinook raced to the battle, a rocket-propelled grenade struck the helicopter, killing all 16 men aboard.

On the ground and nearly out of ammunition, the four SEALs, Murphy, Luttrell, Dietz and Axelson, continued the fight. By the end of the two-hour gunfight that careened through the hills and over cliffs, Murphy, Axelson and Dietz had been killed. An estimated 35 Taliban were also dead.

The fourth SEAL, Luttrell, was blasted over a ridge by a rocket-propelled grenade and was knocked unconscious. Regaining consciousness some time later, Luttrell managed to escape – badly injured – and slowly crawl away down the side of a cliff. Dehydrated, with a bullet wound to one leg, shrapnel embedded in both legs, and three vertebrae cracked, his situation was grim. Rescue helicopters were sent in, but he was too weak and injured to make contact. Traveling seven miles on foot he evaded the enemy for nearly a day. Gratefully, local nationals came to his aid, carrying him to a nearby village where they kept him for three days. The Taliban came to the village several times demanding that Luttrell be turned over to them. The villagers refused. One of the villagers made his way to a Marine outpost with a note from Luttrell, and US forces launched a massive operation that rescued him from enemy territory on July 2.

By his undaunted courage, intrepid fighting spirit and inspirational devotion to his men in the face of certain death, Lt Murphy was able to relay the position of his unit, an act that ultimately led to the rescue of Luttrell and the recovery of the remains of the three who were killed in the battle.[85]

Lieutenant Murphy's Medal of Honor citation noted:

When the primary communicator fell mortally wounded, Lieutenant Murphy repeatedly attempted to call for assistance for his beleaguered teammates. Realizing the impossibility of communicating in the extreme terrain, and in the face of almost certain death, he fought his way into open terrain to gain a better position to transmit a call. This deliberate, heroic act deprived him of cover, exposing him to direct enemy fire. Finally achieving contact with

Navy SEALs operating in Afghanistan in support of Operation *Enduring Freedom*. From left to right: Sonar Technician (Surface) 2nd Class (SEAL) Matthew G. Axelson, 29, of Cupertino, CA; Information Systems Technician Senior Chief (SEAL) Daniel R. Healy, 36, of Exeter, NH; Quartermaster 2nd Class (SEAL) James Suh, 28, of Deerfield Beach, FA; Hospital Corpsman Second Class (SEAL) Marcus Luttrell; Machinist Mate 2nd Class (SEAL) Eric S. Patton, 22, of Boulder City, NV; Lt (SEAL) Michael P. Murphy, 29, of Patchogue, NY. With the exception of Luttrell, all these men were killed June 28, 2005 by enemy forces while supporting Operation *Redwing*. Photograph taken 2005. (Authors' collections)

NSW OPERATION *REDWING* KIAS

Navy SEALs

SEAL Delivery Vehicle Team 1, Pearl Harbor, HI

1. Lt (SEAL) Michael P. Murphy, 29, of Patchogue, NY
2. Sonar Technician (Surface) 2nd Class (SEAL) Matthew G. Axelson, 29, of Cupertino, CA
3. Machinist Mate 2nd Class (SEAL) Eric S. Patton, 22, of Boulder City, NV
4. Senior Chief Information Systems Technician (SEAL) Daniel R. Healy, 36, of Exeter, NH
5. Quartermaster 2nd Class (SEAL) James Suh, 28, of Deerfield Beach, FL

SEAL Delivery Vehicle Team 2, Virginia Beach, VA

1. Gunner's Mate 2nd Class (SEAL) Danny P. Dietz, 25, of Littleton, CO

SEAL Team 10, Virginia Beach, VA

1. Chief Fire Controlman (SEAL) Jacques J. Fontan, 36, of New Orleans, LA
2. Lt Cdr (SEAL) Erik S. Kristensen, 33, of San Diego, CA
3. Electronics Technician 1st Class (SEAL) Jeffery A. Lucas, 33, of Corbett, OR
4. Lt (SEAL) Michael M. McGreevy Jr., 30, of Portville, NY
5. Hospital Corpsman 1st Class (SEAL) Jeffrey S. Taylor, 30, of Midway, WV

Army Night Stalkers

3rd Battalion, 160th Special Operations Aviation Regiment (Airborne), Hunter Army Air Field, GA

1. Staff Sgt Shamus O. Goare, 29, of Danville, OH
2. Chief Warrant Officer Corey J. Goodnature, 35, of Clarks Grove, MN
3. Sgt Kip A. Jacoby, 21, of Pompano Beach, FL
4. Sgt 1st Class Marcus V. Muralles, 33, of Shelbyville, IN
5. Maj Stephen C. Reich, 34, of Washington Depot, CT
6. Sgt 1st Class Michael L. Russell, 31, of Stafford, VA
7. Chief Warrant Officer Chris J. Scherkenbach, 40, of Jacksonville, FL

HQ Company, 160th Special Operations Aviation Regiment (Airborne), Fort Campbell, KY

1. Master Sgt James W. Ponder III, 36, of Franklin, TN

SEAL Jeff Taylor's wife spreads his ashes at his favorite spot in Big Bear, California. (Courtesy Mrs Taylor)

Members of SEAL SDVT- 1. Michael Murphy (Medal of Honor recipient), James Suh, Matthew Axelson, and Marcus Luttrell. (Authors' collections)

his headquarters, Lieutenant Murphy maintained his exposed position while he provided his location and requested immediate support for his team. In his final act of bravery, he continued to engage the enemy until he was mortally wounded.[86]

This was the worst death toll for a single day that US forces have suffered since Operation *Enduring Freedom* began in 1999. It was the single largest loss of life for Naval Special Warfare since World War II.

Opposite:
Insurgents were hiding in the cemetery directly in front of this building in Fallujah. Photograph taken in 2004. (Authors' collections)

PART IV

GLOBAL WAR ON TERRORISM: IRAQ 2003–07

VIET-RAQ

Al Fawbots

AL FAW, MABOT AND KAAOT

Few will forget the apocalyptic visions brought about by massive oil wells on fire, the black tendrils obliterating the sky and, at times, raining black death onto soldier and civilian alike. Nor can one forget the ecological carnage wrought upon the Persian Gulf, the estuaries, animal and marine life ruined for decades. That was the reality of the first war waged against Iraq in 1991 after Saddam Hussein's armies had invaded Kuwait on August 2, 1990. Allied forces under US leadership successfully evicted the Iraqis by 1991. SEALs provided reconnaissance and diversionary operations in this operation.

One key component of Operation *Iraqi Freedom* in March 2003 was the seizure of strategic oil assets. Included on the high value target list were two offshore GOPLATs just south of Al Faw in the Persian Gulf; Mina Al Bakr (MABOT) and Khor Al Amaya (KAAOT) as well as the city of Al Faw itself, as it served as the transfer point of oil to supertankers.[87] It was thought that "demolition of onshore pipeline support valves for each platform and their metering and manifold stations located on the Al Faw could also cause the long-term shutdown of the Iraqi oil spigot."[88] The mission was to seize and hold the economic lifelines of Iraq's oil industry.[89] Part of the funding for the war against Iraq was to have been off-set by the continued flow of crude oil. Seizing the platforms and the port successfully depended on the Iraqis yielding peaceably without destroying KAOOT and MABOT in the process. Funding for the war, Iraq itself, and saving the environment were to be the beneficiaries of a successful maritime special operations mission.

The morning after the operation at Al Faw. Note the Texas flag painted on the satellite dome. Iraq, 2003. (Authors' collections)

Working conditions and the general political situation did not help the Iraqis on the GOPLATs. "The facility was filthy beyond description. Though they were responsible for bringing in millions of dollars of income for their country, the Iraqi workers were often left without food and provisions. Soldiers had to fish. The food left in the storage areas by the workers was infested with cockroaches and other vermin. Out on the platforms, when workers had to relieve themselves, there were no facilities, so they stopped wherever they were and did what they had to do. KAAOT also had a huge rat infestation."[90] Allied planners

Map of Iraq. (CIA)

Map of Al Faw Peninsula in the
Persian Gulf. (DOD)

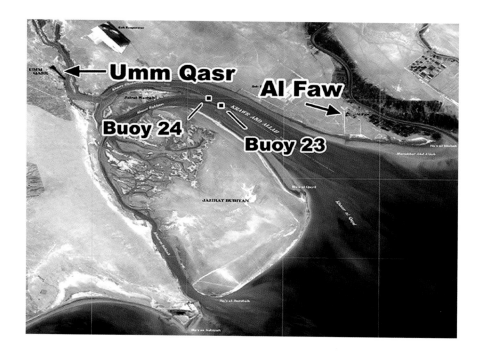

Map of Al Faw Peninsula in the Persian Gulf. (DOD)

were aware of the morale issue and were keen to exploit it. War was coming and everybody knew it; the only thing Iraqis did not know was when the attacks were to begin. With that in mind "thousands of leaflets [were provided] with capitulation instructions as well as phrases dissuading soldiers and workers from destroying oil facilities and equipment: 'You're hurting your family's livelihood of fishing if you destroy the oil.'"[91]

These missions were, of course, tailor-made for NAVSPECWAR. Keen to include allies in the second Iraq war as had previously been done in the First Gulf War, the forces tasked with the capture of the platforms were the US Navy SEALs alongside an excellent Polish naval commando unit known to the West as GROM (Grupa Reagowania Operacyjno-Manewrowego – Operational Mobile Reaction Group).[92] The Polish GROM are considered "bad-asses, top notch operators"[93] by their US SEAL counterparts and SEALs do not praise many.

Combat operations for the SEALs and GROM began on March 20, 2003 when they successfully boarded KAAOT and MABOT during nighttime hours. "There was an SDV platoon and it might have been three platoons in total for both GOPLATS 'cause there was the two of them that took those down but yeah they got those."[94] Neither assault encountered any resistance, although a combat-craft crewman on a high-speed SEAL boat accidentally shot off a .50 cal. at KAAOT, which made the men think they were being shot at. The SEALs and their Polish colleagues found that the platforms had been wired and equipped with explosives.[95] Each platform yielded a dozen or so EPWs [enemy prisoners of war]. The American and Polish commandos were relieved in place by Royal Marines.

The refinery and port of Al Faw were not quite so easy to overcome. Eight MH-53 Pave Low helicopters carried personnel and DPVs to objectives that were code named Coronado and Texaco, while an assortment of British and US Navy and Air Force aircraft provided CAS, as well as simultaneously attacking known enemy troop concentrations and fortifications across the low-lying peninsula. Both insertions were problematic due to the soft and oily ground in their LZs. At Coronado, one enemy vehicle nearby was obliterated by an A-10 Warthog. "The Al Faw pipeline manifold complex was seized and the perimeter reinforced by Royal Marines."[96]

Kyle was involved in the taking of Al Faw refinery in his DPV platoon, "the stuck-in-the-mud platoon":

> We took down Al Faw. Marine 53 helo dropped us off on the ramps, and our intel was by a 21-year-old chick who doesn't know shit. She had aerial photos and claimed the LZ was hard packed. We asked her, and said that ground doesn't look like it can hold our DPVs. She said "Oh no, it's good, it's dry." Of course, we get there, we drive off the ramp, all four of our DPVs get stuck 'cause it's mud and oil… We bottomed out. And those DPVs are not four-wheel drive and they're not set up with mudders [type of tire] or anything so yeah, we got

MABOT. (DOD)

stuck and when they got stuck you know the .50 on top can only pivot so far, and our DPVs weren't even facing in the right direction 'cause we had to drive off and turn around so the .50 was useless. So we had to dismount the DPVs and get out. I had to pull my 60 off the back, the other guys had their M4s and then, the only thing on the DPV that was worth a shit was the, I even forget the name, Mark 19, on the navigators [shot gun rider], 'cause that thing can pivot anywhere so you can shoot that. So we got there and bullets ricocheting off our road cages and everything and we got into a fight there…

Well we started taking fire since we came across the ocean feet dry and our helo started doing evasive maneuvers and you see the "chaf," you know flares shot off the helos to dupe heat-seeking missiles. It's all going off the back and you could see you know, tracers coming off, but I don't know if it was tracer just 'cause we had night vision on you could see a few rounds coming off. The helo never got shot, none of them I know of got shot. Then we all got dropped off there. They [Iraqis] were expecting us to come in. They knew we were coming for that but they had dug in completely surrounding Al Faw. They thought we were coming from the outside. They had no idea we were going to land in the middle. So, of course, when we landed in the middle there were 16 of us in there, surrounded by about 300 dudes dug into the trenches.[97]

KAAOT. (DOD)

However the SEALs had air support: "We had air coming over with us. We had control of them. I guess we had CTT with us. He was doing it from the DPV calling in. He had control over one, Adam our comms guy was controlling Spectre and the CTT guy had control over the A-10s and the A-18s." Due to this and the after actions, the enemy death toll was very high, estimated at: "Over 300 guys, plus there were some from the city of Al Faw. There was armor going out that we never saw since they never made it to us. Actually we had the video of our first platoon and you can, we're in the middle of a firefight, hear the breaks in between the bombs going off and you hear this one guy just screaming bloody murder and it goes on and on for about half an hour." The following day, "… the sun comes up and then what the deal was that, it was the Brits came in, the Royal Marines." 42 Commando came in and took charge of the situation.

LZ Texaco was worse off. All four DPVs got stuck upon exiting the ramp of the helicopters. "Moving out on foot, the SEAL assault team swept the area and then captured its objective, finding no significant weapons or explosives. After securing the south and east gates to the complex, the SEALs called in the Royal Marines, who

Night photo of a SEAL operator with a Carl Gustav anti-armor weapon. The Carl G shown here was dismounted from the DPVs that were stuck in the mud at Al Faw. (Authors' collections)

21 5:24 AM

British commandos arrive in the early hours of the morning after the successful assault onto Al Faw and its oil refineries. (Authors' collections)

REAR ADMIRAL HARWARD

In October 2002, Rear Adm. Harward deployed as Commander, Task Force 561 where he commanded Naval Special Warfare Task Group Central in Iraq. His forces included all the assets in the Naval Special Warfare inventory as well as forces from the Polish Grom, the UK Royal Marines, and the Kuwaiti Navy. His forces conducted Special Reconnaissance and Direct Action missions in the maritime environment and throughout Iraq.

Rear Adm. Harward reported to the Executive Office of the President at the White House in August 2003. He served in the National Security Council staff as the Director of Strategy and Defense Issues where he crafted the National Security Presidential Directive (NSPD-41) on Maritime Security and the National Strategy for Maritime Security. Rear Adm. Harward's portfolio included nuclear counterterrorism for which he implemented policies to prevent terrorist use of Weapons of Mass Destruction.

In April 2005 Rear Adm. Harward was selected for promotion and assigned as a plankowner to the National Counterterrorism Center (NCTC) in Washington.

(Source: http://www.navy.mil/navydata/bios/bio.asp?bioID=338)

Although the SEALs had been briefed that there was no AAA on site, this bunker had an anti-aircraft weapon on top it, and was filled with ammunition for AAA and other small and heavy arms. (Authors' collections)

conducted a thorough search of all structures and took 100 occupants as prisoners of war."[98] CAS missions were flown throughout in support of these missions, striking at pre-designated targets as well as onrushing Iraqi relief columns.

MUKARAYIN DAM

Another concern to military planners was the possibility of dams being destroyed and flooding the surrounding areas. This action would not only have slowed down Allied advances but would have destroyed civilian properties and lives as well. The Mukarayin Hydroelectric Dam, some 57 miles northeast of Baghdad, and close to the Iranian border, was a key installation to capture. To that end a combined special operations task unit comprised of several dozen SEALs and GROM planned and rehearsed the mission, then executed it in April 2003.

Approximately 40 commandos, including SDVT-1, CCTs and two linguists, were tasked with seizing the Mukarayin Dam. The SEALs equipment included chemical suits in addition to "way too much gear."[99] The dam complex had a network of about 3½ miles of tunnels and DPVs were used to establish blocking positions and to keep a wary eye out for Iranian bandits who had been infiltrating and robbing Iraqi villages nearby. German engineers and the CIA provided the primary intelligence gathered for the target. Apart from preventing the dam from being blown up and flooding the area, analysts believed that the site could also be used to house some chemical agents. The local sheikh was unhappy with the

This Iraqi was hit by an AC-130 during nighttime action. He then crawled toward his fighting position at Al Faw screaming until he died. (Authors' collections)

marauding Iranian bandits as well as Iraqis with whom his villagers had been engaged in several firefights in the past.

Part of the analysis revealed an AAA on a ridge overlooking the dam. Some concern was expressed that Iranians might infiltrate and occupy those fighting positions. The ridge was naturally a key area and should have been seized to maintain superiority over the area and and not place the SEALs in danger should enemy forces occupy the ridge. SEAL officer Harward ordered the commandos to leave the ridge alone, potentially exposing and endangering the few commandos.

Six special operations helicopters flew onto the target and allowed the operators to fast-rope the 50ft height. One of the 12–15 GROM commandos broke his ankle. All of the commandos carried too much gear. The breaching stuff weighed a ton by itself. This would be the last time the members of ST-5 would carry this much weight. The blocking teams had a difficult time exiting the rear of the 53 helicopter and the cumbersome and inefficient DPVs were never to be deployed again after this mission. In less than 20 minutes the key structures had been secured; the tactics involved in seizing the dam were very similar to a ship takedown. No resistance was encountered and the SEALs could take several hours to clear the complex tunnel system.

Jim Crawley from the southern California-based *San Diego Union Tribune* noted on June 27, 2003 that:

> the commandos crammed inside several Pave Low special-operations helicopters for a nearly five-hour flight from their Kuwait base to the dam. On the way, each helicopter had to be refueled in midair by a KC-130 tanker. Within minutes, they located and held the

dam's watchmen and power-plant operators, but it would take hours to search the massive structure for explosives and potential saboteurs. However, the Iraqis didn't resist and no enemy troops or bombs were found.[100]

One of the SEAL platoons departed while the others remained in place until relieved by elements of the US Army.

Left:
Iraqi soldiers who had switched into civilian clothing hoping to avoid being captured as enemy combatants. The commandos captured these soldiers after their arrival. The SEALs had pinned down enemy personnel until the arrival of the Brits who in turn captured the Iraqis. (Authors' collections)

Above:
British commandos and US Navy SEALs posing for a photo prior to early missions of Operation *Iraqi Freedom* at Ali Alsalim, Kuwait. The concrete hangars had been built by the French prior to *Desert Storm* (1991) who had claimed that the hangars were indestructible. This was certainly not the case, as demonstrated in this photo. (Authors' collections)

BAGHDAD

Navy SEALs supported Allied forces in the subjugation of the Iraqi capital Baghdad. Much like their comrades fighting the Global War on Terror in the mountains and valleys of Afghanistan, these SEALs had to make do with very little useful equipment at the beginning of each campaign. Indeed they created new standard operating procedures for combat in the twenty-first century urban battle space.[101] These SOPs ranged from joint service operations to sniping and counterinsurgency tactics. In Iraq ST-5 wrote the SOP on personal security detail, now a newly added mission to their doctrinal statement. Traditional SEAL training was discarded, new tactics and procedures were discovered and refined. SEALs created a new paradigm in sniping and counter-sniping throughout their combat operations in Fallujah, Mosul, Tall Afar, and Ramadi.

During their deployments in Iraq the rules of engagement differed from one theater of operation to the next. This meant that the battle space commander in northern Iraq would have a different set of ROE from his fellows elsewhere in the country. The local commanders were not empowered to ease the ROEs; instead, they could only make them more restrictive. These rules could cover anything from when to engage hostiles to the treatment of EPWs. The SEALs noted that the "closer one got to the flagpole [the higher on the chain of command], the more restrictive the rules were."[102]

During the early stages of the Iraq war, the US Navy SEALs were forced to rely on old Navy ambulance Humvees as transportation. The ambulances had no armor, no power, and no doors, but at this time the IEDs (improvised explosive devices) were not yet the threat that they began to become later on in the war. Fortunately, in addition to the Humvees, the SEALs managed to acquire Spanish semi-armored imitation Humvees. The problem with these vehicles was the simple fact that the airbrakes were exposed, so that any bullet or piece of shrapnel

SEAL operators having fun during a little downtime. Guys posing with toy AK-47s and bow and arrow found in Iraq. (Authors' collections)

Get Some! Iraq. (Authors' collections)

could cut the exposed lines, rendering the vehicles useless and possibly creating a nightmare scenario for the SEALs, leaving them stranded and vulnerable in hostile territory. Following the age-old military tradition of begging, borrowing, and stealing, the SEALs also obtained indigenous vehicles, which they could make use of in other missions.

Not all the standard equipment was suitable for all types of mission in Iraq, so the SEALs adapted. For example, the .50-cal. heavy machine gun and the Mark-19 automatic grenade launcher were excellent weapons systems for invading a country, but not so dependable for the precision work required in cities to avoid inflicting unintentional collateral damage. CS grenades, although extremely effective for crowd control, could be not be used either, as they could be regarded as chemical weapons.

Before the invasion, the members of ST-5 were aware that a war in Iraq was rapidly approaching and, consequently, they prepared for it. They concentrated on training in urban warfare as much as possible. Once trained up and ready to deploy they left their West Coast duty station to travel to Kuwait via Rota, Spain. SEAL Team 5 replaced two platoons from ST-3 during the period of April to October, 2003. One said that ST-3's leadership "was the most fucked-up ever."[103]

Both from ST-5, Frank and Paul are physically very different men. One is young, heavily tanned and skinny, the other older and worn looking. When they were interviewed, Frank had just returned from Iraq and Paul had been out of the

Patch of HCS 5, the Firehawks, who provided an aerial platform to the SEALs during Operation *Iraqi Freedom*. (US Navy)

US Navy SEAL cloth patch. (Authors' collections)

Navy for just a very short time. When Frank was queried about how he liked his job he said he was extremely happy. Both men were profound in their observations and in their earnestness.

Based on recent inter-service experiences, some criticism has been expressed about the Navy SEALs' competence. On several occasions, notably during operations in Afghanistan, SEALs were accused of cutting corners and not planning their missions in detail. Frank and Paul countered these criticisms; after all, they argued, SEALs conduct lengthy pre-deployments and their teams' standard operating procedures enabled them to conduct missions within 15 minutes in Iraqi cities such as Baghdad. Unlike some of their other branch counterparts, the SEALs no longer needed 96 hours to prepare, rehearse, and execute a task. The battlefield mechanics of the 21st century require speed. Additionally, the SEALs vetted the individuals in their platoons, fully knowing each team-mate's abilities and limitations. Last but not least, the SEALs could always reject or pick a particular mission depending on their abilities and capabilities.

However, it was not always easy to deploy. When ST-5 first arrived to replace ST-3, Commander Harward denied them direct action missions. The commander of ST-5 therefore described the missions as reconnaissance patrols and received approvals more often than not. SEALs could not deploy alongside their Army counterparts because they lacked the required armored Humvees. For every five or six Army missions, ST-5 might do one and then it "usually was the guy who robbed a store instead of the serial killer."[104]

The SEALs however, achieved some successful mission hits right at the beginning and fortunately for them this occurred at the same time as Harward left the country. His replacement did not change ST-5's operational methods. They had proved their success and going back to restricting their missions would have been political suicide for the new commander. There had been other complaints about the leadership among the SEAL operators interviewed. One story that was often repeated told of an incident when SEAL officer Curtis prevented a SEAL sniper from taking a shot, allowing a Marine sniper the kill instead. Such restrictions and micro-management proved far more detrimental to the SEALs than the enemy did. Fortunately, ST-5 managed to gain control of its own destiny within a month. Finally, now directly responsible to SOCOM, "life was good."[105] Paul felt for the first time like a real SEAL doing what he had trained to do. Ultimately, ST-5 captured or killed 17 HVTs out of the 52 most wanted senior Iraqi leadership.

Frank and Paul bitterly despised their senior leadership, holding them accountable for enlisted men and officers leaving the SEAL community. Their wrath rested primarily on Navy SEAL senior officers Harward and Adam Curtis, the commander of ST-3 and former PDF prisoner in 1989. Both men separately mentioned Curtis' refusal to conduct several missions in Iraq, a decision that caused enormous frustration to the SEALs, and they quoted a British Marine officer who said that SEALs are "lions led by dogs."[106] Navy SEAL Kyle also mentioned the same remark: "The Brits even said that we were lions led by dogs because they would not turn us loose."[107] He said that "we were there at An Nasiriyah when Jessica Lynch was there, and the Marines gave us a free fire zone. They said 'Here this is your sector, just go out, and anyone out there, any male, kill him.' And then Curtis of course said, 'No, we can't do that, you're not going out.'

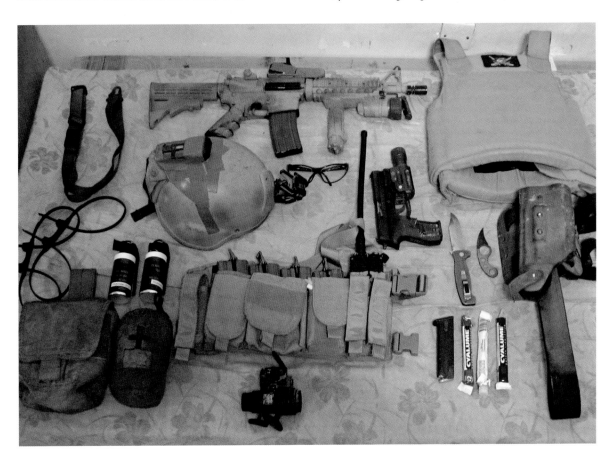

A picture of a typical load out of a SEAL operator in Iraq. (Authors' collections)

So the Marines would come back by after they'd been in town and say, 'Hey, how, many kills did you get today? Oh that's right, y'all didn't go out.'[108] This, of course, upset the SEALs greatly.

Frank and Paul easily identified the true combat leader from the one who was solely interested in promotion. Both noted with dismay the large numbers of commanders who came to Iraq apparently just for the sake of furthering their careers. Nonetheless, both SEALs were very determined to continue to give their best and to succeed in their missions when they were deployed.

The vast majority of interviewees complained bitterly about senior commanders constricting their operational parameters to the point of ineffectiveness. A few SEALs did not defend the actions of their commanders but did present a different perspective on the politics of war. After all, they argued, a maritime special operations unit did deploy to the land-locked country of Afghanistan and that required astute politicking by senior Navy commanders.

However, Robert, a former Navy SEAL from DevGru, did offer a different perspective. When the criticism against officers such as Harward was pointed out he commented easily that:

Commander of Task Force K-Bar, Navy SEAL commander Robert Harward, with a Marine Corps general at Qandahar. (Authors' collections)

Robert Harward can be magnanimous and gregarious and can command that at will and uses it all the time. That Harward took it upon himself without orders to drive up to Qandahar, that is rather bold. Without Admiral Calland and other SEAL commanders, the chances of SEAL teams deploying to Afghanistan were slim to none. The initial invasion of Iraq strained the resources of specwar in that region. Split a team into two others to complement, strained human capital and the planning was unprecedented for West Coast SEAL teams at that time but we pulled it off. Harward knew the Marines from Afghanistan and he got assignments to go with Marines north into Baghdad. Our original plans were only for MABOT and KAAOT but Harward got them more although we really strained them [SEALs] logistically and operationally unit wise.[109]

As in Afghanistan, the terrain in Iraq, and the fact that the area had seen countless wars before, provided additional challenges for the SEALs. Kyle recounts the experience they had on the Shatt al-Arab river between Iraq and Iran, when they came into contact with a legacy of the Iran–Iraq War. ST-5 was tasked with putting SRs on the river to make sure no suicide boats were going out, and they were shot at occasionally by Iranians:

Just 'cause we were in the old Iraqi border station that was up there that had been bombed, demolished to the ground. You know, you tell a couple DPVs to go set up a hide-site but it looks like a couple DPVs trying to hide as it was flat ground. So they knew we were there but they couldn't see us as we hid in the debris. They saw the DPVs with camouflage netting and we knew they were over there. They'd fire a couple of shots at us everyday, just to let us know that they were there watching us.

A patch for Bravo Platoon – ST-5 and an ST-5 pirate patch. (Authors' collections)

… I don't think they were so much trying to hit us, just intimidate us. But the whole thing is I'm getting shot at and I want to return fire. We were told no and it was probably a good thing 'cause they had the border position dialed in long before Americans came in. So they had mortars over there, rockets and everything. In fact, the station that we took over, we had to destroy a bunch of demo – we found a shit ton of RPGs, mortars and everything. So we set it all up, put some C4 on it and blew it and we also called in an F-18 to bomb it just in case there was some unexploded ordnance left.[110]

A further problem that could have been detrimental to any operation was the complete absence of aerial platforms to support the SEALs in Iraq. Although TF-160 was available, their support had to be coordinated through the US Army's elite Delta unit, and, in essence, the SEALs needed dedicated air assets to support their missions. Ultimately, they managed to get Navy reservist helicopter SH-60s attached to them. The SH-60 Seahawk is a twin-engine helicopter used for anti-submarine warfare, search and rescue, drug interdiction, anti-ship warfare, cargo lift, and special operations.[111] The reserve component was HCS-5 that was dis-established on December 3, 2006.[112] "The Naval Air Reserve Squadron HCS-5 was under the command of Commander, Helicopter Wing Reserve, San Diego, California, and Naval Air Reserve Force, New Orleans, Louisiana. HCS-5, along with its sister squadron, HCS-4, were the only Navy squadrons that performed both Combat Search and Rescue (CSAR) and Special Warfare Support (SPECWAR) as their primary missions."[113] The SEALs thought they were "great and incredibly professional."[114]

While the SH-60s were available, the Navy commandos got together with their new aviators and worked out operating procedures for the variety of missions they were to conduct. The SEALs could now have the aerial platforms to hover over or near a target and use it for sniping support. They also taught the aviators shooting techniques and thus ensured competency all the way around. In total three helicopters were attached.

US Navy SEAL platoons in Baghdad, 2004/5. (Authors' collections)

One of the biggest problems for the aviation wing was the complete lack of replacement parts, although the mechanics did an excellent job of salvaging whatever they could. When one of the helicopters had executed an extremely hard night landing, they salvaged it as well and used the parts to maintain the other two helicopters. Reduced to two helicopters, they continued to support ST-5 to the fullest. As their deployment continued HCS-5 needed additional spare parts. Army helicopter mechanics who also used this type of air asset promised to repair one of the SH-60s. It was returned completely repaired, painted in Army green instead of Navy gray, with the tail sporting a proud GO ARMY. Inter-service rivalry was alive and well. Ultimately, the SEALs' aviation team received some paint and the HCS-5's hangar received a proud bright blue GO NAVY on its shelter side. This reserve air component supported ST-5 during their entire deployment. Later on, SOCOM replaced the reservists with an active duty unit. Another air asset available at times was the all-powerful Spectre gunship.

Originally ST-5 stayed at Camp Jenny Pozzi (the camp was named for the eldest daughter of SEAL Chief Warrant Officer William Pozzi) at Baghdad International Airport until they moved to the RPC (Radwaniyah Palace Complex Civil–Military Operations Center) a month later, which became their base of operations. During this time the famous 52 cards were produced that listed and pictured the top 52 people wanted by the US. Seventeen of these were removed from the deck by the SEALs.

Paul and Frank noted that when they first entered Baghdad at the onset of the war in 2003, the city was on fire. Naturally one would assume that the bombs dropped by the Allied forces were the cause of the massive destruction but the SEALs pointed out that the surgical strikes were aimed at reducing collateral damage. The US spent millions of dollars on a bomb just so the strikes could be pinpoint accurate. The subsequent destruction started when the electric grid went

Haifa Street in Baghdad. This is where elections were first held. The US Army asked for help from SEAL snipers as the day before three election officials had been dragged out of their car and shot in the back of the head. (Authors' collections)

out in the ancient city. Many of the fires that burnt out buildings were started by Iraqis, who according to Paul and Frank, would set one room on fire to see what they could loot in the next. Although the American bombing campaign was largely blamed for the problems, in fact there was no infrastructure in place to prevent looting. Most of the looted items soon found their way to the Ali Baba black market.

Outside of conventional forces, various agencies and contractors were in place but they did not constitute a real fighting force capable of urban warfare. It seemed to both SEALs that the Army's special forces and Delta had "done a few things wrong" so that when the SEALs set up shop for the next five months, they became, by default, the primary unit tasked with capturing or killing HVTs, for example enablers of Saddam Hussein. SEAL teams would go out every night, conducting those precarious and aggressive missions. There were times when they would execute three combat missions in a single night.

In any given 24-hour period the SEALs would do a variety of different tasks, which included making re-supply runs to the isolated Polish Embassy; looking for the people on the 52 most wanted playing cards; searching old Iraqi weapons storage facilities; conducting reconnaissance; and searching for WMD storage sites. These searches would be based on information gathered from captured HVT personnel. Often they would discover the entire infrastructure but no actual chemicals. Most of the equipment found was German, French, or Russian.

Hey big spender! Some captured funds were handed over to local Iraqi orphanages by the SEALs. (Authors' collections)

Whenever possible, they would carry out humanitarian work, or add a humanitarian aspect to their missions. Paul recounts that the SEALs hit a house belonging to a Fedayeen leader. The Fedayeen was a paramilitary organization directly responsible to Saddam Hussein. The SEALs captured some Iraqi money, which they handed over to a neighboring orphanage. After each day, they would try to get back to base before night, to catch an hour of sleep if possible or to prepare for live prisoner snatches.

At that time ST-5 was the only SEAL unit in the country and it was tasked with accomplishing a variety of missions throughout Iraq, for example, discovering three mass gravesites. During their deployment, ST-5 created new standards and procedures, such as support, intelligence gathering and analysis, mobility tactics, air asset usage, and joint operations. Subsequent SEAL teams incorporated these valuable lessons into their operational doctrine. These lessons were based on thousands of aggressive targets sets during which the SEALs lost only three members. Other SOF units were not as well trained or as lucky.

One example of such an aggressive target set took place in 2003 and was experienced by Delta Platoon, ST-5. Their target was an Iraqi Air Force general who was funded by an unknown source to conduct hits against US targets. The mission was to seize the HVT and a missile guidance box as identified on the CIA's target list. The agency's source unfortunately identified the wrong house. The SEALs stormed it but because of their superior training and desire and despite the fact that the entire neighborhood was now aware of their presence, they decided to regroup and stormed the correct building. Paul captured the Iraqi officer and his wife but the general's security man hosed down the SEAL platoon and engaged them in a short fight. Then, he dropped his weapon and fled. One of the SEALs was hit in the NVD (night vision device) mount on his helmet but as he was unhurt the saying "Better lucky than good" made its rounds.

After six months ST-7 replaced ST-5. Back from their overseas deployment ST-5 processed and incorporated their

A patch for Delta Platoon, ST-5. (Author's collections)

Naval Special Warfare Task Unit patch produced locally in the Persian Gulf. (Authors' collections)

experiences into their new work-ups, trying to put together a better platoon. Any water-related activity was "shit-canned." There would be no need to focus on their old doctrine of maritime operations.

In the meanwhile, the Iraqi interim government was created at the end of 2004 and early 2005, and the SEALs were tasked with the "ugly" personal security detail (PSD). The focus of their training was now on personal protection, something SEALs had not done previously. Again ST-5 had to reconfigure their deployment training to meet the new requirements.

The second deployment of ST-5 during the Global War on Terrorism saw them back in Iraq from August 2004 through April 2005, replacing ST-1. A number of SEAL snipers also participated in the second battle for Fallujah in November 2004. The remainder of the team was assigned as PSD duty to the President of Iraq, Ghazi Mashal Ajil al-Yawer, who was the principal negotiator between various insurgents, including the Fallujah leaders, and the US. The insurgent cell leaders met with generals and ambassadors among many others.

The SEALs trained Sunni, Shia, and Kurdish Arabs in PSD tactics. Unfortunately, some of them were unable to set aside ethnic and religious backgrounds and fights ensued between them. Some Kurds walked off in the night, while other Iraqis were bribed by al-Qaeda to reveal locations of high value targets, for example.[115] Occasionally a mortar round hit the SEAL compound.

ST-5 traveled everywhere with the president and his various delegations. They accompanied the first Iraqi delegation to enter Kuwait in some 40–45 years. The PSD detail carried millions of dollars with them and foreign intelligence agencies spied on them continuously. Israeli, Iranian, and Russian as well as European agents were hot on their trail, even going so far as to break into the SEALs' hotel rooms, thereby forcing them to carry all classified material in a backpack. The Russians employed a fleet of prostitutes whose mission was to profile the PSD and other personnel and sometimes this information was sold to the highest bidder. The PSD duty lasted three months.

FALLUJAH

Kyle was another SEAL who deployed to Iraq for the opening phases of Operation *Iraqi Freedom*. During his three tours in Iraq, at the time of the writing of this book, he accumulated more kills than any other sniper under SOCOM. In fact he single-handedly killed more insurgents in Iraq than all of DevGru put together. Kyle's story is a rare and insightful look at the 21st-century SEAL.

After training, Kyle joined Charlie Platoon and deployed to the Middle East as a 60-gunner. While there, his platoon "set the record for the most VBSS. We had something like in a month and a half we took down 90 ships in 2001, right after 9/11."[116] After that, Kyle was deployed to Iraq in a DPV platoon where he and other SEALs captured the valuable oil platforms and refinery at Al Faw. He then returned to the US and went through SEAL Team Sniper School during his post-deployment leave. His next deployment took him back to Iraq with Charlie Platoon in 2004 to 2005, this time as a sniper originally to RPC outside of Baghdad: "I got sent overseas, I was sent a month early, most of my guys were going to do the PSD thing but there was a shift in cycles and so I was there for four months before my platoon came in." The Polish GROM were also based there and Kyle worked with them for several months. After the GROM pulled out, plans for Charlie Platoon changed:

My platoon shows up and somehow they decide that since the GROM is leaving they need a direct action force. So my platoon gets to be the DA force so I just get to stay there, and then the other platoon, the 6th Platoon, went up to Baghdad to do PSD. But actually before I had the opportunity to get up there, the assault on Fallujah lit off and they did a call for all SEAL snipers. We had already started to have a good name there, with our own sniper school. They saw how tough it was. Next to BUD/S, the military school with the highest attrition rate is SEAL Sniper School.

Fallujah after it was bombed and American tanks were rolling in. (Authors' collections)

The city of Fallujah lies in the Al Anbar province, roughly 40 miles west of Baghdad on the River Euphrates. Fallujah is the city where, in March 2004, four American Blackwater contractors were killed and burnt after a series of riots initiated by the shooting of Iraqi civilians. It was a tinderbox thereafter, and the coalition forces attempted to gain control of the city, resulting in 1,100 US casualties, including 90 killed. Approximately 1,400 insurgents were killed with an unknown number wounded. Going into Fallujah, Kyle was attached to 3d Battalion, 1st Marines and K and L companies, 3d Battalion, 5th Marines. A number of SEAL snipers went with the Marines:

Fallujah. Top right is Ranger M who helped supply Kyle and other SEAL snipers. This picture was taken the day before the assault began into Fallujah. SEALs' best friends in urban combat are armor and light infantry vehicles, such as this Abrams. (Authors' collections)

There were three different groups of us, and in each group there were six to eight snipers. Basically it was an ST-3 and ST-5 deployment. It was basically ST-3 and one group and then ST-5 had a group. East Coast, ST-8, they didn't have enough to fill a group, and ST-3 had so many snipers, so I was actually attached to the ST-8 guys.

The SEAL snipers had only a week to plan for their insertion with the Marines: "One week is all the time we spent. We integrated with them, we're planning

for it, getting our rounds put together, making sure our guns were good and then basically just making sure our gear was tight." The SEAL snipers were providing sniper overwatch for the Marines as they carried out their mission to seize Fallujah from the insurgents. Though with designated units, they "bounced around quite a bit, whoever needed us, who thought they were in the worst spot would call for us to come over." Kyle started to see action on the very first day of operations, even before the Marines made their first assault on the city: "We took apartments that are about 800yds outside the actual city of Fallujah. We took that down, we set up sniper hides there 'cause we weren't going into the actual city until the next day. So we start taking shots from there." Kyle continues:

> It was my first at being a sniper and being able to really use it and that was a nice feeling to know that you could be able to reach out. Some of those guys were 1000yds out there and to reach out with my .300 and some of the guys had their .50s up, and to reach out and touch them and not have to worry about them reaching you… Not to mention, I'm surrounded by Marines.

Marines and SEALs being inserted via amtracks into Fallujah, 2004. (Authors' collections)

Sniper training being put into practice. This apartment complex was about 800yds north of Fallujah, and was taken down prior to the assault moving into Fallujah proper. The temporary sniping position was made out of a child's crib turned turned on its side. Photograph taken in 2004. (Authors' collections)

During his time in Fallujah Kyle was using his .300 Win Mag and his SR25 (now called a Mark 11). Kyle and Aaron, the SDVT-1 sniper he was working with, were assigned men to provide them with supplies in ammunition:

> We had Ranger M_____ with us, he was with my group, him and Lt K_____, and their only job was they would run supplies and ammo to us in their Humvee; whatever we needed. And they also had our rifles, 'cause we only carried the one rifle, and they had our other rifles in the Humvee.

Kyle recalled that standing ROEs were established quickly:

> I was looking into the city and I could see these guys with AKs and they now know that the Marines have taken that apartment complex. So they're starting to maneuver back into the city more. But we had already had the call that, I forget who the first president of Iraq was, but he actually came out that day, flew out there, and it was funny 'cause I got to see some of my boys in the PSD unit who came out with him, ST-8 guys. And he came and said, "Hey, you see guys out there?" We said, "Yeah." "Well why aren't you shooting them?" We

said "'cause they're not shooting at me and I don't see weapons." He said, "No, they've been given three months to get out of town. Any person in town is to be killed." Also, we were not supposed to shoot anyone carrying a white flag, but then the insurgents started to wave that around and tried to maneuver on us so then we did not shoot at people waving the white flag that came straight at us…

… then we just started letting them fly. So we could see the guys with guns maneuvering back further into the city, trying to get further away from the Marines and probably trying to get into a stronghold somewhere to get set up. We played it by ear trying to make sure nobody got in behind us.

On the very first day in action Kyle got his first confirmed kill, with his .300 Win Mag, and then two more:

That day I got three and Aaron got two so we got five total that first day. The next morning we went in with the Marines, put away the .300, got our SRs and we started doing bounding overwatches. Just going to the rooftops and watching as the Marines went down. We just had one street, two SEAL snipers were divvied up into each group, each group had a street. So we just watched over and we had Marine snipers with us too. We had one crew which was four guys and of the four guys, one is an actual sniper, the other three when they get home are going to sniper school but they pair them up with the snipers. So we have these guys who are awesome; one had a sniper rifle, the other three all had M4s, actually M16s. So we're doing this in the first week, it was awesome. 'Cause we'd be on the scope and the guys [Iraqis] would come out wanting to shoot and everything. After that they knew the

ALLAWI GIVES GREEN LIGHT

[Prime Minister] Allawi said Monday he had given US and Iraqi forces the green light to rid Falluja of insurgents, and he promised to restore law and order. "We are determined to clean Falluja from terrorists," Allawi said at a news conference.

Allawi imposed a curfew for Falluja and Ramadi, and closed Iraq's borders with Syria and Jordan to keep insurgents from escaping to other countries.

Allawi visited Iraqi troops as they waited to enter the city.

"First of all, this is our Iraq, and it is our duty to defend our country. We're counting on you to defend the country and regain its pride and its values," Allawi told them in Arabic. "I'm here to check on you and tell you that all of Iraq is with you."

Allawi announced a state of emergency in Iraq on Sunday – exempting the Kurdish north – and told reporters the terrorists in Falluja "Do not want a peaceful settlement."

(Source: http://www.cnn.com/2004/WORLD/meast/11/08/iraq.main/index.html)

snipers were there. We actually found pamphlets that I actually picked up, that the US dropped, it was saying, you know, it showed the picture of a sniper and it was saying the sniper's going to see you and on the backside showed an insurgent with cross hairs on his head. So the first week the Marines would start with mortars and bombs and then the assault would go. And then at sundown we would stop. And we had a set point that we had to get to so all the Marines would stay online. So if we reached it by noon, we had to stay there. But actually we wouldn't 'cause we kept talking and we didn't want to jump streets so someone [could] come in behind us.

As the Marines moved forward, the sniper team kept in contact to ensure that they were not attacked by their own side as they moved between buildings. There was an established procedure for inserting the scout snipers overwatching in urban hides. The Marines would take a building, the snipers would move in and set up, and the Marines would then leave, and collapse security so that the enemy thought the building was empty:

Spotting for one of the snipers from a hasty position during bounding overwatches. (Authors' collections)

We would pick out the buildings we wanted, we would take it, and then when the Marines got to the next building we wanted, we'd get down and run down to them. And it was a kick

ass week where I had to lose a lot of weight because it was just constant running and gunning. It was November but it was still warm out. The fourth week it finally got cold but for a while it was hot. But the assault would go. And me and Aaron, we'd go out ahead of the Marines. We figured why sit behind, let's go out and that way hopefully we can see them try to maneuver on the Marines before the Marines get there. Twice we'd go out, get contacted and, of course, you've got the walls with the gates, it's a little bit of room where you can suck in there by the gate [the gates are usually set back from the walls by a foot or two and that extra space could be used for cover], and two different times he took off running [away, leaving Kyle alone with the insurgents]. So now I had to call the Marines to come up and get me… the first time they sent a tank, and the second time they sent two Humvees.

After that they split us. Because they knew I wanted to kill him. And also we were in a hide-site, not even a real hide-site, on top of a roof that had maybe a 4in. lip on it, so we had no cover, and we were watching the Marines. We were down in front of them again, and we started taking sniper rounds over our heads. Someone was trying to ping us and as soon as the shot rang out we'd duck, but you duck and it's already too late. But then I kept telling them that it was at night, to look for the muzzle flash. We'd duck, we'd come back up, be scanning again, and I kept asking him, "Do you see the muzzle flash, do you see anything?" "No." "I don't either." The third or fourth time I look at him and he's still got his head down. I said, "Have you even looked up since the first shot?" He goes, "No, I could get killed up here." I said "get the fuck down and send that Marine up here." He went down, the Marine came up. We never did find the guy [shooter]…

During the first week there was a call over the radio that there were Marines down in a nearby building:

> Actually during that first week, when the Marines were assaulting, I was down on the ground moving, and another group, a street over, had come under fire. We got called over the radio that there are men down, men down. So we said "Alright" and we maneuvered on down to where we thought the Marines were. We got up on the roof and found some wounded Marines.

The group had taken small-arms fire, and their corpsmen and one other man had been shot:

> So we carried them off the roof, me and this, I can't remember his name, he's a team-mate, he was corpsman and a sniper but we both carried them down…
>
> I carried one down, he carried the other one down, and then the other Marines followed us down. There were six of them up there, two of them shot, four of them were not. So we carried them downstairs, as soon as we got down we asked them "Hey, where did you take fire from?" And they pointed to this one place across the street, so we figured ok, we're going to go up over here and they'll get some…

The hole in the wall of this building being taken advantage of by a SEAL sniper was created by an American tank or a TOW missile from a Bradley, Fallujah 2004. (Authors' collections)

Navy SEALs and Marine Corps grunts take a break during in joint operations in Fallujah, 2004. Security has been set in place to allow for a few moments of respite. (Authors' collections)

So as we start to maneuver, there was a Marine in an alleyway when a frag came down and blew him up. And I don't even, it was just pure luck because, the alleyway I started to go down, I just turned, just as the wall completely covered me, this blast went off, and I could feel shit blowing behind me, just this black smoke, and I could hear he's still in there so I just ran down there with this corpsmen, and this guy's all fucked up but he's alive, so we drag him out, and then the corpsmen starts working on him 'cause Humvees are starting to roll up and they're the flat-bed Humvee with the tall sides on them. So they were just washing up the blood, coming up to take the wounded 'cause by this time we're taking some heavies on these Marines [Marines were taking casualties]. So then we drag him out, the corpsman works on him. I decide to go down a different alleyway and I see a bunch of Marines on either side looking down the street. So I walked up to them and said "Hey, what the fuck is going on across the street down there?" They said "No, you got it wrong, it's in this house right here." Which it was, you figure an alley that's maybe 50yds long, we're at one end, the house is on the other end, right there on the corner, on the same block that we're on though. Well OK, let's go down and get them but we can't 'cause they're shooting PKC [automatic light machine gun] and they're shooting down the alley at us. No one wanted to move. Well, I come to find out right across that little alleyway there's two Marines pinned down with two reporters. So I said "Ok, well let's at least go get those guys out." Talk to the

Marines they're like "Yeah, we're just going to run down and shoot. We don't care if we aim for anything we're just going to lay down cover fire." So the Marines are like "Yeah, yeah, no problem." So the first time we start to go there's a guy that steps out at the end of the alleyway with a PKC and just starts lighting us up. And it was just like in the movies, like Wyatt Earp, completely missed all of us and we gunned him down. Don't know how it happened, one of the guys actually had a hole through his cammies, in his leg, but it did not touch him. Completely Wyatt Earp style. So then we back off and get situated again and it's like all right, let's go. So I take off, go down there, and all these Marines are like "Get the fuck out of here" and I'm just laying down fire. I have my SR. So I'm just laying it down as fast as I can doing mag changes with this heavy fucking rifle and all of a sudden I turn around and look and I'm the only one that ran down. All the other Marines, they're down there at the end of the alley, watching. So the two reporters get out of there, the two Marines come, and I don't know where this Marine learned this, but he came up, tapped me on the shoulder and said, "Last man." So I was like, holy shit I'm working with a frog man, and just as I'm shooting, I look over my left flank, and there's a Marine laying there on the ground that had been shot up. He'd been shot all through the legs. He was an officer. So I grab him and I'm dragging him as I'm trying to cradle my SR, I'm still shooting to get him down to the

The 21st-century urban battlefield. SEALs and Marines clear streets in Fallujah in 2004 using amtracks. During these intense weeks, they cleared an average of 100 houses a day. (Authors' collections)

end of the alleyway. After that whole deal the Marines put me in for a Silver Star for it, and then they, the Marine Corps, said yeah you're going to get a Silver, that was worth it and S_____ was trying to promote it to make sure they were going to give it but then eventually that new Commandant of the Marine Corps come in and he said none of my Marines got Silvers so I'm not going to give it to a SEAL. I ended up getting a Bronze Star with Valor Device out of that deal. But because of that day I was soaked in blood from the Marines so the Marines actually gave me some Marine digi cammies, so [after that] I was running around looking like a Marine.

The assault on Fallujah lasted four weeks. Kyle and his Marine colleagues were out there the entire time:

Sniper hide-site. This was a SR mission prior to the invasion of Fallujah as an Iraqi sniper called Mustafa, an Olympic shooter, was shooting at the Americans. One of the SEAL snipers killed him subsequently. (Authors' collections)

The first week like I said was all sniper. The second week they quit coming out so I gave a Marine sniper, who wasn't actually a sniper yet, I gave him my SR and took his 16. And there was a staff sergeant there, at this time I was an E-5, he goes, "I'll tell you what – I want you to take charge of my squad." During our little breaks or whatever I was running them through CQC (Close Quarter Combat) to teach them how to do room entries and

everything. I was the point man, the breacher, and the haul boss [not shooting but the controller of the train], and these guys were awesome. We ran out of demo to blow the doors so I started using my loophole charges and lock poppers, cutting them down just to crack the door enough to kick it in. We even got a couple of kills with a Marine's 16, going into a house and the Marines got a bunch of kills going into the houses where we had bad guys set up in there. We ran into Chechens, straight up chocolate chip cammies, Black Hawk Tactical [US mass market manufacturer] gear, ready to fight. We killed them and found their passports. We didn't know they were there and they had no idea we were coming either. We kicked in the doors, cleared rooms and caught them having food at the table. We also found the beheading room and I still got the banner they used in those videos they made. Oh yeah, the Marines had this really hard Iraqi working with them – he got the intel on that one.

… And then the second and third week I was doing that and then the fourth week is when they put me overwatching the river [Euphrates]. Actually a funny story was a group of Tunisians trying to cross the river, broad daylight, there were 12 of them [Marine Corps Intelligence provided data that these were Tunisians trying to join the battle in Fallujah]. So they got on these beach balls like you would see in San Diego… red, yellow, blue, you know

Tools of the trade. This sniper rifle has been broken down to fit into a backpack. (Authors' collections)

the big old beach balls you would see out here on the beaches. These guys catch them, fully jocked-up with all their gear and everything on, four guys per ball hanging on, swimming across the river. They have no idea we're in a sniper hide. So I say "Hey, I've had my fun, I want to get some shots. Here's the deal, we're going to shoot three of the balls, leave one untouched." So we watched these guys drown until they're fighting over the last ball.

Finally I told them it was OK. "I'm going to get on line, I'm going to shoot this last ball, you let them float around in the water for a little while and then you can pop them." So anyway, these Tunisians went all the way down to the bottom. But that's what it was, it averaged out that I got one kill a day that last week in Fallujah just overwatching the river. And we got relieved by the Marines.

Over the four weeks, Kyle got 19 kills. Of that he said, "Well it wasn't anything outstanding. There was a Marine who got 36 in one day when they first went into Fallujah on one street corner." After Fallujah, Kyle was reassigned:

An Army Ranger's SEAL transportation delivery vehicle (ARSTDV). This Humvee was used to supply SEALs in sniper overwatch positions in Fallujah using the power of the pharaohs. Photograph taken in 2004. (Authors' collections)

After Fallujah, I went back to RPC and about this time was when my guys were flying, whipping back into Iraq. So I joined up to be just a DA force. Actually my sister platoon was trying to do some reshuffling because they'd been at PACOM [US Pacific Command] for a while and didn't want to get stuck with just PSD which I don't blame them. They were

trying to even out some experience. So they sent me to go do some PSD, so one of the guys could come over and do some DAs. I did PSD for two weeks, you know how those principals are, fucking stupid, don't tell you shit until the last minute. I was the advance at the Marine checkpoint. They called up, said, "There's this many cars, and there's a Humvee in front and a Humvee behind the convoy." I said "All right, no problem." So they're blowing through, two vehicles flying up behind at high speed so I told the Marines, "Hey those two are not ours. I'll draw down on them, and if they keep coming y'all light them up." So they come closer. Our Marine Humvee pulls up, .50 cal. on top, all the Marines walking loaded, I fire a shot into the radiator, they slam on the brakes and the Marines are pointing at them, they thought they'd turn around and get out of there. Come to find out there's two of the principals' base. So I got fired because he did not tell me that they were coming and that they were flying up behind my convoy. So I got fired trying to protect them but it worked out well 'cause when I got fired, they didn't want to send me back to do DAs cause the Army was screaming they needed snipers. So I went to Haifa Street to go do some more.

This time, Kyle was attached to the 82d Airborne out of Fort Bragg. He was also attached to a reserve component:

Discovered and confiscated by SEALs in Fallujah out of the "torture chamber," this banner was used in al-Qaeda videos of gruesome beheadings of prisoners. Marines and two SEALs pose with the trophy. Two Iraqis were discovered in the chamber; one of them was barely alive having been mutilated, and sadly died after rescue. Photograph taken in 2004. (Authors' collections)

... to a reserve unit out of Arkansas. I had two other SEAL buddies with me. But they [SEALs] would all come to me, being from Texas, and say, "Hey, can you translate what they're saying, 'cause these boys are straight up redneck hillbillies." And no joke, they did not have all their teeth, straight up reserves. But they were good, they were ready to get it. And that 82d, they were good boys too. Haifa Street was awesome, Haifa Street in Baghdad, high-rise apartment buildings. We go take one down and sit up there and the only thing you had to worry about then was your angle 'cause you're shooting from high elevation now. But it worked out great, I got a few kills out there and basically topped off my deployment. Then I went back to do a few DAs with the guys and went home. Actually they moved us out to Hobinea, we went out and set that place up, did a few DAs and came home.

Another sniper overwatch after Fallujah had been taken down. (Authors' collections)

Kyle went home, had a shortened time of leave, then went into work-up for his third platoon. This was a condensed work-up, arranged in order to get the teams back onto their proper schedules. While Kyle was back in the US, he was awarded a Grateful Nation Award and $1,500 by the Jewish Institute for National Security Affairs for his work in SOCOM. One of JINSA's missions is to safeguard Israel.

MOSUL AND TALL AFAR

MOSUL – DECEMBER 2004 – SAW II

Shortly after the concurrent assaults on Fallujah and Mosul in November 2004, a suicide bomber managed to infiltrate a FOB near Mosul where his attack killed 18 US and Iraqi soldiers as well as four Blackwater USA contractors.[117] The urban battles were hard-fought and the suicide assault proved to be the tipping point for the overall commanders. They requested some specific support.

A SEAL Task Unit was put together composed of several platoons from ST-5. SEAL Team 8 replaced them eventually, but in the meanwhile, the TU conducted sniper missions. "The face and name of spec war sniping was established then," Paul and Frank said with a great sense of accomplishment.[118] The SEALs killed well over 100 insurgents in 45 days and helped dramatically to stabilize the volatile city. Mosul was a highly dangerous place because as soon as anyone left the US camp, enemy contact was guaranteed. US battle space commanders lost people quickly.

Once the SEAL snipers arrived at the needed combat outposts, they conferred with each battle space commander to ascertain the most dangerous sectors of the city. The snipers based their hide-site on reports they received from them and then conducted close target reconnaissance missions. The sniper teams were anywhere from five men to the entire platoon in size, depending on their threat analysis. Real-time videos coupled with detailed maps and imagery allowed them to plan out their sniping hide-sites accordingly. At other times they conducted over-flights in helicopters to get a different look at their objectives. The SEALs also conducted reconnaissance missions with their own cameras on the ground.

There were different sniper operations such as overwatch, countersniper, or baiting operations. Yarmuck Square in particular was one of the most dangerous spots in Mosul where attacks occurred frequently. Certainly the insurgents were controlling parts of the city in a brazen fashion.

A much-needed break during a lull in the action. These SEALs spent three hard weeks conducting operations in Tall Afar. (Authors' collections)

SEAL riding in the back seat of a Humvee in Iraq holding an M79 single shot 40mm grenade launcher. Note the platoon's "battering ram" is riding along. (Authors' collections)

The SEALs prosecuted targets from the first night when they killed five hostiles. Word quickly got out within the insurgent camps. Sometimes sniper teams seized positions to let the insurgents know they were in a particular building. Foolish insurgents were killed. Baiting operations included taking out a fake Iraqi truck and putting weapons in it to see if insurgents would attempt to steal those weapons. Other times, they would stage a mock firefight to draw out curious insurgents. Mock firefights sometimes went as far as blowing up a wheel or shooting rounds into an unoccupied building after an American convoy drove by. Blood puddles and drag marks were created by the SEALs with goat blood.

The SEAL-controlled sectors in Mosul shut down for 45 days. There were no more IEDs or mortar rounds to trouble the American forces. The SEAL snipers bounced around from neighborhood to neighborhood during their time in Mosul. They encountered insurgents from Chechnya, Tunisia, and Syria. The sniping game required courage and nerves of steel and the SEALs, interested in learning and improving their craft, told the battle space commander not to send in QRF once they got engaged with hostiles. The SEALs wanted to study the mechanisms of the insurgents, to see the reactions of the hostiles once engaged. Within the prior year two three- or four-man Marine sniper teams had engaged insurgents, then been overrun by superior forces. The SEALs believed that the single loud shot of a sniper's rifle had given away the Marine positions. Because of that the SEAL snipers used suppressor on their sniping rifles but also carried heavy small arms with them to repel any subsequent assaults. The suppressed rifle confused the insurgents as it meant that they could not locate the hide-sites and on occasion they then ran straight into the heavily armed SEALs while attempting to maneuver closer to where they thought the Americans had staged.

At other times the snipers engaged the enemy with an unsuppressed weapon and waited to see what happened next. Occasionally, the Iraqis crowded together to assault the SEALs in numbers, but to no avail. They usually ended up dead. Insurgents might also attempt to flank their positions, only to run into another hidden sniper team. Sometimes the enemy did nothing.

One night the SEALs set up in a four-story building at an intersection where the Army had recently lost two soldiers. They made plenty of noise to let the enemy know "We are here, come and get us." The morning came and went. The snipers were bored, when suddenly, at around 1400 hours, two to three RPG rounds and small-arms fire erupted. The snipers engaged and killed the hostiles, all seven of them, one by one. After the kills, they spotted what seemed to be a

Get some! (Authors' collections)

bald-headed Russian or Chechen with a keffiyeh around his neck, weaponless at the aid station. The hospital was about 800yds away. He was smoking and watching the SEALs, but the ROE did not allow the SEALS to kill him. Only during a subsequent briefing were they given permission to kill him. The SEALs discovered that the Chechen may have helped to set up fake road blocks, dragged people out of their cars, and executed them. They were told during the debrief to go ahead and kill him but the snipers had to have positive identification. He was never sighted again.

STRYKERS

Stryker is a family of eight-wheel-drive combat vehicles, transportable in a C-130 aircraft, being built for the US Army by GM GDLS, a joint venture set up by General Motors Defense of Canada and General Dynamics Land Systems Division of USA. Stryker is based on the GM LAV III 8 x 8 light-armored vehicle, in service since early 2001. The LAV III is itself a version of the Piranha III built by Mowag of Switzerland, now owned by General Motors Defense. GM Defense and GDLS are sharing the fabrication and final assembly of the vehicles among plants at Anniston, AL; Lima, OH; and London, Ontario.

The SBCT combines the capacity for rapid deployment with survivability and tactical mobility. The Stryker vehicle enables the team to maneuver in close and urban terrain, provides protection in open terrain and transports infantry quickly to critical battlefield positions.

(Source: http://www.sbct.army.mil/)

Stryker combat brigades proved their value to the SEALs on many occasions and in many towns across Iraq. (Authors' collections)

The Navy SEALs developed an excellent relationship with the US Army in Mosul. The Stryker Brigade Combat Teams (SBCT) from Fort Lewis were in charge of the town and had divided it into two sectors for command and control purposes. The SEALs thought the Strykers excellent as they, unlike heavy armor, could execute movement-to-contact drills better than the slow-moving and cumbersome tanks.

By April 2005 the SEALS were having fun in Mosul. They put a Stryker in the middle of a field as part of a psychological mission they had previously planned. The mission was to play songs by the heavy metal rock group Metallica for as loud and as long as it took until the insurgents attacked. One sniper position was placed overtly so that the insurgents knew where they were and another team was placed covertly. The SEALs had laid a nice trap. The enemy was unaware of the second team, moved forward and prepared the assault on the Americans in that one known position. Over the next 20–60 minutes, one by one the insurgents maneuvered and lost all their men. The SEALs claimed four to six confirmed kills with a dozen more probables.

SEAL Team 5 pulled 130–150 sniper missions in addition to executing DA missions every two days during the three-month sniping period. Sometimes the

The face of 21st-century urban warfare: highly trained individuals supported by mechanized infantry. (Authors' collections)

America's sons at war. SEALs from ST-5 in Iraq. The ram doubled as mascot and "battering ram." (Authors' collections)

SEALs conducted several missions per night. Certainly these three months were far more rewarding than the three months of PSD duty. The TU Mosul (Task Unit) made life for them easy as well; his focus was on winning the battle space, not winning his next promotion. He knew what the SEALs could do and how to exploit their abilities. The SEALs' tactics forced the insurgents to change their tactics because their freedom of movement was restricted.

TALL AFAR – VOTING BOOTHS, AN OTTOMAN CASTLE AND A SYRIAN SNIPER – SAW III

The town of Tall Afar lies west of Mosul. The area commanders of Tall Afar wanted the Navy SEALs from teams 5 and 8 to protect the voting booths for the upcoming Iraqi elections. The snipers had been so successful in Mosul that they hoped for a similar positive experience during one of the most important events in recent Iraqi history. Paul experienced the best two and a half weeks of his life in Tall Afar.

An American-held Iraqi hospital was one of the official voting stations. This particular area was a hot bed of insurgent activity and needed pacifying. The local commanders briefed the SEAL platoons on the insurgents' training, tactics, and procedures. The SEALs, now well versed in their sniping operations, again used Strykers for the bait and switch operations that had served them so well in Mosul earlier. The snipers also set up unique shooting sites specific to the areas they had to cover. The overall battle space commander of Tall Afar had a great deal of confidence in the snipers and not only permitted them the use of the expensive Strykers, but in effect allowed them to do whatever they needed to accomplish the mission. It was of the utmost urgency to allow Iraqis the ability to live freely and vote during the election.

In the early hours of the combat operations, Paul witnessed one of the greatest shots he had ever seen taken by a fellow SEAL sniper. The "bad guys"[119] were scouting the areas near the sniper hide-sites but could not pinpoint any American positions. Paul mentioned that these insurgents did not wear traditional local Arab clothes and Signal Intelligence (SIGNIT) indicated an impending attack. The three SEAL sniper teams were carefully monitoring the main supply route/road (MSR) when they spotted a man wearing a jacket way down the MSR.

Navy SEALs occupying the 16th-century Ottoman castle of Tall Afar. The castle provided an ideal base of operations for SEAL snipers. (Authors' collections)

Sniper action in Tall Afar. (Authors' collections)

The SEALs knew from previous briefings that weapons were smuggled back and forth by individuals who hid them beneath their clothing. As luck had it, a wind picked up and revealed an AK underneath the man's jacket. The engagement began when one sniper shot one round that struck the man in his leg, putting him down on the street. After a couple of follow-up shots the man was dead. No doubt the insurgents now knew that American snipers were in town. This shooting incident triggered multiple well-coordinated engagements by the insurgents and Paul ranged his shooter at a target of 997 yards. Paul's sniper lit off a round and hit the Iraqi center chest and "laid him out like a fish." The amazing thing was that the SEAL shooter had not attended sniper school. However, he was an Olympic-caliber match 22 shot, and he was probably the best shot from the West Coast teams. Part of the SEALs training also included an in-house, two-week, scout sniping program. ST-5 conducted many such informal training courses in an effort to improve their tactics and procedures.

The multiple sniping engagements lasted for over two weeks until the election finished. According to one SEAL, in Mosul and Tall Afar the SEALs had a 90–100 percent chance of contact when they left the gate. The four Purple Hearts won by SEALs in this time proved how dangerous their work was. Finally, the commander of ST-3, Commander Riley, pulled them out because he was worried that dead SEALs would be bad for his record and promotion.[120] Two American Army soldiers and three Iraqi soldiers had been killed near the old castle of Tall Afar.

One interesting point was that the insurgents soon realized the significance Americans placed on body counts, so they would do their best not to leave dead bodies in the streets. Many times women and children would appear and the body and gun, sometimes on a string, disappeared. If anyone picked up a gun the SEALs shot them. Some Iraqis picked up flat cardboard and built a box

A US Navy SEAL sniper. (Authors' collections)

A US Navy SEAL sniper. (Authors' collections)

around the weapon which they then surreptitiously carried. Some Iraqi women also cleaned the area as well and the snipers saw them carry new dirt to the battle area to cover bloodstains. The SEALs sent Strykers to take a look at those areas and, indeed, they often found bloodstains covered by new dirt. Other times some of those killed were not buried quickly. Those, the SEALs thought, were probably foreign fighters.

The Tall Afar Castle provided a great sniping and counter-sniping position. It was so well situated that the SEALs were able to hit any relief forces that wanted to rush into the areas the SEALs covered for the election. Local Iraqi police and several Strykers supported the position. By 0300 hours the SEALs had set up their fields of fire and the single best sniping position were the lavatories used by the 82d Airborne Division earlier in the war.

On one day, Paul was bored and threw a turd at his buddy just as a coordinated attack was launched on the castle. More than a dozen mortar rounds, RPG rockets, small-arms fire, and carefully aimed sniper shots hit the castle. Coolly, the American snipers found their targets. Many insurgents were dressed in black with white headbands and this made them easy to identify. Air assets tried to add to the insurgents' death toll but some of the CAS support was just not precise enough. Nevertheless, the firefight lasted for six hours. The SEAL snipers learned a lot from trying to hit men sprinting at full speed at a distance of 600 to 1,100yds. Paul estimated that the SEALs hit one out of every six runners. Any insurgent who hesitated usually got hit. "He who hesitates, dies."

Navy SEAL platoon looking menacing at Tall Afar. (Authors' collections)

One particularly tough nut to crack was a well-disciplined sniper who turned out to be Syrian; the SEALs counter-sniped with him repeatedly. Counter-sniping required patience, a keen eye, and luck. It took three days to kill the Syrian sniper and it happened just as the SEALs' mission was about to end. The enemy sniper was so good that a mannequin the SEALs used to draw fire had three head shots. The Syrian used an HK sniping rifle which the Americans ultimately recovered. Paul compared the sniping experiences to the German and Russian WWII snipers locked in mortal combat depicted in the film *Enemy at the Gates*.

Paul tried to draw the Syrian's fire but could not get him to expose himself for even a split second. He was professional and disciplined, and throughout the day small-arms fire intermixed with sniper rounds. So it was tough to isolate the enemy sharpshooter.

The city of Tall Afar is catacombed with a medieval city beneath. Paul spotted children playing soccer, occasionally moving through the underground cave network. Finally, the SEALs figured out that the insurgents were using the network to maneuver into better positions unseen.

The Syrian must have had spotters. The SEAL snipers thought that there was one expert sniper with a support team composed of probably four to five men who helped spot and snipe as well. The Americans did have the advantage of superior technology. The Stryker had excellent optics to scan the areas but the

This dummy took three head shots in the SEALs' attempt to draw out enemy snipers. (Authors' collections)

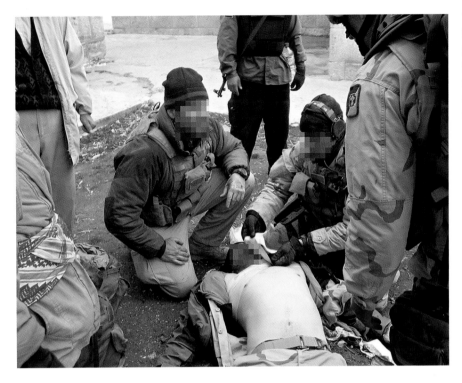

The SEALs in Tall Afar found insurgent snipers to be no slouches. This interpreter learned that the hard way. The bullet just clipped his shoulder, and took a clean slice out of him. (Authors' collections)

Syrian sniper was so good he shot out the optics. The SEALs knew he was close but could not get a precise location on him, only a general area. The snipers put out flank security to lock off particular areas.

SEALs used observation drills to locate the target. They scanned and shot anything suspicious but nothing came of it and it was getting late in the day. Paul looked for an edge. The Stryker commander would not risk another expensive optical system, so Paul thought of using the Iraqi police as bait. He placed them on the top ring of the castle's battlements with orders for them just to shoot.

The day was ending. The mission had been a success. The Iraqis had voted, protected by a small but dedicated force of Americans. The SEALs started to wind down. A few of their snipers were on the walls alongside the Iraqi police. Several men kept shooting, hoping to catch the Syrian sniper trying to get a hit. Maybe he would drop his cover, take a risk to get a kill.

Paul spotted an interpreter exposed at an archer window on the battlement. The SEAL told him to get away from the window but shortly thereafter he got hit in the shoulder and the bullet hit an Iraqi police officer in the spine as well. The SEALs medically evacuated the wounded out of the castle. Finally, one SEAL sniper from ST-8, using the observation drills learned in sniper school, spotted the small movement of a brick at a house closest to the castle, followed by a shot.

 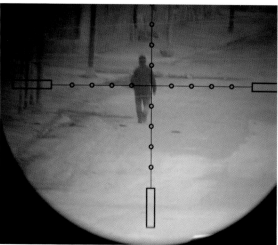

Keeping a close eye on any activity on the streets. No effort was spared to protect voters in Tall Afar. (Authors' collections)

Some of the SEALs assaulted the building but could not find the exact location as more shots rang out. Then they found the place. It was a small false wall hidden inside the building. The spotter would pick out a target and the Syrian sniper would move the brick, fire his weapon, and place the brick back into its hole. Although there was no body, it seemed likely that one of the American snipers had hit the Syrian because the SEALs who assaulted the house found brain and other cerebral matter. Additionally and more importantly, they found the sniper's rifle in an alley as a car sped off.

The Tall Afar mission was a great success. In a speech delivered at Cleveland on March 20, 2006, President George W. Bush referred specifically to Tall Afar as evidence of the new US strategy in Iraq:

The recent elections show us how Iraqis respond when they know they're safe. Tal Afar is the largest city in Western Nineveh Province. In the elections held in January 2005, of about 190,000 registered voters, only 32,000 people went to the polls. Only Fallujah had a lower participation rate. By the time of the October referendum on the constitution and the December elections, Iraqi and coalition forces had secured Tal Afar and surrounding areas. The number of registered voters rose to about 204,000–and more than 175,000 turned out to vote in each election, more than 85 percent of the eligible voters in Western Nineveh Province. These citizens turned out because they were determined to have a say in their nation's future, and they cast their ballots at polling stations that were guarded and secured by fellow Iraqis.

The confidence that has been restored to the people of Tal Afar is crucial to their efforts to rebuild their city. Immediately following the military operations, we helped the Iraqis set up humanitarian relief for the civilian population and by improving infrastructure from the electric grid to sewer and water systems. With their city now more secure, the people of Tal Afar are beginning to rebuild a better future for themselves and their children.

The success of Tal Afar also shows how the three elements of our strategy in Iraq – political, security, and economic – depend on and reinforce one another. By working with local leaders to address community grievances, Iraqi and coalition forces helped build the political support needed to make the military operation a success. The military success against the terrorists helped give the citizens of Tal Afar security, and this allowed them to vote in the elections and begin to rebuild their city. And the economic rebuilding that is beginning to take place is giving Tal Afar residents a real stake in the success of a free Iraq. And as all this happens, the terrorists, those who offer nothing but destruction and death, are becoming marginalized.[121]

RAMADI

SEAL Death Dealers and Casualties

Ramadi lies in the Al Anbar province and is about 70 miles west of Iraq's capital city, Baghdad. American commanders suspected Ramadi of being a staging area for terrorist activity because of its location and the fact that it hosts the main railway line into Syria. In June 2006, American forces assaulted the city in another brutal fight. The SEALs conducted numerous missions for the Marine and Army combat elements involved in the fighting. Kyle went to Ramadi on his third deployment to Iraq. He traveled out a week after the rest of Charlie Platoon, but "somehow the word did not get passed that I was coming in."[122] So he had to make his own way to Ramadi. Here he explains how he managed to get across Iraq:

The dummy in this picture was named after the Tom Hanks' "co-star" in the movie *Cast Away*, Volleyball Wilson. The head was used to draw enemy sniper fire. (Authors' collections)

> So I hooked up with an SF guy, they got me to the helo pad. Then I hooked up with a Ranger who was going to Ramadi too. I was listening to people talk about what they shouldn't be saying, like, I heard there was certain shit going on, that there was an enemy mortar team and all sorts of stuff. I was trying to catch a helo to Alisade Air Base, near the Syrian border, cause from there you can go anywhere. There was a general who was talking about that mortar team at Alisade. I walked up and said "Hey I need to go on this helo." And he turned around and said, "So what makes you so important that some of my guys need to get bumped off?" I said, and I had all my guns and everything, "I'm a sniper and I'm supposed to go to Alisade and take out a mortar team." Of course I was full of shit and I turned to my Ranger guy and said, "And this is another sniper, there's two of us going out." So he turns around and says "Here, these guys get the first two seats. Get to Alisade," and then I told the Ranger, "Hey, come with me, we're going to the CASH."

The CASH (Combat Support Hospital) is the medical center. When Kyle and his Ranger friend arrived there, they found that the only helicopters flying into Ramadi were medevacs, so Kyle managed to persuade a Marine to let them be "medevaced to Ramadi," as if they were returning to duty after being medevaced out. When he got to Ramadi, he went to Camp Ramadi and tried to link up with his platoon.

Actually the platoon had taken off to Camp Corregidor which is on the east side of Ramadi, 'cause they were supposed to be, they were going to do an assault on Ramadi like they did on Fallujah. So everybody's pulled over there, it was just me and two other team guys at Camp Ramadi. So I was pissed off, I was like shit, I just missed the whole thing. So I went and sat on a guard tower one day just thinking I would get the lay of the land, took a sniper rifle with me, I ended up getting two kills. And at this time no one had had any kills out there during this deployment. So they get the word at Corregidor and of course they go, "Oh fuck, Kyle is here." But it worked out great, the assault ended up not getting approved so they all came back and then we just started doing sniper watches, or overwatches. And it was awesome at first 'cause the Army owned the main part of Ramadi and the north portions were owned by the Marines who we'd go to and say, "Hey, where's your hottest spot?" And then they'd point it out and we'd say, "OK, we're going in, will you come QRF us if we need it?" At first they were like, "Um, I'm not taking a tank down there." "Well, if we patrol 200yds will you come pick us up there?" "Yeah." So we started doing that. And then we started having a lot of great success, and then the Army and the Marines both said, "Hey, we'll fucking come get you. Y'all are doing awesome." And then they started coming to us and saying, "Hey, will you go here, will you go here." And we just had a great relationship with them. And, in fact, they decided they were going to start putting the COPs [Combat Out Posts] in Ramadi, and the first one was COP Falcon, and they came to us and said, "Hey,

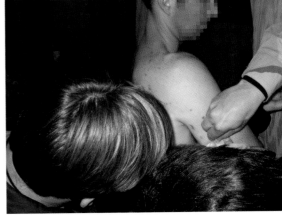

No fighting man wants to win this medal, but Purple Hearts are not unknown to SEALs. (Authors' collections)

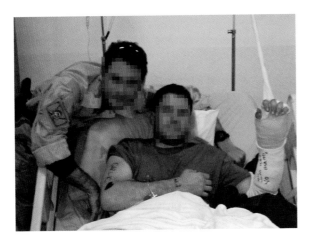

Left:
MRAP V-shaped hull designed to break away to survive the blast of an IED (MRAP vehicles feature a V-shaped hull, which deflects, rather than absorbs, the blast of an IED). The Marine EOD element in the vehicle survived. (Authors' collections)

Right:
An Iraqi counterpart poses with two Navy SEALs and an Iraqi family where someone had taken a shot at the SEALs. Shell casings were found and the family underwent gunpowder residue tests which proved that none of the family had fired a rifle. (Authors' collections)

do you want a part of this," and we said, "yeah, we'll go in before and secure it," and they thought we were just fucking crazy. So we'd go in the night before and secure the place that they wanted to make their COP and they'd come in early in the morning before the sun comes up and we'd do the high five and we'd bump off a couple of hundred yards to overwatch where they were building it up. They thought that was great and turned out to be a great success and no one at the COP got shot at.

Kyle said that "it started to be where the general out there said, you are not going to put a COP in, unless the SEALs are there. They have to go in first." The platoon was working all over the city. They secured buildings for new COPs, then after the Marines had occupied the buildings, they would move out to give them sniper overwatch as they established their base:

We did the next one, was on the west side, right about 300–400yds from the river. I don't even know if that was the Tigris, the Euphrates or what it was, but it's that river right there by Ramadi on the west side. The Marines, the boat drivers, they're the ones that dropped us off and those guys are better than the SBT guys. And they inserted us completely quiet. No one knew we were there, we took it down. The next day all of a sudden the whole town is surprised to see the Army rolling in to set up a COP, 'cause it had already been secured. So we set them up, that was on the west side, then we bumped in a little bit further east and set up another one, went up north, even went in for the Marines and put one in for them. It was a great, great deployment.

During the six-month deployment, the SEALs helped put in five or six COPs, but their mission was broader than just establishing COPs:

We would drive to COP Falcon, 'cause that was the only one you could really drive to, and then from there we would stage. There were a couple of houses in this complex, they gave us our own house, and we spray painted "SEAL House" all over it. They helped us build shelves and cots and everything to make it our home and they would lock it up for us so no one else could get in. And we'd stage out of there and do foot patrols into the city to do sniper overwatches and we would just pick where we wanted to go. And we'd try to find where the most IEDs [improvised explosive devices] were coming from and the most shots and we'd go set up there.

We only caught a few guys setting up IEDs. The most of our kills were either guys maneuvering on the COP or shooting at us. 'Cause if we took a place that was occupied, the rest of the city knew about it by 9–10 o'clock and those people didn't come outside. They got to know there's Americans in there. But usually by 9.30 or so we'd take our first shot anyway, so then they would know that there's snipers out here. So we'd get into usually around an hour-long firefight and then about five in the afternoon another firefight. It got to be where you could set your watch by it. You know you're going to shoot here and you're going to shoot again at this time.

SEALs like to name their vehicles, and earlier names like Goat Rope did not catch on, so GI Joe came to the rescue. (Authors' collections)

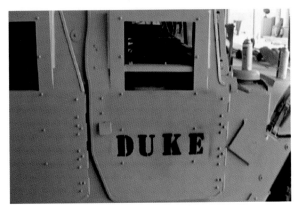

Left:
Camp Marc Lee. One SEAL wanted to feel the weight of the body armor used by EOD technicians. (Authors' collections)

Right:
During a firefight in Ramadi the NVDs were shot off the mount. This is one lucky SEAL. (Authors' collections)

JOB, LEE AND MONSOOR – CASUALTIES OF WAR

The SEALs took casualties. Like all previous wars, men will get wounded, others will die. Kyle's unit was no exception to the rule:

It was real close to 20 Street which was the hottest street in Ramadi. We were standing on the roof doing overwatch, there was just three of us up there. Ryan Job was my 60 gunner running security for me. We were up watching the rest of our guys taking down the blocks with the Army and then all of a sudden a sniper shot rang out and we all went down to the ground and I looked around, saw Ryan on the ground and I said, "Hey, get up, fucking quit being lazy." So we get back up and he's still lying so I say, "Hey, Ryan, get the fuck back up you fat piece of shit." And then I go over there and find out he's been shot. He's the one got shot in the face and he's blinded now. I called it in, "Man down."

He's just laying there trying to cough because all the blood is filling his throat. So as soon as we sit him up he spits the blood out and he's not saying anything, he's just quiet, but you can hear him breathing and everything. So we carry him down a flight of stairs and he's a big guy, and the stairs out there are real narrow. So two guys [are] trying to carry him down and it is kind of a hassle so he finally says, "Let go of me, I'll walk."

You know he was worried for a split second that we were gonna leave him there but just as fast he thought different and we were on top of him real quick, working on him. He said to let him walk by himself, 'cause he didn't want to be a liability to the team. How about that. Good guy! Marc was in the totally exposed stairwell and put on covering fire while they took care of Ryan.

At this point Job could still see out of his left eye. His vision was lost entirely when the swelling in his brain forced fragments from his shattered sunglasses

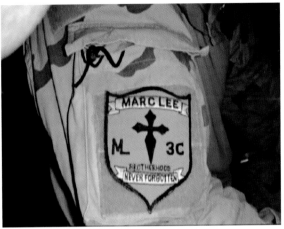

into the wound that severed the optical nerve. Despite his impaired vision, and the pain, it was only a few minutes after he was hit that he was up walking. Kyle said, "I kept his one arm over my shoulder just in case, 'cause he was losing a lot of blood. Went ahead and he walked on down and he walked straight up to the Bradley, he got in there and that's when he went out from loss of blood and I'm sure some shock. That was the last time he saw anything." After this, everybody extracted to the COP:

> We're sitting there, all pissed, and some guys were crying and everything, 'cause we just lost one guy. We think he's going to die. He just got shot in the head. And then the chief comes up to tell me, he goes, "Hey, let's go get the fucker who did it." We got some intel of where the shot came from. So all right, let's go. So we load up in three different Bradleys, we go in and hit the house and what they had done is just sucked us in. We went to the house and it was surrounded on three other sides. Soon as we went in we start taking fire…
>
> The guys still continued clearing the house, the guys stacked on the stairs, and as we started going up, there was a window behind our backs that looked down on us from the rooftop where there had been a guy that popped up with a PKC, and Marc Lee happened to see him, and just as he was raising his gun, and we figure he was starting to say something to warn us to watch our backs, he lit off one or two rounds and at that time a shot came in and went right through his mouth. That's why we think he was trying to say something to us 'cause it didn't hit any of his teeth, his mouth was open, went right through his mouth, hit his spine and killed him instantly.
>
> He was dead before he hit the ground. He hit the ground protecting us, 'cause we were not watching our backs but he was. But everyone did as they were trained. Shot came in, guys kept going up, guys turned around, blasted him, and guys were stepping over his dead body. One corpsman stopped to watch him, the house got taken down and then it was "OK,

Left:
Charlie Platoon, ST-3 around the newly christened US military base named after the first Navy SEAL killed in Iraq, Marc Lee. (Authors' collections)

Right:
A Crusader Cross and patch honoring Marc Lee which was produced in-country. The idea was based on the historical analogy of Knights Templars, an idea which appealed to the SEALs. (Authors' collections)

Left:
Kyle has his eyes on the glass, looking for more targets of opportunity. (Authors' collections)

Right:
These are members of the Iraqi military trained by Navy SEALs. (Authors' collections)

what do we do, let's take care of Marc." And we thought, after seeing Ryan, we thought this guy was going to live. At the time the corpsman had not told us that he was already dead. So we got him out of there, and then we got the guys who were shooting at us, gunned them down, and then we exfiltrated back to the COP, and that's when we got the word that Ryan's going to make it, Marc died.

For his actions, Marc Lee was posthumously awarded the Silver Star:

Petty Officer Lee and his SEAL element maneuvered to assault an identified enemy position. He, his teammates, Bradley Fighting Vehicles and Abrams tanks engaged enemy positions with suppressive fire. During the assault, his team came under heavy enemy fire from an adjacent building to the north. To protect the lives of his teammates, he fearlessly exposed himself to direct enemy fire by engaging the enemy with his machine gun and was mortally wounded in the engagement. His brave actions in the line of fire saved the lives of many of his teammates.[123]

After Marc's death, the remaining men fought in the building for 15–20 minutes before being exfiltrated in Bradleys provided by the Army, who then continued to provide cover: "When we left, I was looking out that portal on the back of the Bradley and the whole city was on fire, black smoke everywhere, dust all over the place. Those guys definitely took care of us." There was by this time a good relationship between the Army and the SEALs, and the Army were happy to use their vehicles to aid the SEALs in their work, and in doing so see action themselves: "When we first went in, the guy who controlled the AO… told us, 'cause he was tank commander, 'I don't care what y'all do, just call me one time, I want to use my main tank round.' And he shot it 37 times when we left, so he got some action in out there, him personally, with his tank." Good relations had also been forged with the two to eight Marines who were stationed up to the north: "If they heard us in a firefight they were on the radio, 'Hey, can we come, can we come?' We'd go 'No, no, we'll tell you when we're not having fun anymore.' After that whole little friendship was made we had to beat them to make them stay back at base."

During that six month deployment, Kyle achieved a good number of kills:

I got a lot. I have 137 in total including the 19 from Fallujah. The rest of them came from Ramadi. And the gun I got it all with was my .300 Win Mag. I know for urban sniping it's not preferred 'cause it's bolt action and most of the guys would take their SRs but most of the buildings we were taking, there was an opportunity to take a shot out to 1,000yds and I figured if I'm going to take a shot out to that distance, and an SR can reach out to 1,100yds but with a .300 Win Mag I know I can drill them. So I aimed up and I still got a shot at 1,600yds. That was my furthest.

Kyle has the highest kill score in SOCOM. A SOCOM historian was sent to interview him in Ramadi because of his record-breaking score. Of this, Kyle says "I don't care if I break the record or if someone else beats me... I would rather be the guy who didn't get the record and someone else gets all the attention." Due to his work sniping, Kyle has been awarded one Silver Star, and five Bronze Stars, and is pleased to have never received a Purple Heart.

SEAL Team 3 Charlie Platoon achieved over 300 known kills in six months. "Actually we looked at it and out of the whole theater since the time the war kicked off until we left, the SEALs have accounted for 25 percent of kills in Iraq."

The Navy SEALs raised the flag similar to the fashion of the Marines at Iwo Jima. One half of the platoon had been engaged by insurgents and the other platoon on the roof top raised Old Glory to draw fire away from the other half of the SEAL platoon, thus enabling them to find cover. (Authors' collections)

The front man is Michael Monsoor, the second Navy SEAL killed in Iraq. This photo was taken during an extraction after a firefight and the smoke was used to conceal their movements to the enemy. (Authors' collections)

On April 8, 2008 President George Bush awarded Navy SEAL Michael A. Monsoor posthumously the Medal of Honor. While engaged in a firefight in Ramadi on September 29, 2006, Monsoor sacrificed his life to save his beloved comrades. The official Navy summary describes his actions on that day:

Petty Officer Michael A. Monsoor, United States Navy, distinguished himself through conspicuous gallantry and intrepidity at the risk of his life above and beyond the call of duty as a Combat Advisor and Automatic Weapons Gunner for Naval Special Warfare Task Group Arabian Peninsula in support of Operation *Iraqi Freedom* on 29 September 2006. He displayed great personal courage and exceptional bravery while conducting operations in enemy held territory at Ar Ramadi Iraq.

During Operation *Kentucky Jumper*, a combined coalition battalion clearance and isolation operation in southern Ar Ramadi, he served as automatic weapons gunner in a combined SEAL and Iraqi Army (IA) sniper overwatch element positioned on a residential rooftop in a violent sector and historical stronghold for insurgents. In the morning, his

The Medal of Honor. Two SEALs have thus far earned the nation's highest honor in the Global War on Terrorism. (DOD)

team observed four enemy fighters armed with AK-47s reconnoitering from roads in the sector to conduct follow-on attacks. SEAL snipers from his roof engaged two of them which resulted in one enemy wounded in action and one enemy killed in action. A mutually supporting SEAL/IA position also killed an enemy fighter during the morning hours. After the engagements, the local populace blocked off the roads in the area with rocks to keep civilians away and to warn insurgents of the presence of his coalition sniper element. Additionally, a nearby mosque called insurgents to arms to fight coalition forces.

Left:
.50cal. heavy machine gun with Pope glass similar to the vehicle used by the highest Navy SEAL commander in the world, the Pope. (Authors' collections)

Right:
All of the SEALs in Ramadi carried guns and magazines with the Punisher logo on it. (Authors' collections)

In the early afternoon, enemy fighters attacked his position with automatic weapons fire from a moving vehicle. The SEALs fired back and stood their ground. Shortly thereafter, an enemy fighter shot a rocket-propelled grenade at his building. Though well-acquainted with enemy tactics in Ar Ramadi, and keenly aware that the enemy would continue to attack, the SEALs remained on the battlefield in order to carry out the mission of guarding the western flank of the main effort.

Due to expected enemy action, the officer in charge repositioned him with his automatic heavy machine gun in the direction of the enemy's most likely avenue of approach. He placed him in a small, confined sniper hide-sight between two SEAL snipers on an outcropping of the roof, which allowed the three SEALs maximum coverage of the area. He was located closest to the egress route out of the sniper hide-sight watching for enemy activity through a tactical periscope over the parapet wall. While vigilantly watching for enemy activity, an enemy fighter hurled a hand grenade onto the roof from an unseen location. The grenade hit him in the chest and bounced onto the deck. He immediately leapt to his feet and yelled "grenade" to alert his teammates of impending danger, but they could not evacuate the sniper hide-sight in time to escape harm. Without hesitation and showing no regard for his own life, he threw himself onto the grenade, smothering it to protect his teammates who were lying in close proximity. The grenade detonated as he came down on top of it, mortally wounding him.

Petty Officer Monsoor's actions could not have been more selfless or clearly intentional. Of the three SEALs on that rooftop corner, he had the only avenue of escape away from the blast, and if he had so chosen, he could have easily escaped. Instead, Monsoor chose to protect his comrades by the sacrifice of his own life. By his courageous and selfless actions, he saved the lives of his two fellow SEALs and he is the most deserving of the special recognition afforded by awarding the Medal of Honor.[124]

THE FUTURE OF THE SEALS

Almost all the Navy SEALs believe that the United States cannot win the war on terrorism. Not one offered a solution, although in a hasty comment one said, "We apply the Rule of Fifty."[125] When queried, he explained by saying that the Israelis destroy a suicide bomber's house as well as each neighboring home, thereby sending a warning to any supporter and potential bomber. That is the "Rule of Three" and the SEALs would make it 50 instead of just three. It was pointed out that Israel is far from peaceful and secure and this particular ruthlessness has alienated and hardened the Palestinians even more. The SEAL agreed.

Iraqi counterparts with Navy SEALs conducting building clearing in the streets of Ramadi. The SEALs are clearing the building and the Iraqis are providing security. (Authors' collections)

There is no magic ball to foretell the future. Americans can take pride in their armed forces who have always served their country faithfully. Our soldiers, sailors, Marines, and airmen are not only warriors but are also our ambassadors and we ought to remember that no military can win any war without clear-cut political objectives.

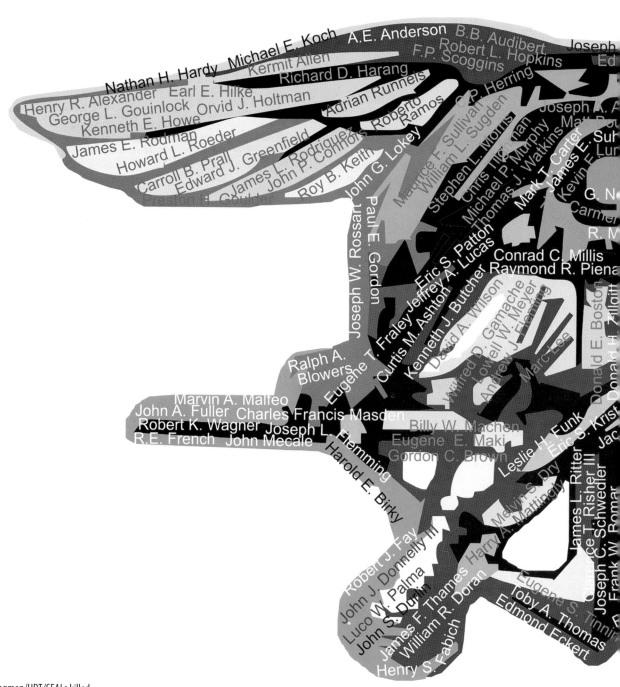

All Frogmen/UDT/SEALs killed
since 1942. (Tactical Assault Gear)

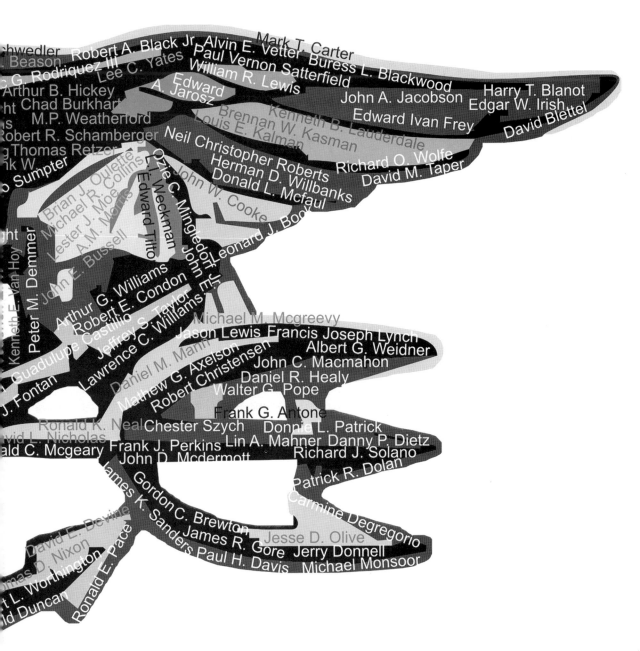

APPENDIX 1

ORGANIZATION OF US NAVAL SPECIAL OPERATIONS FORCES 1999–2000

The United States Army Command and General Staff College's *The Special Operations Force Reference Manual* of 1999/2000 describes the organization of the United States Naval Special Operations Forces (Chapter 4) as follows:

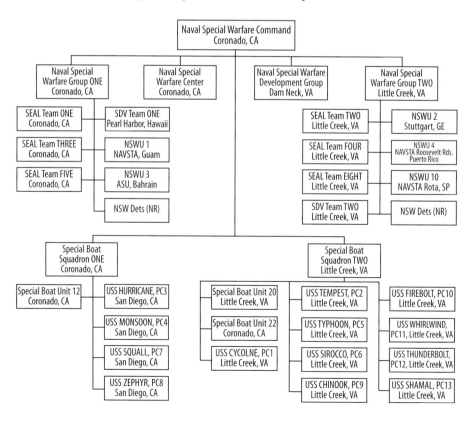

NAVAL SPECIAL WARFARE CENTER

The Naval Special Warfare Center, Naval Amphibious Base (NAB) Coronado, CA.
- Commanded by a captain (O-6).
- Schoolhouse for Naval Special Warfare training.
- 26-week BUD/S course.
- Nine-week Special Warfare Combatant Crewman (SWCC) course.
- Advanced maritime special operations training.
- Maintains a detachment at the NAB, Little Creek, VA, for training of East Coast personnel.

NAVAL SPECIAL WARFARE DEVELOPMENT GROUP

The Naval Special Warfare Development Group, Little Creek, VA.
- Commanded by a Navy captain (O-6).
- Conducts tests, evaluations, and development of current and emerging technology.
- Develops maritime ground and airborne tactics.

NAVAL SPECIAL WARFARE GROUPS

Two NSW Groups, One and Two, at NABs Coronado, CA and Little Creek, VA.
- Echelon II captain (O6).
- Equip, support, and provide command and control elements.
- Provide SEAL and SDV platoons and forces.

NSW Groups One and Two are organized into:
- Three SEAL teams, each composed of eight 16-man platoons.
- One SDV team.
- Small command and control elements outside the continental US, to support NSW forces during operations.

NAVAL SPECIAL WARFARE COMMAND COMBAT SERVICE SUPPORT TEAMS (CSST)

One CSST is assigned to each NSW Group.

CSST includes three primary mission elements:

- O(perational)PLAN/CON(tingency)PLAN and crisis-action logistic planning and coordination.
- In-theater contracting, small purchase and lease actions.
- Forward operating base support.

Additional tasks include:

- Force embarkation.
- Load-planning.
- Multi-modal transport coordination.
- Combat cargo handling.
- In-theater logistic coordination.
- Military Liaison Officer/Defense Attaché Officer liaison.
- Exercise-related construction.
- Infrastructure support.
- Contingency engineering.
- Expeditionary camp siting and development.
- Camp maintenance.
- NBC decontamination.
- Defensive combat planning and execution.

NAVAL SPECIAL WARFARE TASK GROUPS AND TASK UNITS

Naval Special Warfare Task Groups (NSWTG) and Task Units (NSWTU) are tailored to particular missions and can operate independently, jointly, or in combined operations. Their missions include:

- Provision of command and control elements.
- Administrative support.
- Logistical support.

SPECIAL BOAT SQUADRONS (SBRs)

Commanded by Echelon II captain at NABs Coronado, CA, and Little Creek, VA.

- Provide special operations ships and craft.
- One or more active duty or reserve component Special Boat Units (SBUs) and CYCLONE Class Patrol Coastal (PC) ships.

SPECIAL BOAT UNITS (SBUs)

Organized, trained, and equipped to operate a variety of special operations surface craft in maritime and riverine environments.

SEAL DELIVERY VEHICLE TASK UNIT

Submersible systems operations from specially configured submarines equipped with Dry Deck Shelters (DDS).
- Commanded by an SDV team commanding officer or executive officer.
- Comprised of one or more SDV or SEAL platoons.

SEAL PLATOON

- Commanded by a Navy lieutenant (O-3).
- A platoon consists of 16 SEALs and can be divided into two squads or four elements.
- All SEALs are dive, parachute, and demolitions qualified.

MOBILE COMMUNICATIONS TEAM

- Communications–electronics departments of the Naval Special Warfare Groups One and Two. Provides operational communications support for NSW forces.
- Provide new equipment and develop tactics for communications operations and support.
- Prepare, implement, and review communications plans.

NAVAL SPECIAL WARFARE GROUP ONE (NSWG-1)

NSWG-1 is located in Coronado, CA, and is one of the six major operational components of the Naval Special Warfare Command:
- Commanded by a captain (O-6).
- Operational and administrative control, of ST-1, ST-3, ST-5, and SEAL Delivery Vehicle Team One (SDVT-1).
- Administrative control of NSWU-1 (Naval Special Warfare Unit One) and NSWU-3.
- NSWG-1's geographic area of concentrations is the Pacific and Central Commands.

SEAL TEAM ONE (ST-1)

ST-1 is based in Coronado, CA.

- Commanded by a Navy commander (O-5).
- It has eight operational platoons and a headquarters element.
- ST-1's geographic area of concentration is Southeast Asia.
- ST-1 deploys platoons to NSWU-1 in Guam and conducts Deployments for Training (DFTs) throughout the Pacific and Central theaters.

SEAL TEAM THREE (ST-3)

ST-3 is based in Coronado, CA.

- Commanded by a Navy commander (O-5).
- It has eight operational platoons and a headquarters element.
- ST-3's geographic area of concentration is Southwest Asia.
- ST-3 deploys platoons to NSWU-1 in Guam aboard amphibious ships deployed to Seventh, Fifth, and Third Fleets, and conducts DFTs throughout the Pacific and Central Theaters.

SEAL TEAM FIVE (ST-5)

ST-5 is based in Coronado, CA.

- Commanded by a Navy commander (O-5).
- It has eight operational platoons and a headquarters element.
- ST-5's geographic area of concentration is the Northern Pacific.
- ST-5 deploys platoons to NSWU-1 in Guam, aboard amphibious ships deployed to Seventh, Fifth, and Third Fleets, and conducts DFTs throughout the Pacific and Central Theaters.

SEAL DELIVERY VEHICLE TEAM ONE (SDVT-1)

SDVT-1 is based in Pearl Harbor, HI.

- Commanded by a Navy commander (O-5).
- It has three operational SEAL Delivery Vehicle (SDV), Dry Deck Shelter (DDS) Task Units and a headquarters element.
- Each SDV/DDS Task Unit is designed to operate independently from a host submarine in the conduct of Naval Special Warfare missions.
- SDV/DDS Task Units normally deploy only aboard host submarines, but may be deployed from shore or surface ships.

- SDVT-1 conducts operations throughout the Pacific and Central commands geographic areas of responsibility.

NAVAL SPECIAL WARFARE UNIT ONE (NSWU-1)

NSWU-1 is based in Guam.
- Commanded by a Navy commander (O-5).
- Consists of a headquarters element and has operational control of SEAL platoons and SBU detachments from NSWG-1 and from SBS-1 that forward deploy to NSWU-1 on a six-month rotational duty.
- NSWU-1 maintains operational control of five forward-deployed SEAL platoons and two SBU Rigid Hull Inflatable Boat (RHIB) detachments.
- NSWU-1 is under the administrative command of NSWG-1, but operationally reports to Special Operations Command, Pacific and US Navy Seventh Fleet for operational tasking.
- Provides operational support to forward-deployed platoons and conducts theater planning for contingencies and exercises for Naval Special Warfare forces in the Pacific.
- NSWU-1 is capable of forming the nucleus of a Naval Special Warfare Task Unit (NSWTU).

NAVAL SPECIAL WARFARE – GROUP ONE DETACHMENT KODIAK

Detachment Kodiak is located in Kodiak, AL.
- Six-man training cadre that specializes in training SEAL platoons and Special Boat Unit Detachments in maritime cold-weather operations.

NAVAL SPECIAL WARFARE UNIT THREE (NSWU-3)

NSWU-3 is based in Bahrain and is under the administrative control of NSWG-1.
- Commanded by an NSW commander (O5).
- It consists of a small headquarters and forms the core of a NSWTU when deployed.
- It plans, coordinates, and supports the activities of SEAL platoons and SBU detachments deployed to the US Central Command, exclusive of those organic to amphibious ready groups (ARG) and carrier battle groups (CVBG).

- In view of the maritime character of the area of responsibility and nature of the operations supported, day-to-day operational control (OPCON) is exercised by COMNAVCENT (Commander, Naval forces, Central Command). OPCON may be shifted to Special Operations Command, Central (SOCCENT) when required by operational tasking.

NAVAL SPECIAL WARFARE GROUP TWO (NSWG-2)

NSWG-2 is located in Little Creek, VA, and is one of the six major operational components of the Naval Special Warfare Command.

- Commanded by a Navy captain (O-6).
- Operational and administrative control of ST-2, ST-4, ST-8, SDVT-2, NSWU-4 and NSWU-10.
- Administrative control of NSWU-4 and NSWU-8.
- NSWG-2's geographic area of concentration is the Atlantic, Europe and Southern Command.

SEAL TEAM TWO (ST-2)

ST-2 is based at Little Creek, VA.

- Commanded by a Navy commander (O-5).
- It has eight operational platoons and a headquarters element.
- ST-2's geographic area of concentration is Europe.
- ST-2 deploys platoons to NSWU-2 in Germany, aboard amphibious ships deployed to Second and Sixth Fleets, and conducts DFTs throughout the European theater.
- ST-2 is the only SEAL team with an arctic warfare capability.

SEAL TEAM FOUR (ST-4)

ST-4 is based at Little Creek, VA.

- Commanded by a Navy commander (O-5).
- It has ten operational platoons and a headquarters element.
- ST-4's geographic area of concentration is Central and South America.
- ST-4 deploys platoons to NSWU-8 in Panama, aboard amphibious ships deployed to Second Fleet, and in support of the annual UNITAS cruise, and conducts DFTs throughout the Central and South American theater.
- ST-4 is the only SEAL team with a viable standing language capability, Spanish.

SEAL TEAM EIGHT (ST-8)

ST-8 is based at Little Creek, VA.
- Commanded by a Navy commander (O-5).
- It has eight operational platoons and a headquarters element.
- ST-8's geographic area of concentration is the Caribbean, Africa, and the Mediterranean.
- ST-8 deploys platoons with CVBGs and amphibious ships in support of Second, Fifth, and Sixth Fleet commanders, and conducts DFTs throughout the Caribbean, Africa, and the Mediterranean.

NAVAL SPECIAL WARFARE UNIT TWO (NSWU-2)

NSWU-2 is based in Stuttgart, Germany.
- Commanded by a Navy commander (O-5).
- It consists of a headquarters element and has operational SEAL platoons and SBU detachments from NSWG-2 and from SBS-2 that forward deploy to NSWU-2 on a six-month rotational duty.
- NSWU-2 maintains operational control of two forward-deployed SEAL platoons and an SBU RHIB detachment.
- NSWU-2 is under the administrative control of NSWG-2, but operationally reports to Special Operations Command, Europe.
- NSWU-2 can form the nucleus of an NSWTU.

NAVAL SPECIAL WARFARE UNIT FOUR (NSWU-4)

NSWU-4 is based at Naval Station Roosevelt Roads, Puerto Rico.
- Commanded by a Navy lieutenant commander (O-4).
- It consists of a headquarters element and an integrated SBU detachment.
- NSWU-4 is a training command that provides training support to SEAL platoons, SDV Task Units, SBU detachments, and other special operations forces conducting training in the Puerto Rico operational areas.
- NSWU-4 is under the operational and administrative control of NSWG-2.

NAVAL SPECIAL WARFARE UNIT EIGHT (NSWU-8)

NSWU-8 is based in Rodman, Panama.
- Commanded by a Navy commander (O-5).

- It consists of a headquarters element and has operational SEAL platoons from NSWU-2 that forward deploy to NSWU-8 on a six-month rotational duty.
- NSWU-8 maintains operational control of two SEAL platoons and SBU-26.
- NSWU-8 is under the administrative control of NSWG-2, and operational control of Special Operations South and Atlantic Fleet, South.
- NSWU-8 is capable of forming the nucleus of an NSWTU.

NAVAL SPECIAL WARFARE UNIT TEN (NSWU-10)

NSWU-10 is based at Naval Station Rota, Spain.
- Commanded by a NSW commander (O-5).
- It has three operational SDV Task Units and a headquarters element.
- SDVT-2 conducts operations throughout the US Atlantic, Southern, and European commands.
- Provides tactical training opportunities for NSW forces deployed aboard Sixth Fleet ships during slack periods while on routine deployments, so NSW forces can maintain perishable skills.
- NSWU-10 is responsible for all NSW exercises conducted in Spain.
- NSWU-10 is under the operational and administrative command of NSWG-2.
- NSWU-10 conducts close coordination with Special Operations Command, Europe.

SEAL DELIVERY VEHICLE TEAM TWO (SDVT-2)

SDVT-2 is based at Little Creek, VA.
- Commanded by a Navy commander (O-5).
- It has three operational SDV/DDS Task Units and a headquarters element.
- SDVT-2 conducts operations throughout the Atlantic, Southern, and European command.
- SDVT-2 places special emphasis on providing the Sixth Fleet Commander a SDV/DDS capability.

SPECIAL BOAT SQUADRON ONE (SBR-1)

SBR-1 is located in Coronado, CA, and is one of the six major operational components of Naval Special Warfare Command.

- Commanded by a Navy captain (O-6).
- SBR-1 has under its operational and administrative control SBU-12 and four Patrol Coastal Class (PC) ships, USS *Hurricane* (PC-3), USS *Monsoon* (PC-4), USS *Squall* (PC-7), and USS *Zephyr* (PC-8).
- SBR-1 deploys PCs and SBU detachments worldwide.
- SBR-1's geographic area of concentration is the Pacific and Central areas of responsibility.

SPECIAL BOAT UNIT TWELVE (SBU-12)

SBU-12 is based at Coronado, CA.

- Commanded by a Navy commander (O-5),
- Consists of a headquarters element and eight Rigid Hull Inflatable Boat (RHIB) detachments.
- SBU-12 will have 5 MK V Special Operations Craft (SOC) detachments by Fiscal Year 1998. Each detachment normally consists of two boats with crews.
- SBU-12 supports open-water special operations missions for West Coast Naval Special Warfare forces and deploys detachments aboard amphibious ships, to NSWU-1, and on DFTs throughout the Pacific and Central areas of operation.
- SBU-12 is under the operational and administrative control of SBR-1.

SPECIAL BOAT SQUADRON TWO (SBR-2)

SBR-2 is based at Little Creek, VA and is one of the six major operational components of Naval Special Warfare Command.

- Commanded by a Navy captain (O-6).
- Administrative and operational control over SBU-20, SBU-22, and 9 PC ships.
- The PCs under SBR-2 are USS *Cyclone* (PC-1), USS *Tempest* (PC-2), USS *Typhoon* (PC-5), USS *Sirocco* (PC-6), USS *Chinook* (PC-9), USS *Firebolt* (PC-10), USS *Whirlwind* (PC-11), USS *Thunderbolt* (PC-12) and USS *Shamal* (PC-13).
- SBU-26 reports administratively to SBR-2.
- SBR-2 concentrates on the Atlantic, Southern, and European areas of responsibility.

SPECIAL BOAT UNIT TWENTY (SBU-20)

SBU-20 is based at Little Creek, VA.

- Commanded by a Navy commander (O-5).
- Consists of a headquarters element and 13 RHIB detachments and two MK V Special Operations Craft (SOC) detachments.
- By the end of FY98, SBU-20 will have 5 MK V SOC detachments. Each detachment consists of two boats.
- SBU-20 supports open-water special operations missions for East Coast Naval Special Warfare forces and deploys detachments aboard amphibious ships and to NSWU-2 and NSWU-10.
- SBU-20 focuses on providing operational support to the European and Atlantic theaters of operations.
- SBU-20 is under the operational and administrative control of SBR-2.

SPECIAL BOAT UNIT TWENTY-TWO (SBU-22)

SBU-22 is based in New Orleans, LA.

- Commanded by a Navy commander (O-5).
- Consists of a headquarters element and 2 Patrol Boat Riverine (PBR) detachments, 2 Mini Armored Troop Carrier (MATC) detachments and 2 Patrol Boat Light (PBL) detachments. Each detachment normally consists of two boats with crews.
- SBU-22 is mainly a reserve organization with over 70 percent of the command being naval reservists.
- SBU-22 focuses on providing riverine support in Southern and European theaters of operations.
- SBU-22 is under the operational and administrative control of SBR-2.

SPECIAL BOAT UNIT TWENTY-SIX (SBU-26)

SBU-26 is based in Rodman, Panama.

- Commanded by a Navy lieutenant commander (O-4),
- Consists of a headquarters element and 10 PBL detachments. Each detachment normally consists of two boats with crews.
- SBU-26 is dedicated to conducting operations in the riverine environment in support of the Southern commands.
- SBU-26 is under the operational control of NSWU-8 and under administrative control of SBR-2.

US NAVAL PSYCHOLOGICAL OPERATIONS FORCES

The US Navy possesses the capability to produce audiovisual products in the Fleet Audiovisual Command, Pacific.

- The Fleet Tactical Readiness Group (FTRG) provides equipment and technical support to conduct civil radio broadcasts and broadcast jamming in the amplitude modulation (AM) frequency band.
- This unit is not trained to produce PSYOP products and must be augmented with PSYOP personnel or linguists when necessary.
- The unit is capable of being fully operational within 48 hours of receipt of tasking.
- The unit's equipment consists of a 10.6kw AM band broadcast radio transmitter; a broadcast studio van; antenna tuner; two antennas (a pneumatically raised 100ft top-loaded antenna mast and a 500ft wire helium balloon antenna); and a 30kw generator that provides power to the system.

US MARINE CORPS (USMC) PSYCHOLOGICAL OPERATIONS FORCES

The USMC has the capability to execute observable actions to convey selected impressions to support PSYOP objectives:

- Aerial and artillery leaflet dissemination.
- Combat camera documentation.
- Motion picture projection equipment.

APPENDIX 2

ORGANIZATION OF US NAVAL SPECIAL OPERATIONS FORCES 2003–04

ORGANIZATION OF US NAVAL SPECIAL OPERATIONS FORCES 2003 (BRIEF)

CNSWG-1 Commander Naval Special Warfare Group One
Group One Det Training

- Group One Logistics and Support Unit
- Group One Logistics and Support Unit CSST
- Naval Special Warfare Unit One (NSWU-1)
- Naval Special Warfare Unit Three (NSWU-3)
- SEAL Team One (ST-1)
- SEAL Team Three (ST-3)
- SEAL Team Five (ST-5)
- SEAL Team Seven (ST-7)

CNSWG-2 Commander Naval Special Warfare Group Two
Group Two Det Training

- Group Two Logistics and Support Unit
- Group Two Logistics and Support Unit CSST
- Naval Special Warfare Unit Two (NSWU-2)
- Naval Special Warfare Unit Four (NSWU-4)
- Naval Special Warfare Unit Ten (NSWU-10)
- SEAL Team Two (ST-2)

- SEAL Team Four (ST-4)
- SEAL Team Eight (ST-8)
- SEAL Team Ten (ST-10)

CNSWG-3 Commander Naval Special Warfare Group Three
- Special Boat Team Twelve (SBT-12)
- SEAL Delivery Vehicle Team One (SDVT-1)
- SEAL Delivery Vehicle Team One Advanced SEAL Delivery System (ASDS)

CNSWG-4 Commander Naval Special Warfare Group Four
- Special Boat Team Twenty (SBT-20)
- Special Boat Team Twenty Det Caribbean
- Special Boat Team Twenty-Two (SBT-22)
- Special Boat Team Twenty-Two Det Sacramento
- SEAL Delivery Vehicle Team Two (SDVT-2)

NSWC Naval Special Warfare Center
- Naval Special Warfare Center SDV Training Det Panama City
- Naval Special Warfare Center Training Det Key West
- Naval Special Warfare Center Advanced Training Det Little Creek
- Naval Special Warfare Center Det Hawaii
- Naval Special Warfare Center Det Yuma
- Naval Special Warfare Center Det Hurlburt
- Naval Special Warfare Center Det Kodiak
- Naval Small Craft Instruction and Technical Training School (NAVSCIATTS)

APPENDIX 3

ORGANIZATION OF US NAVAL SPECIAL OPERATIONS FORCES 2007

NAVAL SPECIAL WARFARE CENTER

The Naval Special Warfare Center is based at Naval Amphibious Base (NAB) Coronado, CA.

- Commanded by a captain (O-6).
- Schoolhouse for Naval Special Warfare training.
- 26-week BUD/S course.
- Nine-week Special Warfare Combatant Crewman (SWCC) course.
- Advanced maritime special operations training.
- Maintains a detachment at the NAB, Little Creek, VA for training of East Coast personnel.

NAVAL SPECIAL WARFARE DEVELOPMENT GROUP

The Naval Special Warfare Development Group is located in Dam Neck Naval Base, VA.

- Commanded by a Navy captain (O-6).
- Conducts tests, evaluations, and development of current and emerging technology.
- Develops maritime ground and airborne tactics.

NAVAL SPECIAL WARFARE GROUPS

Two NSW Groups, One and Two, at NABs Coronado, CA and Little Creek, VA:
- Commanded by an Echelon II captain (O-6).
- Equip, support, and provide command and control elements.
- Provide SEAL and SDV (Seal Delivery Vehicle) platoons and Task Units.

NSW Groups One and Two are organized into:
- Four SEAL teams, each composed of six 14–16-man platoons.
- One SDV team.
- Small command and control elements outside the continental US, to support NSW forces during operations.

NAVAL SPECIAL WARFARE COMMAND COMBAT SERVICE SUPPORT TEAMS (CSST)

One CSST is assigned to each NSW group.
CSST includes three primary mission elements:

- O(perational)PLAN/CON(tingency)PLAN and crisis-action logistic planning and coordination.
- In-theater contracting, small purchase and lease actions.
- Forward operating base support.

Additional tasks include:
- Force embarkation.
- Load-planning.
- Multi-modal transport coordination.
- Combat cargo handling.
- In-theater logistic coordination.
- Military Liaison Officer/Defense Attaché Officer liaison.
- Exercise-related construction.
- Infrastructure support.
- Contingency engineering.
- Expeditionary camp siting and development.
- Camp maintenance.
- NBC decontamination.
- Defensive combat planning and execution.

NAVAL SPECIAL WARFARE TASK UNITS

Naval Special Warfare Task Units (NSWTU) are tailored to particular missions and can operate independently, jointly, or in combined operations. They are made up by combining 2 operational platoons, creating 3 task units per team. Each TU trains together throughout the entire work-up.

SPECIAL BOAT SQUADRONS (SBRs)

Organized, trained, and equipped to operate a variety of special operations surface craft in maritime and riverine environments.

SEAL Delivery Vehicle Team
Submersible systems operations from specially configured submarines equipped with Dry Deck Shelters (DDS).
- Commanded by a SDV team commanding officer or executive officer.

SEAL Platoon
- Commanded by a Navy Lieutenant (O-3).
- A platoon consists of 14–16 SEALs and can be divided into two squads or four elements.
- All SEALs are dive, parachute, and demolitions qualified.

Mobile Communications Detachment (MCD)
- Communications-electronics departments of the Naval Special Warfare Groups One and Two. Provide operational communications support NSW forces.
- Provide new equipment and develop tactics for communications operations and support.
- Prepare, implement, and review communications plans.

NAVAL SPECIAL WARFARE GROUP ONE (NSWG-1)

NSWG-1 is located in Coronado, CA, and is one of the six major operational components of the Naval Special Warfare Command.
- Commanded by a captain (O-6).
- Operational and administrative control, of ST-1, ST-3, ST-5, and ST-7, and SDVT-1 (Hawaii).
- Administrative control of NSWU-1 and NSWU-3.
- NSWG-1 geographically concentrates on the Pacific and Central Commands.

SEAL TEAM ONE (ST-1)

ST-1 is based in Coronado, CA.

- Commanded by a Navy commander (O-5).
- It has six operational SEAL platoons and a headquarters element. Two Task Units CENTCOM, and one TU PACOM.

SEAL TEAM THREE (ST-3)

ST-3 is based in Coronado, CA.

- Commanded by a Navy commander (O-5).
- It has six operational platoons and a headquarters element.

SEAL TEAM FIVE (ST-5)

ST-5 is based in Coronado, CA.

- Commanded by a Navy commander (O-5).
- It has six operational platoons and a headquarters element.

SEAL TEAM SEVEN (ST-7)

ST-7 is based in Coronado, CA.

- Commanded by a Navy commander (O-5).
- It has six operational platoons and a headquarters element.

SEAL DELIVERY VEHICLE TEAM ONE (SDVT-1)

SDVT-1 is based in Pearl Harbor, HI.

- Commanded by a Navy commander (O-5).
- It has three operational SDV, Dry Deck Shelter (DDS) task units and a headquarters element.
- Each SDV/DDS task unit is designed to operate independently from a host submarine in the conduct of Naval Special Warfare missions.
- SDV/DDS task units normally deploy only aboard host submarines, but may be deployed from shore or surface ships.
- SDVT-1 conducts operations throughout the Pacific and Central commands geographic areas or responsibility.

NAVAL SPECIAL WARFARE UNIT ONE (NSWU-1)

NSWU-1 is based in Guam.

- Commanded by a Navy commander (O-5).
- Consists of a headquarters element and has operational control of SEAL platoons and Special Boat Unit (SBU) detachments from NSWG-1 forward deploy to NSWU-1 on a six-month rotational duty.

- NSWU-1 maintains operational control of two forward-deployed SEAL platoons (one TU) and two SBU Rigid Hull Inflatable Boat (RHIB) detachments.
- NSWU-1 is under the administrative command of NSWG-1, but operationally reports to Special Operations Command, Pacific and US Navy Seventh Fleet for operational tasking.
- Provides operational support to forward-deployed platoons and conducts theater planning for contingencies and exercises for Naval Special Warfare forces in the Pacific.
- NSWU-1 is capable of forming the nucleus of an NSWTU.

NAVAL SPECIAL WARFARE — GROUP ONE DETACHMENT KODIAK

Detachment Kodiak is located in Kodiak, Alaska.
- Training cadre that specializes in training SEAL platoons and SBU teams in maritime cold-weather operations.

NAVAL SPECIAL WARFARE UNIT THREE (NSWU-3)

NSWU-3 is based in Bahrain.
- Commanded by a NSW commander (O5).
- It consists of a small headquarters and forms the core of a NSWTU when deployed.
- It plans, coordinates, and supports the activities of SEAL TU and Special Boat Team (SBT) detachments deployed to the US Central Command, exclusive of those organic to amphibious ready groups (ARG) and carrier battle groups (CVBG).
- In view of the maritime character of the area of responsibility and nature of the operations supported, day-to-day operational control (OPCON) is exercised by COMNAVCENT (Commander, Naval forces, Central Command). OPCON may be shifted to Special Operations Command, Central (SOCCENT) when required by operational tasking.

NAVAL SPECIAL WARFARE GROUP TWO (NSWG-2)

NSWG-2 is located in Little Creek, VA, and is the one of the six major operational components of the Naval Special Warfare Command.
- NSWG-2 is commanded by a Navy captain (O-6).
- Operational and administrative control of ST-2, ST4, ST-8, ST-10, and SDVT-2.
- NSWG-2 geographically concentrates on the Atlantic, Europe, Southern, and Central Command.

SEAL TEAM TWO (ST-2)

ST-2 is based at Little Creek, VA.
- Commanded by a Navy commander (O-5).
- It has six operational platoons and a headquarters element.

SEAL TEAM FOUR (ST-4)

ST-4 is based at Little Creek, VA.
- Commanded by a Navy commander (O-5).
- It has ten operational platoons and a headquarters element.

SEAL TEAM EIGHT (ST-8)

ST-8 is based at Little Creek, VA.
- Commanded by a Navy commander (O-5).
- It has six operational platoons and a headquarters element (3 Tus).

SEAL TEAM TEN (ST-10)

ST-10 is based in Coronado, CA.
- Commanded by a Navy commander (O-5).
- It has six operational platoons and a headquarters element.

NAVAL SPECIAL WARFARE UNIT TWO (NSWU-2)

NSWU-2 is based in Stuttgart, Germany.
- Commanded by a Navy commander (O-5).
- It consists of a headquarters element and has operational platoons and SBR detachments from NSWG-2 that forward deploy to NSWU-2 on a six-month rotational duty.
- NSWU-2 maintains operational control of two forward-deployed SEAL platoons (one TU) and a SBR RHIB detachment.
- NSWU-2 is under the administrative control of NSWG-2, but operationally reports to Special Operations Command, Europe.
- NSWU-2 can form the nucleus of an NSWTU.

SEAL DELIVERY VEHICLE TEAM TWO (SDVT-2)

SDVT-2 is based at Little Creek, VA.
- Commanded by a Navy commander (O-5).
- It has three operational SDV/DDS task units and a headquarters element.
- SDVT-2 conducts operations throughout the Atlantic and Southern, and European command.

- SDVT-2 places special emphasis on providing the Sixth Fleet Commander with a SDV/DDS capability.

SPECIAL BOAT SQUADRON ONE (SBR-1)

SBR-1 is located in Coronado, CA, and is one of the six major operational components of Naval Special Warfare Command.
- It is commanded by a Navy captain (O-6).
- SBR-1 has under its operational and administrative control SBU-12.
- SBR-1 deploys PCs and SBU detachments worldwide.
- SBR-1 geographically concentrates on the Pacific and Central areas of responsibility.

SPECIAL BOAT UNIT TWELVE (SBU-12)

SBU-12 is based in Coronado, CA.
- Commanded by a Navy commander (O-5).
- Consists of a headquarters element and eight RHIB detachments.
- SBU-12 will have 5 MK V Special Operations Craft (SOC) detachments by Fiscal Year 1998. Each detachment normally consists of two boats with crews.
- SBU-12 supports open-water special operations missions for West Coast Naval Special Warfare forces and deploys detachments aboard amphibious ships, to NSWU-1, and on DFTs throughout the Pacific and Central areas of operation.
- SBU-12 is under the operational and administrative control of SBR-1.

SPECIAL BOAT SQUADRON TWO (SBR-2)

SBR-2 is based at Little Creek, VA and is one of the six major operational components of Naval Special Warfare Command.
- Commanded by a Navy captain (O-6).
- Administrative and operational control over SBU-20, SBU-22, and 9 Patrol Coastal Class (PC) ships.
- The PCs under SBR-2 are USS *Cyclone* (PC-1), USS *Tempest* (PC-2), USS *Typhoon* (PC-5), USS *Sirocco* (PC-6), USS *Chinook* (PC-9), USS *Firebolt* (PC-10), USS *Whirlwind* (PC-11), USS *Thunderbolt* (PC-12) and USS *Shamal* (PC-13).
- SBU-26 reports administratively to SBR-2.
- SBR-2 geographically concentrates on the Atlantic, Southern and Europe areas of responsibility.

SPECIAL BOAT UNIT TWENTY (SBU-20)

SBU-20 is based at Little Creek, VA.
- Commanded by a Navy commander (O-5).
- Consists of a headquarters element, 13 RHIB detachments and two MK V (SOC) detachments.
- By the end of Fiscal Year 1998, SBU-20 will have 5 MK V SOC detachments. Each detachment consists of two boats.
- SBU-20 supports open-water special operations missions for East Coast Naval Special Warfare forces and deploys detachments aboard amphibious ships and to NSWU-2 and NSWU-10.
- SBU-20 focuses on providing operational support to the European and Atlantic theaters of operations.
- SBU-20 is under the operational and administrative control of SBR-2.

SPECIAL BOAT UNIT TWENTY-TWO (SBU-22)

SBU-22 is based in New Orleans, LA.
- Commanded by a Navy commander (O-5).
- Consists of a headquarters element and 2 Patrol Boat Riverine (PBR) detachments, 2 Mini Armored Troop Carrier (MATC) detachments and 2 Patrol Boat Light (PBL) detachment. Each detachment normally consists of two boats with crews.
- SBU-22 is mainly a reserve organization with over 70 percent of the command being naval reservists.
- SBU-22 focuses on providing riverine support in Southern and European theaters of operations.
- SBU-22 is under the operational and administrative control of SBR-2.

APPENDIX 4

US NAVY SEAL EQUIPMENT

NAVAL SPECIAL WARFARE WEAPONS SYSTEMS

MK V SPECIAL OPERATIONS CRAFT (SOC)

Primary and secondary missions include:

- Medium range insertion and extraction for special operations forces, and limited duration Coastal Patrol and Interdiction (CP&I).
- Operate in a two-craft detachment with a Mobile Support Team (MST).
- MST provides technical assistance and maintenance support during mission turnaround.
- The Mk V SOC is a single sortie system with a 24-hour turn-around time.
- The typical Mk V SOC mission duration is 12 hours.
- The Mk V SOC is fully interoperable with the PC (Patrol Coastal) ships and NSW RHIBs (Rigid Hull Inflatable Boats).
- A Mk V SOC detachment, consisting of two craft and support equipment.
- Deployable on two United States Air Force (USAF) C-5 aircraft within 48 hours of notification.

DESIGN CHARACTERISTICS

Length: 81ft 2in.
Beam: 17ft 5¾in.
Draft: 5ft
Displacement: 57 tons (full load)

Fuel capacity: 2,600 gallons
Propulsion: 2 MTU 12V396 diesels (2,285hp each)
2 KaMeWa water jets
Aluminum hull with five watertight compartments
Radar, full suite communications (HF, UHF, HF, SATCOM), GPS, IFF
Complement: 1 officer, 5 enlisted
Detachment: 16 SOF combat loaded operators with 4 CRRCs

PERFORMANCE CRITERIA

Maximum speed: 45–48 knots for 250 nm in Sea State 2
Cruising speed: 25–40 knots in Sea State 3
Seaworthiness: Survive through Sea State five
Maximum range: 500nm (2 engines at 45 knots)

ARMAMENT

Stinger Station
5 pintles supporting any combination of: .50cal. machine guns; M60 machine guns
MK19 grenade launchers
Small arms
Pre-planned product improvement: Mounting stations for GAU-17 Minigun, MK95 twin .50 cal. machine gun, MK38 chain gun

ROLLING STOCK PER TWO-BOAT DETACHMENT

2 Mk V SOC transporters
2 M9161A prime movers
2 M1083 5-ton trucks
4 M1097 Humvees with S250 shelters
1 5-ton forklift

RIVER PATROL BOAT

- Designed for high-speed riverine patrol operations.
- Insertion/extraction of SEAL teams.
- Since 1966 500 units were built during the Vietnam War.
- Transported in C-5 aircraft.
- Heavily armed.
- Vital crew areas protected with ceramic armor.
- The unit can operate in shallow, debris-filled water.

- The craft is highly maneuverable and can turn 180 degrees and reverse course within the distance of its own length while operating at full power.
- Engine noise silencing techniques incorporated into the design.

DESIGN CHARACTERISTICS

Length: 32ft
Beam (including guard rails): 11ft 7in.
Weight: 8¾ tons
Draft: 2ft
Propulsion: 2 GM 6V53N diesel engines (215hp each)
2 Jacuzzi 14YJ water jet pumps
Radar, VHF/UHF radios
Complement: 4 crew and 6 passengers
Fiberglass-reinforced hull

PERFORMANCE CHARACTERISTICS

Speed: 24 knots
Seaworthiness: Sea State 3
Max Range: 300nm at full speed

ARMAMENT

Standard:
Twin mount .50-cal. machine gun
.50-cal. machine gun, stand mounted
MK19 40mm grenade launcher
Options:
40mm/.50-cal. machine gun, stand mounted
60mm mortar
M60 machine guns

MINI-ARMORED TROOP CARRIER

- Designed for high-speed patrol.
- Interdiction.
- Combat assault missions in rivers, harbors, and protected coastal areas.
- Transporting combat-equipped troops, carrying cargo.
- Seven organic weapon stations.

- Beaching operations.
- Hydraulic bow ramp is designed to aid the insertion and extraction of troops and equipment.

DESIGN CHARACTERISTICS

Length: 36ft
Beam (including guard rails): 12ft 9in.
Draft: 2ft
Displacement: 12½ tons
Propulsion: 2 GM 8V53N diesel engines (283 hp each)
2 Jacuzzi 20YJ water jet pumps
Aluminum hull, flat bottom
Radar, VHF/UHF radios
Complement: 4 crew and 8 passengers

PERFORMANCE CRITERIA

Maximum speed: 25+ knots
Seaworthiness: Sea State 3
Maximum range: 350nm

ARMAMENT

7 pintle-mounted weapons to include .50 cal., M60, MK19
60mm mortar

LIGHT PATROL BOAT

- Lightly armed Boston Whaler-type craft with no armor.
- Useful in interdicting a lightly armed adversary.
- Not to be used to engage a heavily-armed or well-organized enemy.
- Policing actions.
- Harbor control.
- Diving and surveillance operations.
- Riverine warfare.
- Drug interdiction.
- Displaces 6,500lb fully loaded.
- Transportable via its own trailer, helicopter sling, or C-130 aircraft.

DESIGN CHARACTERISTICS

Length: 25ft
Max beam: 8ft 7in.
Draft: 18in.
Propulsion: Twin 155-HP outboards
Fiberglass hull
VHF, UHF, and SATCOM radios
Complement: 3 crew and 8 passengers

PERFORMANCE CRITERIA

Speed: 30+ knots
Seaworthiness: Sea State 2
Range: 150 nm

ARMAMENT

Three weapons stations, one forward and two aft
Combination of .50 cal. or M60

RIGID HULL INFLATABLE BOAT

- Primary mission of insertion/extraction of SEAL tactical elements from enemy occupied beaches.
- Constructed of glass reinforced plastic with an inflatable tube gunwale made of a new hypalon neoprene/nylon reinforced fabric.
- Two types of RHIBs in the inventory, a 24ft RHIB and a 30ft RHIB.
- 24-ft RHIB carries a crew of three and a SEAL element.
- 30-ft RHIB, NSW RHIB, 10m RHIB carries a crew of three.
- Allows for a SEAL squad delivery capability.

DESIGN CHARACTERISTICS

24ft RHIB; 10m RHIB
Length: 24ft; 30ft
Beam: 9ft; 11ft
Draft: 2ft; 3ft
Weight: 9,300lb; 14,700lb
Propulsion: Single Volvo Penta Two Iveco diesels with waterjets
Complement: 3 crew/4 passengers; 3 crew/8 passengers
Radar, HF, UHF, VHF radios; radar, HF, UHF, VHF, SATCOM radios

PERFORMANCE CRITERIA

Speed: 25+ knots; 35+ knots
Seaworthiness: Sea State 5
Maximum range: 170nm; 200nm

ARMAMENT

Forward, after forward and after mounts
Mounts capable of M60; capable of M60, M2, or MK19

COMBAT RUBBER RAIDING CRAFT

- Clandestine surface insertion and extraction of lightly armed SOF forces.
- Land and recover SOF forces.
- Capable of surf passages.
- Launched by air (airdrop/helo-cast), or by landing craft.
- Deck launched or locked out from submarines.

DESIGN CHARACTERISTICS

Length: 15ft 5in.
Beam: 6ft 3in.
Draft: 2ft
Weight: 265 lb without motor or fuel
Speed: 18 knots, no load
Maximum range: Dependent on fuel carried
Complement: 8

SEAL DELIVERY VEHICLE MK VIII

- Is a "wet" submersible, designed to carry combat swimmers and their cargo in fully flooded compartments.
- Submerged, operators and passengers are sustained by the individually worn underwater breathing apparatus (UBA).
- Underwater mapping and terrain exploration.
- Location and recovery of lost or downed objects.
- Reconnaissance missions.
- Limited direct action missions.
- Propelled by an all-electric propulsion subsystem powered by rechargeable silver-zinc batteries.

- Buoyancy and pitch attitude are controlled by a ballast and trim system; control in both the horizontal and vertical planes is provided through a manual control stick to the rudder, elevator, and bow planes.
- A computerized Doppler navigation sonar displays speed, distance, heading, altitude, and other piloting functions.
- Instruments and other electronics units are housed in dry, watertight canisters.
- The special modular construction provides easy removal for maintenance. Major subsystems are Hull, Propulsion, Ballast/Trim, Control, Auxiliary Life Support, Navigation, Communications and Docking Sonar.

DRY DECK SHELTER

- Launch and recovery of an SDV or combat rubber raiding craft (CRRC) with personnel from a submerged submarine.
- It consists of three modules constructed as one integral unit. The first module is a hangar in which an SDV or CRRC is stowed. The second module is a transfer trunk to allow passage between the modules and the submarine. The third module is a hyperbaric (higher than normal atmospheric pressure) recompression chamber.
- Provides a dry working environment for mission preparations.
- The DDS hangar module will be flooded, pressurized to the surrounding sea pressure, and a large door is opened to allow for launch and recovery of the vehicle.
- Can be transported by USAF C-5/C-17 aircraft, rail, highway, or sealift.
- 40ft long; weighs 65,000lb.

Current submarines capable of single DDS employment:
USS *L. Mendel Rivers*
USS *Bates*
Current submarines capable of dual DDS employment:
USS *Kamehameh*
USS *Polk*

DESIGN CHARACTERISTICS
Length: 39ft
Width: 10ft
Weight: 65,000lb.
Volume: 3,705 cubic feet

ADVANCED SEAL DELIVERY SYSTEM

- A "dry" mini-submersible that transports a SEAL squad from a host platform, either surface ship or submarine, to an objective area.
- Takes SEALs over longer distance with more equipment and without getting wet.
- Has a lock-out chamber that is controlled by operators for lock-out from an anchored position.
- Exit from the ASDS is accomplished through a chamber in the floor of the craft, which has also been manufactured so that it can dock with a parent submarine, much like a deep submergence rescue vehicle.
- Anchors above the bottom between 2 and 190ft.
- Transportable by land, sea, or C-5/17 aircraft.

DESIGN CHARACTERISTICS

Length: 65ft
Beam: 6ft 9in.
Height: 8ft 3in.
Displacement: 55 tons
Propulsion: 67hp electric motor (Ag-Zn battery)

Current vessels capable of single ASDS employment (1999):
USS *Charlotte*
USS *Greenville*
New Virginia-class submarines

PERSONAL WEAPONS SYSTEMS

HAND GUNS

9mm SIG Sauer P226 hand gun
Revolver 357 Magnum S&W

RIFLES

M16s plus derivatives
Carbine automatic M4A1, 5.56mm rifle
Chicom Type 56 (AK47)
7.62 M14 semi or automatic rifle

GRENADE LAUNCHERS

40mm, M203
MK19 40mm Mod 3

MORTAR

60mm M224

SHOTGUNS

12 GA Mossberg shotgun, pump
Remington 870 Wingmaster 12-gauge shotgun

MACHINE GUNS

MK43, 7.62mm
M2HB, .50 cal.
MK48 SAW, 5.56mm

SUBMACHINE GUN

MP5 series, 9mm

ROCKETS

M136 anti-tank rocket, AT4
M72 LAW rocket
M3 Carl Gustaf Recoilless rifle, anti-tank/anti-material rocket assist, 84mm
Stinger anti-aircraft missile launcher (FIM92A)

SNIPER WEAPONS

M14 sniper kit, sniper rifle
SR25 semi-automatic, sniper rifle
300 Win Mag bolt gun, sniper rifle
M88 .50 PIP, bolt gun, magazine fed, sniper rifle
Carbine M4 5.56mm

SCUBA AND UNDERWATER DIVE SYSTEMS

Navy commandos utilize three primary types of underwater breathing apparatuses:

OPEN-CIRCUIT COMPRESSED AIR SYSTEMS

Open-circuit systems allow air to be breathed from a supply tank and then exhaled directly into the surrounding water. The traditional supply tank(s) can be worn on the diver's back (SCUBA). SDVs feature tanks as well, so that in the event the diver is using an SDV he may utilize those tanks instead. As with all dives, deep dives may require diver decompression in conformation with the US Navy Standard Air Decompression Table.

CLOSED-CIRCUIT (100% PURE OXYGEN) LAR V DRÄGER UNDERWATER BREATHING APPARATUS (UBA)

The LAR V Dräger is a German manufactured self-contained closed-circuit double-hosed underwater breathing apparatus that is designed to work exclusively on oxygen, which it recycles after use. Closed-circuit systems such as the Dräger are intended for underwater operations in shallow water where traditional bubble-generating open-circuit systems could prove deadly. The LAR V is worn on the diver's chest. Numerous factors need to be considered by the user, including depth, rate of work, and temperature. Dive teams that used the Dräger in combat in 1989 stated that 20ft was considered the safety limit but that they had dived as deep as 50ft.

CLOSED-CIRCUIT(MIXED GAS) MK 15 UBA

"The MK15 is a self-contained, closed-circuit mixed-gas, underwater breathing apparatus. The breathing gas is completely retained within the apparatus except during ascent when excess pressure is vented. In the MK15, oxygen is mixed with a diluent gas (normally air) to maintain a present partial pressure of oxygen (PPO$_2$) level. The constantly preset PPO$_2$ level provides greater depth and duration capability than a 100% oxygen system could. The duration of the MK15 is limited by the carbon dioxide scrubber canister. Long duration or deep dives may require diver decompression in accordance with the US Navy MK15 Decompression Tables."

APPENDIX 5

FROGMEN, UDTS AND SEALS KILLED IN ACTION

SECOND WORLD WAR

Henry R. Alexander
Kermit Allen
A. E. Anderson
B. B. Audibert
Edwin A. Beason
Robert A. Black Jr.
Buress L. Blackwood
Harry T. Blanot
David Blettel
Ralph A. Blowers
Leonard J. Bock
John E. Bussell
Guadulupe Castillio
Robert Christensen
John W. Cooke
Paul H. Davis
Carmine DeGregorio
Peter M. Demmer
Jerry Donnell
Patrick R. Dolan
William R. Doran
Harold Duncan
Edmond Eckert

Henry S. Fabich
Andrew J. Fleming
Joseph L. Flemming
R. E. French
John A. Fuller
Wilfred D. Gamache
Paul E. Gordon
George L. Gouinlock
Preston H. Goulder
Edward J. Greenfield
Richard D. Harang
C. P. Herring
Arthur B. Hickey
Earl E. Hilke
Orvid J. Holtman
Robert L. Hopkins
Kenneth E. Howe
Edgar W. Irish
John A. Jacobson
Edward A. Jarosz
Louis E. Kalman
Brennan W. Kasman
Kenneth B. Lauderdale

William R. Lewis
John G. Lokey
Francis Joseph Lynch
John C. MacMahon
Eugene E. Maki
Marvin A. Malfeo
Charles Francis Masden
John D. McDermott
Donald C. McGeary
Thomas R. McKnight
John Mecale
Conrad C. Millis
Ozie C. Mingledorf Jr.
A. M. Morris
Louis G. Netz
Thomas D. Nixon
Jesse D. Olive
Frank J. Perkins
Raymond R. Pienack
Carmen F. Pirro

Carroll B. Prall
James E. Rodman
James L. Rodriquez
Howard L. Roeder
Joseph W. Rossart
Adrian Runnels
F. P. Scoggins
William L. Sugden
Maurice F. Sullivan
Frank W. Sumpter
Chester Szych
Edward Tilton
Alvin E. Vetter
Thomas J. Watkins
M. P. Weatherford
L. I. Weckman
Albert G. Weidner
Herman D. Willbanks
Lee C. Yates

KOREA

Edward Ivan Frey

Paul Vernon Satterfield

VIETNAM

Joseph A. Albrecht
Frank G. Antone
Curtis M. Ashton
Harold E. Birky
Frank W. Bomar
Donald E. Boston
Gordon C. Brewton
Gordon C. Brown
Michael R. Collins
Robert E. Condon
David E. Devine
John J. Donnelly III
Melvin S. Dry
John S. Durlin

Robert J. Fay
Eugene T. Fraley
Leslie H. Funk
James R. Gore
Roy B. Keith
Billy W. Machen
Lin A. Mahner
Daniel M. Mann
Harry A. Mattingly
Lowell W. Meyer
Lester J. Moe
Ronald K. Neal
David L. Nicholas
Ronald E. Pace

Luco W. Palma
Donnie L. Patrick
Walter G. Pope
Roberto Ramos
Clarence T. Risher III
James L. Ritter
James K. Sanders
Richard J. Solano
James F. Thames
Toby A. Thomas

Eugene S. Tinnin
Frederick E. Trani
Kenneth E. Van Hoy
Robert K. Wagner
Arthur G. Williams
Lawrence C. Williams
David A. Wilson
Richard O. Wolfe
Robert L. Worthington
Donald H. Zillgitt

GRENADA

Kenneth J. Butcher
Kevin E. Lundburg

Stephen L. Morris
Robert R. Schamberger

PANAMA

John P. Connors
Donald L. McFaul

Isaac G. Rodriquez III
Chris Tilghman

KOSOVO

Chad Burkhart

AFGHANISTAN

Mathew G. Axelson
Matt Bourgeois
Danny P. Dietz
Jacques J. Fontan
Daniel R. Healy
Eric S. Kristensen
Jeffrey A. Lucas
Michael M. McGreevy
Michael P. Murphy

Brian J. Oulette
Eric S. Patton (also listed as Shane E. Patton)
Thomas Retzer
Neil Christopher Roberts
James E. Suh
David M. Taper
Jeffrey S. Taylor

IRAQ

Mark Carter
Nathan H. Hardy
Michael E. Koch
Marc Lee

Jason Lewis
Michael Monsoor
Joseph C. Schwedler

ENDNOTES

1. Carl von Clausewitz, *On War,* translated by Michael Howard and Peter Paret, Princeton University Press, Princeton, 1984, p.69.

2. https://www.navsoc.navy.mil/history.htm.

3. Ibid.

4. Ibid.

5. http://www.af.mil/news/airman/0401/hostage.html.

6. http://www.socom.mil/Docs/USSOCOM_Posture_Statement_2007.pdf.

7. Richard R. Burgess, "SEAL force restructured to stabilize deployments," *Sea Power,* May 2002, http://findarticles.com/p/articles/mi_qa3738/is_200205/ai_n9043908.

8. http://www.navyleague.org/sea_power/dec_02_41.php.

9. https://www.navsoc.navy.mil/

10. Gary J. Richard, LCDR, USN, "Naval Special Warfare's Contribution to Global Joint Operations in Support of Sea Power 21, the United States Navy's Vision for the Twenty-First Century," US Army Command and General Staff College, 2004, p.10, http://stinet.dtic.mil/cgi-bin/GetTRDoc?AD= ADA429072&Location=U2&doc=GetTRDoc.pdf.

11. https://www.navsoc.navy.mil/

12. Graphic from Naval Special Warfare's Contribution to Global Joint Operations, http://www.navy.mil/navydata/navy_legacy_hr.asp?id=266.

13. Interview with member of DevGru, 2007, conducted by Mir Bahmanyar/Chris Osman.

14. https://www.navsoc.navy.mil/

15. Ibid.

16. Interview with Marcus Luttrell, November 2007, Bahmanyar/Osman.

17. Roy Boehm, *The First Seal*, Pocket Star, 1998, p.124.

18. Interview with Marcus Luttrell, November 2007, Bahmanyar/Osman.

19. Ibid.

20. Ibid.

21. https://www.navsoc.navy.mil/

22. http://www.sealchallenge.navy.mil/seal/contractinstructions.aspx.

23. Interview with Richard Whiteside, Bahmanyar/Osman.

24. All quotes in this section are from interviewing Kyle, Bahmanyar/Osman, unless otherwise stated.

25. The Rigid Hull Inflatable Boat (RHIB) is used by SEALs for insertion and extraction onto enemy-occupied beaches. Extremely fast, this inflatable boat with a solid hull comes in two sizes – 24- and 30-foot versions – both stressing high buoyancy that can handle even the most extreme weather. The 30-foot model utilizes the water jet propulsion system, allowing for the beaching of the craft and close-to the-beach work if the SEAL platoon requires fire support. http://www.navy.com/about/navylife/onduty/seals/equipment/

26. http://www.americanrhetoric.com/speeches/ghwbushpanamainvasion.htm.

27. Lt Gen Edward Flanagan, *The Battle for Panama*, Brassey's Inc, 1993, p.82.

28. Ibid.

29. Ibid. The *Presidente Porras* was actually docked at Pier 17.

30. Ibid.

31. All quotes in this section are from the Bahmanyar/Osman interviews with Chris Dye, 2007/8, unless otherwise noted.

32. Home of the Air Commandos since 1961, Hurlburt Field today accommodates the 1st Special Operations Wing (1 SOW), Headquarters Air Force Special Operations Command (AFSOC), an Air Force major command, and a number of associate units. The field is named for First Lieutenant Donald Wilson Hurlburt who was killed in an aircraft crash at Eglin Auxiliary Field #9 in 1943. http://www2.hurlburt.af.mil/

33. Flanagan, *The Battle for Panama*, p.83.

34. Ibid.

35. Ibid.

36. Ibid.

37. All quotes in this section are from the Bahmanyar/Osman interviews with Tony Duchi, 2007/8, unless otherwise noted.

38. Flanagan, *The Battle for Panama*, p.85.

39. http://www.deamuseum.org/dea_history_book/1985_1990.htm.

40. James L. Pate, "Death to the Tyrant Cocaine" in *Soldier of Fortune*, July 1991.

41. http://www.gwu.edu/~nsarchiv/NSAEBB/NSAEBB69/col02.pdf.

42. http://www.gwu.edu/~nsarchiv/NSAEBB/NSAEBB69/col13.pdf.

43. Interview with Tony Duchi, 2007, Bahmanyar/Osman.

44. Ibid.

45. See Mir Bahmanyar's *Shadow Warriors: A History of the US Army Rangers*, Osprey Publishing, Oxford, 2005, and Mark Bowden, *Black Hawk Down: A Story of Modern War*, Atlantic Monthly Press, 1999.

46. Numerous SEALs expressed their frustration during peacetime training.

47. http://en.wikipedia.org/wiki/Yugoslav_wars.

48. Alastair Finlan, *The Collapse of Yugoslavia 1991–99*, Osprey Publishing, Oxford, 2004, pp.17–18, 23–25.

49. The camp is named after the Vietnam War Medal of Honor winner, James Leroy Bondsteel, http://en.wikipedia.org/wiki/Camp_Bondsteel.

50. http://www.nato.int/issues/kosovo/index.html.

51. http://www.huffingtonpost.com/richard-shepard/capturing-radovan-karadzi_b_61327.html.

52. http://www.cfr.org/publication/9126/, http://en.wikipedia.org/wiki/Maktab_al-Khidamat.

53. http://www.globalsecurity.org/security/profiles/abdullah_azzam.htm.

54. Interviews, various, 2007/8, Bahmanyar/Osman.

55. http://transcripts.cnn.com/TRANSCRIPTS/0507/07/ldt.01.html.

56. http://www.harpers.org/archive/2006/08/sb-seven-michael-scheuer-1156277744.

57. Niall Ferguson, interview, *Conversations with History*, Institute of International Studies, UC Berkeley.

58. http://www.whitehouse.gov/news/releases/2001/12/20011228-1.html.

59. Interview with Chris Osman, 2007/8, Bahmanyar.

60. Interview with Darrick, 2007/8, Bahmanyar/Osman.

61. Interview with Marcus Luttrell, 2007, Bahmanyar/Osman.

62. Ibid.

63. Otto Kreisher and Albert M Calland III, "In the Forefront of the War on Terror," *Sea Power*, December 2002.

64. http://www.navy.mil/navydata/bios/bio.asp?bioID=338.

65. Kreisher and Calland, "In the Forefront of the War on Terror."

66. Mir Bahmanyar, *Shadow Warriors*, pp.195–240.

67. Soft compromise occurs when the detachment is seen or discovered by non-threatening indigenous people. There is no immediate threat of attack or death.

68. Interview with Darrick, 2007, Bahmanyar/Osman.

69. Ibid.

70. Interview with Michael, 2007, Bahmanyar/Osman.

71. Interview with Chris Osman, 2007, Bahmanyar.

72. SOCOM briefing, in-country Afghanistan, 2001.

73. Ibid.

74. Ibid.

75. Ibid.

76. Ibid.

77. Ibid.

78. Ibid.

79. Interview with Chris Osman, 2007, Bahmanyar.

80. SOCOM briefing, in-country Afghanistan, 2001.

81. Interview with Chris Osman, 2007, Bahmanyar. All further quotes in this section are from Chris Osman unless otherwise noted.

82. For an account of the Ranger part of the rescue operation see Mir Bahmanyar, *Shadow Warriors*, pp.195–240. See also Sean Naylor's *Not a Good Day to Die*, Berkley, New York, 2005.

83. http://www.navy.mil/moh/mpmurphy/soa.html.

84. Interview with Marcus Luttrell, November 2007, Bahmanyar/Osman.

85. http://www.navy.mil/moh/mpmurphy/soa.html.

86. www.navy.mil/moh/mpmurphy/

87. David F. Winkler, "Navy SEALs' Action May Have Prevented Iraqi Oil Disaster," *Sea Power*, February 2007, p.1.

88. Ibid., p.1.

89. http://www.uscg.mil/reserve/magazine/mag2003/MayJun03/OpIraqFreedom.htm.

90. Ibid.

91. Ibid.

92. http://www.grom.wp.mil.pl/home.htm.

93. Every SEAL operator interviewed said good things about their Polish counterparts.

94. Interview with Kyle, 2007, Bahmanyar/Osman.

95. Ibid.

96. Winkler, "Navy SEALs' Action May Have Prevented Iraqi Oil Disaster", p.1.

97. Interview with Kyle, 2007, Bahmanyar/Osman. All further quotes in this section are from Kyle unless otherwise noted.

98. Winkler, "Navy SEALs' Action May Have Prevented Iraqi Oil Disaster," p.1.

99. Interview with Paul and Frank, July 2007, Bahmanyar/Osman.

100. Jim Crawley, "Seals Give Glimpse of Missions in Iraq," *San Diego Union Tribune*, June 27, 2003.

101. "Battle Space": The environment, factors, and conditions that must be understood to successfully apply combat power, protect the force, or complete the mission. This includes the air, land, sea, space, and the enemy and friendly forces; facilities; weather; terrain; the electromagnetic spectrum; and the information environment within the operational areas and areas of interest. (http://stinet.dtic.mil/cgi-bin/GetTRDoc?AD=ADA429072&Location=U2&doc=GetTRDoc.pdf)

102. Interview with Paul and Frank, 2007, Bahmanyar/Osman.

103. Several SEALs independently made this point.

104. Interview with Paul and Frank, 2007, Bahmanyar/Osman.

105. Interview with Paul, 2007, Bahmanyar/Osman.

106. Interview with Paul and Frank, 2007, Bahmanyar/Osman.

107. Interview with Kyle, 2007, Bahmanyar/Osman.

108. Ibid.

109. Interview with member of DevGru, 2007, Bahmanyar/Osman.

110. Interview with Kyle, 2007, Bahmanyar/Osman.

111. http://www.navybuddies.com/planes/sh60.htm.

112. http://www.navy.mil/search/display.asp?story_id=26887.

113. http://navyreserve.navy.mil/Public/Staff/Centers/Forces+Command/Centers/Helicopter+Reserve+Wing/Centers/HCS-5/WelcomeAboard/default.htm, accessed December 2007.

114. Interview with Paul and Frank, 2007, Bahmanyar/Osman.

115. Interview with Paul, 2007, Bahmanyar/Osman.

116. All quotes in this section from interview with Kyle, 2007, Bahmanyar/Osman, unless otherwise indicated.

117. http://en.wikipedia.org/wiki/Mosul#Mosul_after_Saddam.

118. Interview with Paul and Frank, 2007, Bahmanyar/Osman.

119. All quotes in this section from interview with Paul, 2007, Bahmanyar/Osman, unless otherwise indicated.

120. Interviews, 2007, Bahmanyar/Osman.

121. http://www.whitehouse.gov/news/releases/2006/03/20060320-7.html.

122. All quotes in this section from interview with Kyle, 2007, Bahmanyar/Osman, unless otherwise indicated.

123. www.navyseals.com/marc-lee.

124. http://www.navy.mil/moh/Monsoor/

125. Interviews, Bahmanyar/Osman.

INDEX